Change or Continuity Policy

While *evidence-based* policy is an emerging rhetoric of the desire by and for governments to develop policies based on the best available evidence, drug policy is an area where particular challenges abound. This book is a detailed and comprehensive examination of the contours of drug policy development through the consideration of the particular roles of science, media, and interest groups. Using Belgium as the primary case-study, supplemented by insights gathered from other countries, the author contributes to a richer understanding of the science-policy nexus in the messy, real-world complexities of drug policy. *Change or Continuity in Drug Policy: The Roles of Science, Media, and Interest Groups* is the first book to bring together policy and media theories, knowledge utilisation models, and public scholarship literature. As such, the book provides unique insights relevant to aspects of change or continuity in drug policies in Europe and beyond.

This book will be of great value to undergraduate and graduate students, as well as to academics, practitioners, and policy-makers with interest in the science-policy nexus with a particular focus on the drug policy domain.

Julie Tieberghien is currently a post-doctoral fellow of FWO – Research Foundation Flanders – at the Department of Criminology, Criminal Law & Social Law (Ghent University). Her main areas of research are drug policy analysis, newsmaking, and public criminology, and she has published widely in these areas.

Routledge Frontiers of Criminal Justice

34 **Improving Criminal Justice Workplaces**
Translating Theory and Research into Evidence-based Practice
Paula Brough, Jennifer Brown and Amanda Biggs

35 **Experiencing Imprisonment**
Research on the Experience of Living and Working in Carceral Institutions
Edited by Carla Reeves

36 **Restorative Justice in Transitional Settings**
Edited by Kerry Clamp

37 **Prisoner Radicalization and Terrorism Detention Policy**
Institutionalized Fear or Evidence-Based Policy-Making?
Tinka M. Veldhuis

38 **Change or Continuity in Drug Policy**
The Roles of Science, Media, and Interest Groups
Julie Tieberghien

39 **Restorative Policing**
Concepts, Theory and Practice
Kerry Clamp and Craig Paterson

40 **The Penal Voluntary Sector**
Philippa Tomczak

41 **Transforming Summary Justice**
Modernisation in the Lower Criminal Courts
Jennifer Ward

42 **Stop and Search and Police Legitimacy**
Ben Bradford

43 **Young Offenders and Open Custody**
Tove Pettersson

44 **Restorative Responses to Sexual Violence**
Legal, Social and Therapeutic Dimensions
Edited by Estelle Zinsstag and Marie Keenan

45 **Policing Hate Crime**
Understanding Communities and Prejudice
Gail Mason, JaneMaree Maher, Jude McCulloch, Sharon Pickering, Rebecca Wickes and Carolyn McKay

Change or Continuity in Drug Policy

The Roles of Science, Media, and Interest Groups

Julie Tieberghien

Routledge
Taylor & Francis Group
LONDON AND NEW YORK

First published 2017 by Routledge

2 Park Square, Milton Park, Abingdon, Oxfordshire OX14 4RN
52 Vanderbilt Avenue, New York, NY 10017

Routledge is an imprint of the Taylor & Francis Group an informa business

First issued in paperback 2019

Library of Congress Cataloging in Publication Data
Names: Tieberghien, Julie, author.
Title: Change or continuity in drug policy : the roles of science, media, and interest groups / Julie Tieberghien.
Description: 1 Edition. | New York : Routledge, 2017. | Series: Routledge frontiers of criminal justice | Includes bibliographical references.
Identifiers: LCCN 2016055454| ISBN 9781138203068 (hardback) | ISBN 9781315472379 (eISBN)
Subjects: LCSH: Drug abuse–Government policy. | Drug control. | Drug legalization.
Classification: LCC HV5801 .T54 2017 | DDC 362.29/1561–dc23
LC record available at https://lccn.loc.gov/2016055454

ISBN: 978-1-138-20306-8 (hbk)
ISBN: 978-0-367-13644-4 (pbk)

Typeset in Sabon
by Wearset Ltd, Boldon, Tyne and Wear

For Bruno, Mette, and Klara

Contents

Tables

Preface

Researchers often wonder what becomes of the results of their research. So did I. The idea for this book came from drug research that I have been working on in recent years. My initial research work focused on local drug/alcohol monitoring systems and comparative assessments of drug-policy strategies. In this context, I was involved in monitoring drug use trends at the local level for the city of Antwerp, which aimed to provide information for an *evidence-based* policy concerning prevention, harm reduction, and treatment, as well as to stimulate the (ongoing) dialogue between policy-makers and a broad range of stakeholders. Over the course of my involvement in this research, I presented findings to a broad range of stakeholders including police officers, treatment practitioners, and local policy-makers, and I felt optimistic about inspiring some small policy changes. However, through informal conversations with some stakeholders and drug users, I had an increasing number of reservations about the potential impact of my research findings on the local (drug) policy context. Generally, I started to wonder *if* and *how* scientific knowledge can play a role in the drug policy-making process or, in other words, how the science-policy nexus in the drug policy field actually works. From these first research experiences onwards, I became fascinated with the complex processes that underpin the development of criminal justice and public policy, and the debates around expert knowledge and the policy process. This book is devoted to these particular issues and reflects my attempt to create further insight about the links between science and policy in the field of drugs by moving beyond zero-sum statements of policy-making being *evidence-based* or *evidence-free*. Analysing the roles of science, media, and interest groups in the context of Belgian drug policy development – but with insights gathered from other countries – this book discusses theoretical perspectives and presents new evidence that can be used to challenge the way you think about the link between science and policy and, more broadly, about the underlying aspects of change or continuity in drug policies.

Acknowledgements

This book has depended on the goodwill of all those who participated in the research, particularly the interviewees, and on the research funding provided by Ghent University, for which I am thankful. Furthermore, I would like to thank Tom Decorte, Brice De Ruyver, Carl Devos, Simon Lenton, Susanne MacGregor, Mark Monaghan, Guido Van Hal, and Wouter Vanderplasschen for their critical and enriching comments on various aspects of this work and for their ongoing support. Thanks are also due to Ellen Boyne at Routledge for her practical support for the book. As always, I most thankfully acknowledge the endless support of my family. This book is dedicated to them, with love.

Finally, grateful acknowledgement is made to the following sources for the permission to reproduce material in this book:

'The role of the media in the science-policy nexus. Some critical reflections based on an analysis of the Belgian drug policy debate (1996–2003)', Julie Tieberghien, *International Journal of Drug Policy*, 25(2014), 276–281. Reprinted by permission of the publisher, Elsevier.

'Understanding the science-policy nexus in Belgium: an analysis of the drug policy debate (1996–2003)', Julie Tieberghien, *Drugs: Education, Prevention and Policy*, 20(2013), 241–248. Reprinted by permission of the publisher, Taylor & Francis Ltd (www.tandfonline.com).

'Challenges and opportunities of "good governance" for drug policy: the case of the development of Belgian drug policy between 1996 and 2003', Julie Tieberghien, *Drugs: Education, Prevention and Policy* (2016). Reprinted by permission of the publisher, Taylor & Francis Ltd (www.tandfonline.com).

Abbreviations

ACF	Advocacy Coalition Framework
AGALEV	Flemish Green party
BIRN	Belgian Information Reitox Network
CA	Conversation Analysis
CDA	Critical Discourse Analysis
CDH	French-speaking Christian Democrats
CVP/CD&V	Flemish Christian Democrats
DP	Discursive Psychology
EBM	Evidence-Based Medicine
EBP	Evidence-Based Policy
ECOLO	French-speaking Green party
EMCDDA	European Monitoring Centre for Drugs and Drug Addiction
EU	European Union
FEDITO	Fédération Wallonne des Institutions pour Toxicomanes
FPS	Federal Public Services
ICWG	Inter-Cabinet Working Group
IDPC	International Drug Policy Consortium
INCB	International Narcotics Control Board
MC	Ministerial Circular Letter
MP	Member of Parliament
MSOC	Medical-Social Treatment Centres for drug users
PRL-FDF-MCC	French-speaking Liberals
PS	French-speaking Socialist party
PSC	French-speaking Christian Democrats
PWG	Parliamentary Working Group on drugs
RCT	Randomised Controlled Trials
SP/SP.A	Flemish Socialist party
UKDPC	United Kingdom Drug Policy Commission
UN	United Nations
UNGASS	United Nations General Assembly Special Sessions

UNODC	United Nations Office on Drugs and Crime
VAD	Association for Alcohol and other Drug Problems [Vereniging voor Alcohol- en andere Drugsproblemen]
VLD/OpenVLD	Flemish Liberals
VU/VU&ID	Flemish Nationalists
WHO	World Health Organization

Chapter 1

Introduction

Over the past decades, drugs and drug use have shifted from marginal phenomena to a situation in which they are widely sampled and used (South, 1999; Levine, 2003; Boland, 2008). As long as drug use was seen as pertaining to marginalised and minority groups, it was possible to confine it to a limited place on the policy agenda (Gusfield, 1975). Over the years, serious drug problems have become increasingly connected with a number of other social issues, such as crime, disorder, or poverty (Garland, 2001; Seddon, Ralphs, & Williams, 2008). Gradually, it was also recognised that drugs were pervasive in society and particularly among young people (instead of among marginalised populations only). Drug use moved from exceptional to being part of everyday life (Parker, Aldridge, & Measham, 1998; South, 1999). Referring to drugs as a problem of everyday life or by magnifying existing problems (e.g. crime rates, poverty), politicians soon exploited and inflamed feelings of unease and made it a political issue (MacCoun & Reuter, 2001).

Governments around the world have developed a variety of policies intended to influence whether or not individuals decide to use drugs and to affect the consequences for the individual and the society (Tops, 2001; Eisenbach-Stangl, Moskalewicz, & Thom, 2009; Babor et al., 2010; Pompidou Group, 2011; Hughes & Stevens, 2012; Muscat & Pike, 2012). Drug policies, not only in European nations but also in Australia or the USA, usually comprise a mix of three or four ways of regulating drugs: drug control, treatment, prevention, and harm reduction (MacCoun & Reuter, 2001). Nonetheless, the strategic direction of national drug policies is often discussed in terms of two opposing ideological positions (Kleiman & Hawdon, 2011). As Chatwin (2011) notes in her analysis of European drug policy, policies in Sweden and the Netherlands represent both ends of the restrictive-liberal spectrum: the liberal, pragmatic policy of the Netherlands with the primary aim of harm reduction for the users, and the more moralistic and restrictive zero-tolerance policy of Sweden that aims to eradicate drug use from society. In between these two extremes, countries lie at different points along the continuum. The depth of commitment to these paradigms varies and may evolve among countries. The Netherlands may now be moving towards a more restrictive interpretation of its national liberal drug policy than previously seen (Wouters, 2013; Brewster, 2014). In 2001, Portugal made a radical change towards a more liberal policy based firmly on harm reduction principles. By far the most famous element in this national drug strategy was to decriminalise the personal use of all illicit drugs (Hughes & Stevens, 2012). In contrast, Danish drug policy which used to be known as rather liberal compared with other Nordic countries, is now increasingly saturated with a 'zero-tolerance' and 'tough on crimes' rhetoric (Asmussen, 2008). In the UK, lately, the crime reduction discourse has shifted more towards a recovery and reintegration discourse (Duke, 2012). Simultaneously, the re-classification of cannabis from Class C to Class B by British policy-makers in 2009 seemed to show a toughening attitude (Seddon et al., 2008; Monaghan, 2011). And, according to Stevens and Measham (2014), the toughening has been extended recently by the practice of banning new psychoactive substances such as mephedrone. Finally, in the light of current debates on reforms in national and global drug control policies (Global Commission on Drug Policy, 2011; UNGASS, 2016), some new approaches to drug control are being tested, for example the legalisation of the cannabis supply in Uruguay and some US states (Singleton & Rubin, 2014; Caulkins et al., 2015). Thus, where drug policy strategies are involved, glimmers of hope to reduce drug-related violence or harms come from several directions. In this context, it is unsurprising that increasing attention has been paid to questions of evidence and effectiveness (Strang et al., 2012): which policies are most effective at reducing harm? What evidence is there of a particular policy's success or failure? And is evidence, after all, integrated into development or change of drug policies? Exploring the last question, the contribution of scientific knowledge to drug policy development, is this book's central task.

One of the early visions of how evidence could impact policy was advanced by the American political scientist Lasswell (1951), but expectations about the intersection between scientific knowledge and policy-making have been more widely discussed in the (knowledge utilisation) literature since the 1970s (Caplan, 1979; Weiss, 1979). The term *evidence-based* policy is, however, relatively new: it was popularised in 1997 in the UK when the Blair Labour government, as part of its strategy of modernisation, put forward the notion that "what counts is what works" (Monaghan, 2011). Since then, it has remained an integral element of public management strategies and policy practice (Clear, 2010; Strassheim & Kettunen, 2014). An *evidence-based* account assumes that scientific knowledge in policy-making is a given, and that if only policy-makers paid more attention to evidence, society would see better policy (Pearce, 2014). The ideal of *evidence-based* policy became a global movement and has been echoed in other countries such as Australia, the USA, and Belgium (Verhofstadt, 1999; Rudd 2008; Obama, 2009). Also, international networks such as the *Cochrane Collaboration* have been developed with this in mind (Devroe, Deschamps, & Hannes, 2008).

The concept of *evidence-based* policy has become part of the common policy lexicon in the drug policy field too. Throughout the USA, Europe, and further afield, a range of initiatives has been developed with the mission to monitor, review, or broker evidence to better inform policy-making. An important push for the European context was provided with the installation of the European Monitoring Centre for Drugs and Drug Addiction (EMCDDA) during the 1990s. One of its aims is to identify gaps in knowledge to strengthen the research base for promoting *evidence-based* policy (Stimson, 1997; Hartnoll, 2004; EMCDDA, 2008). More recently, the European Commission has also been a progressive factor in pushing for balanced, *evidence-based* drug policies and programmes, as set out in the EU Drugs Strategy 2013–2020:

> the drug strategy aims to protect and improve the well-being of society and of the individual, to protect public health, to offer a high level of security for the general public and to take a balanced, integrated and evidence-based approach to the drugs phenomenon.
>
> (Council of the European Union, 2012)

Similarly, such an approach has also been endorsed by the United Nations General Assembly at the latest meeting on the future of global drug control: "We recognize that civil society, as well as the scientific community and academia, plays an important role in addressing and countering the world drug problem" (UNGASS, 2016). Clearly, this plethora has become the benchmark by which drug policies are made and judged.

Endorsing the *evidence-based* rhetoric is one thing – actually adopting and implementing *evidence-based* policies is another. The role of evidence within drug policy has already been the focus of considerable criticism (Bourgois 2000; Bennett & Holloway, 2010; Stevens & Rhodes, 2011; Monaghan, 2011; Stevens & Ritter, 2013). Several case-studies have pointed out that scientific knowledge is often called on to provide the facts after value choices have been made by the ruling party, paradoxically to be seen to objectify and de-politicise decisions; in this context, drug policy is often called an '*un-evidenced-based mess*' (Room, 2005; Hall, 2008; Ritter, 2009; Monaghan, 2011). Drug policy seems to be an area where particular challenges abound, if only because the importance of control of legislative and governmental institutions limits the possibility of new approaches (Houborg & Asmussen, 2014) and (il)licit drugs is one of the most polarised subjects of media coverage. Its often distorted or inaccurate construction has been a recurrent concern (Lancaster, Hughes, Spicer,

Matthew-Simmons, & Dillon, 2011). Therefore, as in other fields, attempts (particularly in Australia and the UK) have been made to identify elements of policy-making associated with successful drug policy development or, in other words, 'good governance' (Hughes, Lodge, & Ritter, 2010; UKDPC, 2012; MacGregor, Singleton, & Trautmann, 2014; Duke & Thom, 2014; Singleton & Rubin, 2014). A multi-actor, pluralistic perspective is now being embraced, acknowledging that a variety of stakeholders (scientists, practitioners, media, interest groups) frame their views, claims, and interests too, and as such, have opportunities to influence the policy-making process through promotion of *evidence-based* ideas (MacGregor et al., 2014). However, in this context, drug scholars indicate the need for further theoretical and empirical reflection on the mechanisms, processes, and structures through which policy is informed, made, implemented, and assessed rather than what drug policy is, especially because the political, social, economic context may differ between countries (Tonry, 2010; Hyder et al., 2011; El-Jardall, Lavis, Ataya, & Jarnal, 2012; Monaghan, 2011; MacGregor, 2013; Sznitman, Lewis, & Taubman, 2014; MacGregor et al., 2014).

With the stated desire in mind by and for governments to formulate policies based on the best available scientific evidence, there has recently been a revival of academic dialogue discussing the need for social scientists to shape the representation of 'newsworthy' items and to engage in well-informed public and policy debates (Rock, 2010; Wacquant, 2011). Running almost in parallel to the emergence of *evidence-based* policy is the endeavour that can collectively be termed 'public sociology' or 'public criminology'. It is just over 10 years since Michael Burawoy (2005) proclaimed his manifesto for *public sociology* making the plea for sociology to reconnect with civil society as its ongoing project. Over succeeding years, there have emerged variants on the theme including calls for more *public criminology* (e.g. Loader & Sparks, 2011). Public criminology tends to have a narrower focus than its sociological counterpart, focusing mainly on the idea that criminology's purpose is to contribute to a 'better' politics of crime and its regulation. This is considered essential in that criminal justice policy discussions often occur in a febrile atmosphere where 'penal populism' (Bottoms, 1995) or 'totemic toughness' (Stevens, 2011) have tended to trump rational debate. In an era in which *evidence-based* policy is promoted, the prospects of a 'public' role for scientists are paramount given the 'hot' climate in which they operate. There is, however, limited knowledge about whether and how different types of public engagement meaningfully impact on and shape knowledge utilisation in policy-making and whether it stands any chance of producing 'better' politics. Understanding the mechanisms through which scientists engage with policy and the roles they take, requires a critical appraisal of the way in which that process actually unfolds in a particular case. As Rhodes (2000) argues, it is interesting to connect analyses of governance processes with the narratives of individuals (such as public scholars).

The aim of the book is to gain a richer understanding of the complexities of the relationship between evidence and drug policy processes, considering this through the lenses of policy and media theories and knowledge utilisation/public scholarship literature. With the reforms of national and global drug control policies currently high on the international agenda (Global Commission on Drug Policy, 2011; Edwards & Galla, 2014; UNGASS, 2016), the science-policy nexus is a matter of much attention for policy-makers and researchers in the drug policy field. However, the tradition of research on the role and nature of evidence use in the context of drug policy is mainly situated in the UK and Australia. Despite a global discourse on *evidence-based* policies, illuminating policy processes in other countries is still relevant to provide a better understanding of how drug policy processes work and how scientific knowledge is constructed, used or not used in relation to drug policy-making. The few comparative studies in this field have shown that, in a variety of socio-economic, cultural, and political environments, countries may strongly differ in how they do, or do not, value and use scientific research in formulating or shaping drug policy (Nutley, Morton, Jung, & Boaz, 2010; Ritter, Livingston, Chalmers, Berends, & Reuter, 2016).

Belgian drug policy makes an interesting case to examine the complexities of the science-policy nexus, although it neither encompasses a radical or trendsetting policy on the spectrum, nor has it undergone a number of significant changes recently. In most countries the first discussions on drugs and drug policy came into being in the 1960s and 1970s, or, at least, drug policies really came into focus during the HIV epidemic of the 1980s (EMCDDA, 2004; UNODC, 2008; Muscat & Pike, 2012). In contrast, in Belgium, the drug phenomenon was 'discovered' very late (De Ruyver, Vander Laenen, & Eelen, 2012). Although the basic Belgian drug law dates back to 24 February 1921 (as a result of Belgium's ratification of the International Opium Convention in 1912), the Parliamentary Working Group on drugs (PWG) in 1996 actually brought the first serious discussion on how to responsibly deal with the problems of drugs. Thus, drugs did not emerge as a priority for governmental decision-making in Belgium until the mid-1990s and even then there was much less national cohesion on how to best deal with the issue (EMCDDA, 1995). The beginnings of the development of Belgian drug policy were caught between toleration of drug users and understanding of the societal problems they face, and efforts to control the drug problem (Cartuyvels & Hebberecht, 2002). Relations were particularly strained with the Netherlands and debates about the success or failure of the liberal model in the neighbouring country were rife (Fijnaut & De Ruyver, 2014). And, while in this period EMCDDA's monitoring activities were further elaborated, Belgium appeared to be one of the few countries which had not yet developed any insight into the nature and extent of the drug phenomenon in the country (Kenis, 1997; Decorte, Mortelmans, Tieberghien, & De Moor, 2009). However, by the end of the 1990s, interest in this area expanded quickly and the drugs issue was brought into the public arena. Drug policy became the subject of contested debates among policy-makers, professionals, scientists, journalists, and the public. Widespread non-government stakeholder consultation at multiple levels (a *bottom-up* approach) became apparent in the Belgian case and can be considered vital in drug policy governance processes. This occurred in parallel with an emergence of the rhetoric of *evidence-based* policy by which Belgian policy-makers showed commitment to the use of evidence in policy-making (Verhofstadt, 1999). So, clearly, Belgian policy-makers were able and willing to learn from a variety of evidence including scientific knowledge, practice-based knowledge, and (inter)national experiences or evaluations of drug policies, negative as well as positive. Therefore, development of national drug policy in Belgium is of importance and worthy of further investigation. In addition, given the current overall objective of an *evidence-based* approach to the drugs problem (Council of the European Union, 2012; International Drug Policy Consortium, 2016), there is also a practical reason to review the Belgian case. The principles underlying Belgian drug policy today date back to the late-1990s. Drug policy has not been a contentious issue in Belgium since. During this 20-year period, only some elements of the policy have been reviewed internally (Inter-Ministerial Conference on Drugs, 2010), while the foundations of current Belgian drug policy have never been analysed externally in their entirety.

In what follows, Belgian drug policy development between 1996 and 2003 is used as a critical case for looking at and discussing the *mechanisms and processes through which policy is (not) informed by scientific knowledge*, with a particular focus on the *practices of public scholars* and the *roles of the media and interest groups*. This book attempts to place the national perspective in an international context and may offer useful lessons for other contexts, including the importance of scientific knowledge and non-government stakeholder involvement in drug policy-making; bringing different ways of regulating together under a coherent policy framework; and standing up to ideological criticisms, domestic and international, with evidence and pragmatism. In this context, Belgian policy-makers and other non-governmental actors faced some challenges that are faced the world over. Readers from the USA, Australia, and Europe will be able to apply the analyses presented to their own national contexts. The exploratory value of leading theories from political sciences and media studies is assessed and relevant historical and contemporary examples originating from other countries are presented and discussed. As such, this book uses a historical case-study in a media sensitive and politically charged area to move forward the current thinking about *evidence-based* policy, knowledge utilisation, and the discourses of public scholarship.

The Case of Belgian Drugs Policy-Making (1996–2003)

The foundations of modern Belgian drug policy were laid down in the second half of the 1990s, although the drug issue entered the legislative framework with Belgian law criminalising certain drugs and drugs possession in 1921. In the mid-1990s, a *window of opportunity* – defined as a confluence of events that allows advocates to push their policy solutions to problems onto the political agenda (Kingdon, 2002) – opened up when a Parliamentary Working Group on drugs (1996–1997) was established by the Federal Parliament to develop a clear and timely view of all aspects of the Belgian drug phenomenon. The Parliamentary Working Group on drugs (PWG) asked national and international experts, working in all domains of drug policy, to convey their analysis and to give clear recommendations to the Federal Government. Its recommendations encompassed a comprehensive move towards a national drug strategy based firmly on public health principles (e.g. the improvement of the prevention and treatment system, or the introduction of new harm reduction measures). At the same time, the PWG resoundingly rejected a proposal for decriminalisation of cannabis, illustrating the complex political environment from which Belgian drug policy has emerged. After a silent intermezzo between 1997 and 2000, the drug issue re-emerged on the political agenda. The new Belgian Government further elaborated the principles and recommendations of the Parliamentary Working Group (1996–1997) and established the first national drug strategy in 2001. The first national drug strategy, called the 'Federal Drug Policy Note' (Federal Government, 2001), determined the policy priorities and thus the legislative and prosecution framework. Belgium favoured a 'balanced' approach and officially considered the drug problem to be primarily a problem of public health (Federal Government, 2001), similar to countries like Australia, Switzerland, Spain, France, Portugal, and the UK — as well as the European Union itself — which demonstrated a trend towards viewing the drug problem in a broader context encompassing issues of poverty, unemployment, and social exclusion (EMCDDA, 2004; Ritter & McDonald, 2008; Standring, 2016). The approval of the Federal Drug Policy Note (2001) was followed by two years of pervasive uncertainty and legal insecurity concerning what was effectively permitted, as the Narcotic Drug Act of 1921 was not altered by Parliament until 4 April and 3 May 2003. This legislative shift separated cannabis from other drugs and granted prosecution more discretion regarding the enforcement of cannabis-related offences. The changes in the prosecution framework made the possession of three grams by adults and the cultivation of one female plant for personal use tolerable (not meaning 'decriminalised') offences (Decorte, 2007). In other words, by modifying the way the law is used or applied in the various stages of the criminal justice system, Belgium introduced the possibility of waiving prosecution in the case of possession of cannabis for personal use (de facto *depenalisation*) (Room et al., 2010). This reform, together with the election of a new Government, marked the closing of the *window of opportunity* in 2003. Both the 2001 drug strategy and the 2003 drug law form the foundations of the Belgian drug policy today (Table 1.1).

A Note on Terminology

Here is what is meant by the most important terms the reader will encounter in this book. The central topic of the book is the *knowledge utilisation process*. The book draws on the three-fold typology of Weiss (1979), a commonly cited theoretical framework, who identified in her work on knowledge utilisation and policy-making three models of knowledge utilisation (*instrumental*, *conceptual*, *political/symbolic*). The notions of *contribution* or *utilisation* (instead of *impact*) are adopted to encompass not only the direct, instrumental use (i.e. scientific knowledge has a direct bearing on policy), but also its more indirect/conceptual uses (i.e. scientific knowledge can be conceived as part of the process of policy-making). In addition to Weiss' political/symbolic model (i.e. scientific knowledge is considered to be ammunition for political sides), and of particular interest in a media sensitive and politically charged area, the book examines the characteristics of the scientific knowledge which has been included (e.g. How do policy-makers see the role of scientific knowledge? What counts as scientific knowledge?) (*processual model*; Monaghan, 2011), and, if and how power mechanisms play a role in the knowledge utilisation process (*evolutionary model*; Stevens, 2007a). Each of these notions are also elaborated in detail in Chapter 2 of this book.

The complexity of knowledge utilisation processes is assumed to be related to the *characteristics of scientific knowledge* (e.g. unsuitability to

Table 1.1 Timeline of Key Events Leading up to Policy Change in Belgium (1996–2003)

Date	*Key Events*
1996–1997	Parliamentary Working Group on Drugs (PWG): expert hearings and working visits
1999	Election of a new six-party coalition led by Prime Minister Guy Verhofstadt (1999–2003)
2001	Federal Drug Policy Note
2003	Reform of the original Belgian drug law of 24 February 1921 and endorsement of a new Ministerial Circular Letter Election of a new four-party coalition led by Prime Minister Guy Verhofstadt (2003–2007)

policy-makers' needs, academic format of communication, and contradictory findings) and the *levels of engagement of scientists* (Rich, 2001; Haines, Kuruvilla, & Borchert, 2004). This book applies the notion of scientific knowledge to refer to scientific research executed by academics who work in university or college departments as well as to the scientific discourse of an academic. Reflecting on the notion of *public scholarship*, scientists may take different positions in the policy-making process: they may refrain from involvement or they may play a more active role. The typology of modes of criminological engagement, as developed by Loader and Sparks (2011), offers a useful and commonly cited description of varying stances of public engagement. Consistent with Loader and Sparks (2011), as described in detail in the second chapter, the book elaborates on the types of public engagements as *scientific experts*, *policy advisors*, *observer-turned-players*, or *social movement theorists/activists* as a way to make sense of the involvement and influence of different actors in the process. By exploring these accounts, the book highlights the relatively unexplored role of public scholars in the science-policy nexus.

As the book is focusing on the *policy-making process*, it is also important to stress that policy-making is considered here as a pluralist, complex process (policy-making as a *structured interaction*) and these elements are fleshed out in Chapter 2. This involves getting away from the idea that there is authoritative power, implicit in many discussions of policy-making. Rather, against the backdrop of the drug policy governance framework, there are many policy-makers and other actors involved. Initially, *policy-makers* were broadly defined to include all (elected and unelected) stakeholders with political responsibility for shaping policy, or in a position to influence its direction. However, because of the historical characteristics of the case-study, it has been very difficult to access unelected participants with informal influence such as civil servants. In spite of some interviews with retired policy actors and the accessibility of some internal documents, this book primarily discusses the visible parts (or layers) of the policy process. In particular, the book presents a study of fairly high politics or strategic policy-making – above the radar and in terms of strategic/policy documents – and the place of scientific knowledge in discussions on drugs policy at this level and in these forums, rather than a focus on bureaucratic or administrative routine day-to-day policy-making 'behind the scenes' (e.g. by civil servants). Such underrepresentation of civil servants is a clear limitation of the sample.

In empirically exploring knowledge utilisation, the book also draws attention to the broad networks of actors involved in the science-policy nexus including, for example, journalists or interest groups. The *media* can be seen as a rather ambiguous concept which includes several forms of communication: newspapers, television, radio, or internet (McCombs & Reynolds, 2009). In this book, the concept of media is used to refer specifically to the print media, newspapers/magazines in particular. Newspapers and magazines offer practical advantages, for example they are easier to collect than audio-visual data, and they have a more permanent character than web material which is particularly significant when studying policy-making processes from a historical perspective (Mautner, 2008). Furthermore, newspapers are deemed a useful proxy for news reporting, as they often set the agenda for other news formats (Hughes, Lancaster, & Spicer, 2011).

Interest (or advocacy) groups give voice to a particular segment of the general public (Marteache, 2013; Matthew-Simmons, Sunderland, & Ritter, 2013). This concept refers to a variety of groups of people with shared beliefs and goals in a particular policy area: civil society associations, NGOs or third sector organisations, alliances, coalitions and networks of existing organisations, professional associations of lawyers or law enforcement officers, and user groups (Tops, 2001; Hall, 2004; Lancaster, Ritter, & Stafford, 2013; EMCDDA, 2013). In this book, interest groups include the associations advocating for drug users' rights as well as groups representing parents or ex-drug users who advocate against drug use. This type of interest group may be of particular interest to the study of the science-policy nexus in the drug policy field, especially because (ex-)drug users are the direct objects of drug policy (Lenton, 2004; Bergin, 2013).

Outline of This Book

The book is organised in the following way. Chapter 2 is directed at readers who have little previous knowledge of the historical origins and evolution of the thinking on the relationship between science and policy. This chapter offers an overview of the *evidence-based* movement and the renewed discussion that sparked across social science disciplines such as sociology and criminology about the need to engage with the public domain. It also describes the key policy-making theories that political scientists and other policy-making scholars have advanced, exploring whether these theories offer insight into drug policy-making. The literature on the barriers and facilitators of the relationship between science and policy, in the field of drugs in particular, is also reviewed in depth. Such information has also been covered to different extents in other works, but is presented here as it is essential for understanding the analysis and case-study discussed in this book.

Chapter 3 explores the research design and the methods (including the Critical Discourse Analysis of Norman Fairclough and elite interviews) through which the data for this study are collected. Finally, a description is presented of the limitations and the challenges the researcher was faced with during data-collection and data-analysis.

Drawing on documentary material and interview data, Chapters 4 to 8 form the core of the analysis. These chapters explore the role of scientific knowledge – as well as political, economic, and other factors – in the drug policy-making process. The book chronologically addresses the history of Belgian drug policy and legislative framework before 1996 (Chapter 4), the Parliamentary Working Group on drugs (1996–1997) (Chapter 5), the intermezzo between 1997 and 2000 (Chapter 6), the Federal Drug Policy Note (2001) (Chapter 7), and the reform of Belgian drug law (2002–2003) (Chapter 8).

The main conclusions and considerations summarise and integrate the key findings of the case-study and also add reflections on its international relevance and comparability. Leading policy and media theories as well as knowledge utilisation and public scholarship literature are used as sound frameworks for analysis. Specific directions for future research on this under-examined but deeply important issue are proposed.

Chapter 2

The Science-Policy Nexus

From Knowledge Utilisation Models to the *Evidence* Movement

Attention to the relationship between science and policy is not new. Historically, there has been an interest in the political and social relations of knowledge production (Walters, 2003; Allen, 2007). More recently, in association with an *evidence-based* movement, discussion was revived across social science disciplines such as sociology, criminology, and anthropology on the need to engage with the public domain (Burawoy, 2005; Loader & Sparks, 2011). In this section, the origins of the interest in the science-policy nexus as well as more recent debates about *evidence-based* policy and *public scholarship* are addressed. Furthermore, the chapter critically examines theories of policy-making to demonstrate the different ways in which scientific knowledge can be used in the policy-making process. The linkages between these theoretical models and their shortcomings are identified and debated. In addition, this chapter outlines the barriers and facilitators of the relationship between science and policy. This chapter does not focus solely on the general literature about the science-policy nexus and policy-making but also looks more specifically at the drug policy-making literature related to these accounts.

Historical Origins of the Interest in the Science-Policy Nexus

An early view of the science-policy nexus included the idea that scientific rationality could serve as a key to problem-solving (Hoppe, 1999). For some time, the idea of an independent, truth-seeking scientist who conducts his or her work in virtual isolation from societal and political influences was instrumental in the protection of scientists from political interventions (Hoppe, 1999; Jasanoff, 2006). As a result, scientists attempted to establish scientific objectivity in the measurement and quantification of social phenomena (e.g. criminal behaviour) and sought to identify explanations for individual or social causes that determined this behaviour. This was a time of great optimism about the positive influence of 'technocrats' on the policy-making process (Lasswell, 1951). However, enthusiasm was followed by increasing disillusionment about science's capacity to address complex social issues. In particular, the notion of scientific knowledge as the driving force of policy-making and social progress was challenged as early as the mid-twentieth century when both World Wars and an economic crisis strongly impacted on public belief in scientific rationality (Walters, 2003; Hammersley, 2013). As the 1960s progressed, it was gradually acknowledged that scientific knowledge was fallible as a result of its frequently inconclusive and ambiguous conclusions. In other words, there was a relative consensus that scientists do not possess absolute *truth* about social phenomena: in fact, their assumptions can have a strong effect on the results they find (Head, 2010). Furthermore, it was more strongly argued that policy was being determined by powerful groups rather than by scientific rationality (Walters, 2003). This shift initiated a change in critical thinking about the role of the state, society, and the public at large (Carrabine, Iganski, Lee, Plummer, & South, 2004) as well as the role that scientific knowledge could – or should – play in the policy-making process. Weiss (1991) characterised the increasing interest in the science-policy connection as follows: "If they (social scientists) no longer claim to find 'truth' about 'reality', what is their role in the policy process?" (p. 309). Within this context, the tradition of knowledge utilisation literature began to develop.

The Two Communities Thesis and Utilisation as an Outcome

In the mid-1970s social scientists started to study the use or non-use of research in policy decisions (Webber, 1991; Weiss, 1995). In the first examples, researchers tried to determine the direct effects and to establish causal links without trying to understand how scientific knowledge may have a particular influence (Carden, 2004). Although this is a reductive approach, many of the researchers who worked on the original empirical studies held such beliefs. These early international studies were skewed strongly towards quantitative research methods, thereby focusing on surveys among policy-makers and/or scientists or bibliometric analyses of academic citations in policy documents. The underlying assumption is that if an idea/finding is good enough, it will be used (Nutley, Walter, & Davies, 2003). Utilisation is considered to be the specific (direct or rational) impact of research on policy (Webber, 1991; Lampinen, 1992). Utilisation as an *outcome* can be considered as a narrow and deterministic view on knowledge utilisation. The principle is that knowledge automatically produces an effect on a policy or decision. Through these early studies, researchers identified that research was not having much influence on policy decisions. Many disillusioned scientists published articles in professional journals bemoaning the neglect of their work. Explanations for the failure of the connection between science and policy were dedicated to the gap between researchers and policy-makers. In particular, the earliest paradigm concerning the science-policy connection, developed by Caplan (1979), describes scientists and policy-makers as part of *two communities* with different world views, values, and language, separated by a huge gap. Although it provided the basis for much thinking about the science-policy nexus (Weiss, 1979; Nutley et al., 2003; Landry, Amara, & Lamari, 2001; Hoppe, 2005), it utilises a rather simplistic model which ignores other actors (e.g. media and interest groups). Along with these concerns came the recognition that measurements of research *impact* cannot be limited to examples of direct, instrumental use of research within a single decision point. Neither can it rely on the traditional mechanisms of measuring academic success, such as academic citations or publications and memberships of advisory groups (Brambila, Ottolenghi, Marin, & Bertrand, 2007). Gradually, utilisation was interpreted in a more broad sense, whereby scientific knowledge plays a role in the process of policy-making rather than just in the outcome of policy formulation.

Utilisation as a Process

Unlike the *two communities* thesis, several authors refused to accept the simple dichotomy between use and non-use, aiming to uncover alternative modes of knowledge utilisation (Landry et al., 2001; Hoppe, 2005; Ottoson & Hawe, 2009). From this perspective, researchers look out for any unexpected and more subtle, indirect ways in which scientific knowledge may seep into the policy-making process (utilisation as *process*). In other words, the main point of the *process* approach is that scientific knowledge has been received and read, and that information is judged to be relevant or valuable. It does not imply that action has been undertaken but rather that scientific knowledge in some way has contributed to new or advanced thinking about a problem (Krastev, 2000; Neilson, 2001). Such a broad definition offers a more realistic approach to utilisation as a consideration with an indirect, more subtle impact (Rich, 1997).

At the same time, in a response to the two communities thesis, it was acknowledged that a different set of actors is involved in the policy-making process especially when studying how knowledge is (not) used in the policy-making process (Sabatier, 1998; Sutton, 1999; Kingdon, 2002). Lindquist (2001) introduced the concept of the *third community*. In an attempt to embrace more actors with an interest in policy, the *third community* includes intermediary institutions standing alongside the knowledge producers (academic worlds) and knowledge consumers (decision community) such as think tanks, political consultants or advisors, commissions, councils, media, or journalists. Accordingly, the perspectives of and the interactions between policy-makers, as well as researchers and the third community (e.g. media, think tanks), were also integrated. However, treating two or three communities as separate entities, still minimises the heterogeneity among scientists and policy-makers. Ginsburg and Gorostiaga (2001) claimed that a focus on communities can be seen as an ideal-type and does not take into account simultaneous memberships of these groups. Researchers can potentially perform a variety of influencing roles within the policy process such as acting as experts or advisors (see also *public criminology*; Loader & Sparks, 2011). For example, both professors of criminology Petersilia (2008) and Stevens (2007b and 2011) worked in a government department for a particular length of time.

Parallel to these reconsiderations came a rethinking of methods for studying knowledge utilisation. Scientists began to realise that the fixed survey form, with its fixed questions and constrained choices of answers, was not necessarily the only way to go. As a consequence, scientists increasingly favoured qualitative inquiry and interviews in particular (Lindquist, 2001; Carden, 2004; see also Chapter 3).

Modelling Knowledge Utilisation

While the early paradigm of the *two communities* thesis offered a rather pessimistic view on the connection between two fundamentally different worlds separated by a huge gap (Caplan, 1979), Carol Weiss, a prominent author in this field, identified seven meanings (or models of knowledge utilisation): the knowledge-driven and the problem-solving model, the political and tactical model, the interactive, the enlightenment and the intellectual model (Weiss, 1979; Nutley, 2003) (Table 2.1). She believed that the utilisation of social sciences in policy development is a highly complex phenomenon that can be perceived in a large number of different ways.

The Three-fold Knowledge Utilisation Typology

These seven meanings of knowledge utilisation have, however, mainly been operationalised by developing a three-fold classification system distinguishing the *instrumental model* representing an approach where scientific knowledge has a direct bearing on policy, the *political/symbolic model* (i.e. policy-makers using scientific knowledge in a selective way to delay actions, for example waiting for research results or convincing sceptics about the value of a measure) and the *enlightenment model* (i.e. delayed and diffused use of information in policy-making). Weiss' three-fold knowledge utilisation typology (1979) (Table 2.2) has proven to be very influential in the knowledge utilisation literature and has been applied widely to studies of the science-policy nexus in the drug policy field and elsewhere (Lester, 1993; Chan, 1995; Brereton, 1996; Rich, 1997; Oh, 1997;

Table 2.1 Overview of Meanings of Use

	Outcome/Process	*Scientific Knowledge: Only Guiding Factor*	*Meanings of Use*
Knowledge-driven	outcome	yes	Scientific knowledge provides the necessary pressure for policy to develop in line with new knowledge
Problem-solving	outcome	yes	A policy problem is first recognised, prompting research with the aim of providing evidence on which to base policy solutions
Political	outcome	no	Scientific knowledge is used in a predetermined manner to support policies that have already been considered for implementation
Tactical	outcome	no	Scientific knowledge is used as a method of delaying the decision-making process
Enlightenment	process	yes	Scientific knowledge influences policy through indirect processes over long periods
Interactive	process	no	Scientific knowledge is just one factor among many that have the ability to influence policy
Intellectual	process	no	Scientific knowledge is considered as a part of the intellectual pursuits of the society

Table 2.2 Three-Fold Typology of Knowledge Utilisation

Three-Fold Typology	*Meanings of Utilisation*	*Description*
Instrumental	• knowledge driven model • problem-solving model	This model represents the typical understanding, a rather static approach, of the science-policy nexus. It assumes that scientific knowledge has a direct bearing on policy
Enlightenment/conceptual	• interactive model • enlightenment model • intellectual model	A dynamic perspective of the science-policy nexus is supported in this model. Scientific knowledge can be conceived as part of the process of policy-making. Utilisation must be considered as a series of events or processes which may (not) lead to a specific action/ decision
Political/symbolic	• political model • tactical model	Offering a more strategic approach of knowledge utilisation, in this model, scientific knowledge is considered as ammunition for political sides. It can be used to silence the arguments of the opposition or to support ideas, which the policy-makers have already adopted

Sorian & Baugh, 2002; Hanney, Gonzalez-Block, Buxton, & Kogan, 2003; Amara, Ouimet, & Landry, 2004; Smet, 2013; Stevens, 2007a; Monaghan, 2008a; Head, 2010; Freiberg & Carson, 2010).

Even though the typology may be very helpful in structuring data analysis and interpretation, some caveats must be borne in mind. First of all, these models assume a voluntarist attitude of policy-makers and scientists: both have the intention to maximise the use of scientific knowledge. Of course, in reality such an approach rather ignores the institutional context of policy-making (e.g. party hierarchies) (Flitcroft, Gillespie, Salkeld, Carter, & Trevena, 2011) as well as the levels of engagement of scientists (Haynes et al., 2011).

Second, utilisation cannot be readily classified into types, for example a single study may be used in different ways. These models must be interpreted as parallel processes rather than contrasting classifications. Therefore, some authors started to view knowledge utilisation as a continuum rather than in terms of static types. Placing the types of utilisation along a spectrum, Greenberg and Mandell (1991) suggested a continuum across two dimensions: (1) a concrete/conceptual dimension (i.e. ranging from the use of findings to make decisions to the intangible and conceptual influence) and (2) a substantive/elaborative/strategic dimension (i.e. defining the extent to which research influences an action or serves to legitimate a decision). Nutley et al. (2007) also supported the idea of a two-way continuum ranging from conceptual to instrumental uses of research. However, even though they recognise the dynamic nature of knowledge utilisation, they overlook the importance of strategic or political ways of utilisation.

Finally, the *political/tactical* model leaves unanswered the question of what constitutes proper use. Some authors support the view that symbolic use reflects the *bad* use of knowledge while instrumental and conceptual use includes *good* ways of utilisation (Souchon & Dianmantopoulos, 1994). However, in general, knowledge utilisation models have been focused only on addressing selective ways of use and far less attention has been paid to *misuse* of scientific knowledge (Nutley et al., 2007).

Accordingly, some authors took on the task of refining Weiss' work on the meanings of knowledge utilisation (Landry et al., 2001; Nutley, 2003; Hoppe, 2005; Hoppe 2009). Some efforts have proved to be very fruitful in remodelling the science-policy nexus. Cross, Henke, Oberknezev, and Pouilias (2000) further developed the *political* and *tactical* model with the introduction of the *status* model, which refers to the use of a well-stocked portfolio of commissioned research as a status symbol for policy agencies. However, in many cases, these elaborations remained limited to the implementation of another terminology. For instance, Nutley (2003) identified four main types of knowledge utilisation. Next to the instrumental and conceptual use (comparable with Weiss' classification), she distinguishes

(1) *mobilisation of support* whereby research is an instrument of persuasion and (2) *wider influence*, which refers to the impact of research for policy paradigms or belief communities. Nevertheless, it is clear that the first addition is strongly linked with the *political* model, while the second shows similarities with the *conceptual* or *enlightenment* model.

The Evolutionary–Processual Model

Of particular relevance to the drug policy field is that some newer models have been advocated by Stevens (2007a and 2011) and Monaghan (2011). According to Stevens (2011), existing theoretical models "do not include issues of power in the filtering process through which research passes into policy and so does not predict systematic bias in the use of evidence" (p. 70). In a similar vein to the *conceptual* model (*enlightenment*), the evolutionary model views utilisation as a *process* and not just as an outcome. Unlike the *political* and *tactical* model, this model tends to focus not only on the policy-makers but also on the social structure as important in supporting selection in the use of scientific knowledge. In this respect, there is recognition that the media or interest groups may play a role in influencing what is permissible in policy-making. Furthermore, one of the strengths of the model is that it pays attention to the power dynamics in the policy-making process; an issue largely neglected in existing models of knowledge utilisation or policy-making. The evolutionary model assumes that there is a Darwinian *survival of the fittest* evidence in the policy-making process, for example as some evidence may fit the interests of the powerful groups, and others may not, evidence without a powerful supporter will not be used. Several arguments and processes of selection of scientific knowledge are distinguished, which may help to explain the (preservation of the) relative power of some groups (Stevens, 2007a). A first mechanism is *trawling*, which means that policy-makers select the beneficial evidence and ignore the rest (which is similar to what others have called *cherry-picking*). Second, policy-makers can *farm* for evidence, whereby powerful actors focus attention on evidence that supports a given policy. A third mechanism is called *flak*, creating disquiet about evidence which is detrimental to a particular policy direction. Finally, a *strain* mechanism includes the imposition of strain on researchers who produce irrelevant evidence. Monaghan (2011) puts forward an important downside of this evolutionary model. He argued that the evolutionary model has an understanding of a linear deterministic form of utilisation and policy-making as an *authoritative choice*. He argues that even evidence that fits with the interests of the powerful groups may not be used if the political conditions are not favourable. In other words, Monaghan refutes that policies move towards a fixed point, *evidence-based* or not.

Based on a case-study of the (re)classification of cannabis in the UK, Monaghan (2011) tentatively advocated a synthesis of the *enlightenment* and *evolutionary* models. Drawing on the evolutionary model, the processual model shares the approach of the selection mechanisms (Stevens, 2007b). However, it does not support the deterministic view of utilisation focussing on the outcome of policy formulation. Instead, as this model accepts that evidence is not the only player in the policy-making process and that the policy process is of an ad hoc, back and forth nature, with multiple groups interacting and competing in shaping policy (policy-making as *structured interaction*; see below), the model can be thought of as related to the *enlightenment* model (Monaghan, 2009; Ingold & Monaghan, 2016). Additionally, the processual model also provides a more nuanced account of the nature of evidence. It is put forward that the concept of evidence itself must be seen as contested and in a constant state of flux. Taking each of these considerations into account, the science-policy nexus in a heavily politicised policy area is described as uncertain and unpredictable.

Evidence-Based Policy (EBP) and its Challenges

In more recent years, the expectations for the influence of scientific knowledge on policy development or change have been consolidated under the banner of *evidence-based* policy and practice. The *evidence-based* policy concept is actually derived from the 1970s *evidence-based medicine* framework, the philosophical origins of which go back to the mid-nineteenth century (Reimer, Sawka, & James, 2005). *Evidence-based medicine* (*EBM*) includes the thoughtful integration of the best available evidence coupled with best practices of medical expertise. This original framework gained prominence as the *what works* approach (Sackett, Rosenberg, Gray, Haynes, & Richardson, 1996; Marston & Watts, 2003; Behague, Tawiah, Rosato, Some, & Morrison, 2009). Gradually, this approach has also been advocated for and adopted in other fields of professional activity, such as nursing, social work, probation, human resource management, education, and substance abuse treatment (*evidence-based practice*) (Miller, Sorensen, Selzer, & Brigham, 2006; Santisteban, Vega, & Suarez-Morales, 2006; Jack et al., 2011).

Since the late 1990s, the focus changed from *evidence-based practice* to evidence's influence in non-clinical arenas, such as public policy. A prominent role has been played by the UK New Labour government's commitment to *evidence-based* policy-making as a key part of its strategy of 'Modernization through managerialization' in 1997 (Monaghan, 2011). From then onwards, the popular label *evidence-based* policy has strongly influenced the discourse on the relationship between science and policy. In the twenty-first century, the ideal of *evidence-based* policy became a global movement and has also been echoed in other countries such as Australia, the USA, and Belgium (Federal Government, 2001; Rudd 2008; Obama, 2009). Davies (2004) defined *evidence-based* policy as "an approach that helps people make well-informed decisions about policies, programmes and projects by putting the best available evidence from research at the heart of policy development and implementation" (p. 3). Marston and Watts (2003) suggested that the concept of *evidence-based* policy is "a powerful metaphor in shaping what forms of knowledge are considered closest to the 'truth' in decision-making processes" (p. 145). This distinguishes it from policy governed by intuitive appeal, tradition, or politics (O'Dwyer, 2004).

The growing interest in the area of *evidence-based* policy led to several additions to the literature. The interface between policy and knowledge has been studied in social, economic, and environmental policy domains (Carden, 2004; Hoppe, 2009), criminal (juvenile) justice policy (Brereton, 1996; Marston & Watts, 2003; Petersilia, 2008; Freiberg & Carson, 2010; Devroe, 2010; Vande Walle, 2010), and migration policy (Brans et al., 2004; Scholten, 2011). Drug policy has also gradually shared these tendencies, especially in the UK, Australia, and Canada (Berridge, 2002; Musto & Sloboda, 2003; Lenton & Allsop, 2010; Macleod & Hickman, 2010; Hughes & Stevens, 2012; Stevens & Measham, 2014).

The goal of basing a policy on scientific knowledge is to eliminate decisions based on bias or arbitrary grounds (Montuschi, 2009). But despite its popular appeal, several critics have countered the notion of *evidence-based* policy-making. First, a common critique has been that the EBP account assumes a linear, rational connection between science and policy while, in fact, it is far more complex, and involves actors outside the domain of evidence and policy. In particular, the EBP paradigm ignores the realities of policy-making (such as e.g. parliamentary terms and timetables, and policy-making procedures) and the scientific community. Policy-makers are not always able to act rationally, a foundational concept in EBP (Head, 2010). The decisions they have to make are often more complex and affected by institutional, cultural, or political factors (Hammersley, 2013). At the same time, researchers do not always communicate their findings clearly or prefer to remain distant from public debates (Head, 2010). Taking these criticisms into account, some authors have advocated replacing the *evidence-based* ideal with softer approaches such as *evidence-informed*, *evidence-aware*, *evidence-influenced*, or *evidence-inspired* to underline a more reasonable view of the science-policy nexus (Sanderson, 2009; Hammersley, 2013). This reassessment of EBP concludes that evidence can *inform* policy rather than constitute a foundation for policy-makers (Head, 2010). However, some advocates of this more pragmatic position caution of the risk of undermining efforts for stronger use of scientific knowledge in the policy-making process (Sanderson, 2009).

Second, what constitutes *best evidence* is based on the assumption that some types of research provide more and better scientific knowledge than others (*evidence hierarchy*) (Nelen, 2008, 2010a; Hammersley, 2013). Emerging as it has from *evidence-based* medicine, the concept of *evidence-based* policy assumes that policy-makers are generally best served by studies that use *experimental and quasi-experimental research designs* with good measures (randomised control trials – RCT). A softer variant is the claim that a better understanding may emerge from *systematic reviews*. Some hierarchies place this type above RCTs, as these often combine data from multiple RCTs (Pawson, 2006; Head, 2010). Systematic reviews (Farrington, 2006; Devroe et al., 2008; Freiberg & Carson, 2010; McNeill, Farrall, Lightowler, & Maruna, 2012) can be particularly well used because they are a high-level overview of the best available evidence about the effectiveness of policy and programmes ('what matters is what works'). Organisations such as the *Campbell Collaboration* (C2) have been developed with this in mind.[1] With this emphasis on evaluation, innovative strategies to *mandate* the use of this type of evidence have been adopted recently: for example, some applicants for federal programme funds in the USA are required to show that their programme has been scientifically evaluated and proved successful (Weiss, Murphy-Graham, Petrosino, & Gandhi, 2008).

While experimental trials and systematic reviews have been and continue to be perceived as providing reliable sources of evidence, some forms of scientific research as well as knowledge derived from practitioners' experiences are automatically portrayed as unsystematic and lacking rigor. Although controlled studies and systematic reviews might be useful in evaluating a given intervention or policy and such research is increasingly popular in the social research field, too many policy questions cannot be answered with this approach (Burssens, 2008; Clear, 2010). For instance, like other criminological topics, drug use is a complex phenomenon that cannot be studied and fully understood using only (quasi-)experimental designs or systematic reviews (Kraus & Korf, 2005). These methods disregard the context or sociological meaning of a finding (Stevens, 2011). For instance, qualitative research and expert opinions are required to analyse how different drug policies create, recreate, and reinforce social inequality and power structures (Snertingdal & Basberg Neuman, 2010).

Furthermore, the notion of *evidence-based* policy-making, with the centrality of its evidence hierarchy, can be perceived as a kind of reaffirmation of the positivist view (Marston & Watts, 2003; Naughton, 2005; Hammersley, 2013). Lancaster (2014, 2016) questioned the fixed and stable premise of *evidence-based* policy endeavour, suggesting that the concepts of evidence and thus *evidence-based* policy are always social constructs. From the postmodernist or social constructivist point of view in social research, social reality can never be objectively known. It is argued that the concept of evidence is more contested than it appears: it often fails to cumulate systematically resulting in fragmented data or yields contradictory or otherwise untrustworthy findings (Naughton, 2005; Weiss et al., 2008; Monaghan, 2008b). Formulating conclusions or setting operational goals in research will always remain a somewhat uncertain task (Fountain & Korf, 2007; Burssens, 2008). Thus, a strong research base with rigorous findings is simply not viable in many areas (Head, 2010).

The *Evidence* Movement and Public Scholarship

There is a long-standing tradition of interest in public scholarship (Carrier, 2014; Carlen, 2011). Against the backdrop of the evidence movement, social scientists again became more and more concerned with the nature of their own commitment to the policy-making process (Van Swaaningen, 2009). According to Wacquant (2011), the new engagement with publics outside of the academy is simply a variation on the time-honoured question of the relationship between social knowledge and public action. Braithwaite (2005) termed this connection between the evidence movement and public scholarship *public social science*. However, it was sociology as a discipline that played a pioneering role in the recent rise of the debate on public scholarship. In particular, Michael Burawoy (2005) championed initiatives to give sociology a public voice. A public sociology has to translate scientific knowledge to other arenas (e.g. public, policy-makers, and professionals) to establish a dialectical relationship. On the one hand, it allows a scientist to contribute to public and political discussions, while, on the other hand, scientists can learn from the experiences of their public to broaden their insights and ideas about social phenomena. However, it is assumed that public sociology is but one of four different types of sociology that also include: *professional sociology* (i.e. focus is on academic peers and producing/discussing academic knowledge and theoretical paradigms; instrumental knowledge), *policy sociology* (i.e. focus is on serving clients in solving a problem, mostly involving a contract), and *critical sociology* (i.e. focus is on examining the fundamental assumptions of the professional approach; reflexive knowledge). Professional and critical sociology focus on an academic audience while policy and public sociology have an extra-academic audience. Nevertheless, the distinctions made are less straightforward than they have been portrayed: scientists can belong to more than one type and they may change their approach during their career (Niemeijer, 2009; Loader & Sparks, 2010). Indeed, Burawoy's typology has incited much criticism. For instance, critics feared that the discipline of sociology was being diminished by the contaminations of the public/policy side. At the same time, it has been argued that all engaged in sociology ought to be critical, as this is a core element of professionalism (Ericson, 2005). This thinking was incorporated into debates across different social science disciplines. However, while the understanding of 'public sociology' as defined by Burawoy is that he advocates that sociologists should contribute to broad public debates, engaging in dialogue as part of a pluralist democratic polity, criminologists have adopted a narrower stance articulating the idea that criminology's purpose is to contribute to a 'better' politics of crime and its regulation (Wacquant, 2011; Loader & Sparks, 2011). In particular, most reflections on public criminology focus primarily on the discipline's contribution to the policy-making process (as an exception, Fichtelberg & Kupchik (2011) have studied the discipline's contribution to the public opinion at-large). This focus is of particular interest when studying the science-policy nexus.

The Rise of 'Public Criminology'

The current public criminology debate is not entirely new but rather reinvigorated several older debates. First of all, criminological research does not take place in a political vacuum; it has always found itself in close proximity to the state and its political needs (Walters, 2003; Garland, 2011; Bauwens, De Koster, Enhus, & Evenepoel, 2013). The relationship between *knowledge and power* has explicitly been studied in the work of Michel Foucault.[2] In the later work of Michel Foucault (*genealogy*), the government is understood to be not simply a political institution but rather a form of activity aiming to shape, guide, or affect the conduct of some person or persons (Gordon, 1991). The criteria of what constitutes knowledge, what is to be excluded, and who is designated as qualified to know, involves acts of power. For instance, the selective management of scientific knowledge in the government is a vital component in the manufacture of legitimate authority (Naughton, 2005; Foucault, 1972). Researchers form part of the regime of power/knowledge/truth for each society, because they constitute the space that produces, reproduces, legitimates, and disseminates knowledge/discourse approved as true. Influenced by this work, authors such as Garland (2001),[3] Walters (2003), and Moore (2008) supported the concept of *deviant knowledge* to make a distinction between knowledge upheld as sophisticated, relevant, and useful, and knowledge upheld as marginalised, neutralised, and disregarded by policy-makers. Thus, deviant knowledge refers to knowledge that is critical of the state crime-control apparatus or challenges the existing social and political order (Walters, 2003). As a result, these types of knowledge may be systematically neutralised or marginalised by social controls/ powers (e.g. state controlled research institutions or funds). In other words, it is suggested that policy-makers may use techniques of neutralisation to rationalise their position choosing to neglect or dismiss findings which do not support their political agenda (see also above). These techniques can be contextualised within political frameworks (macro-level) and within day-to-day problems that researchers endure (micro-level). They include the politics of winning grants and contracts; restricted and proceduralised access to information; negotiating and bargaining for independence; the use of contracts to legalise control and restrict academic freedom; censorship of written work; and failure to publicly release research findings (Walters, 2003).

Second, the debate about public engagement is associated with a heating up of the public and media discourse in relation to crime in recent years. Media are accused of failing to provide the public with objective and complete accounts of criminality and of distorting policy-makers' understanding of the direction of public opinion (Green, 2008). Barak's (1988) call for a *newsmaking criminology* aimed to encourage criminologists to share their knowledge with the general public through the media, to increase the public's exposure to overlooked crime topics, alternative perspectives on existing problems, and informing and altering the discourses of crime, justice, and punishment to influence the shape of policy (Barak, 1988; McLaughlin & Muncie, 2013). Within this framework, Groombridge (2007) argued that "if criminologists don't do criminology in public – which means the media now – then the media will do it for them" (p. 473). Likewise, Henry and Milovanovic (1996) argued that criminologists must use media to ensure maximum impact of scientific knowledge on policy development. Criminologists can do this by "actively challenging silences, identifying omissions and resurrecting the eliminated through participating in the making news stories about crime" (p. 216). According to Barak (2007) criminologists may take four roles: as an expert, as a crime reporter or journalist, as a subject, or as a critic towards media representations. The concept of public criminology goes beyond the traditional concerns with the role of media, but this point may raise questions about the public role of scientists as well as the role of the media in the science-policy nexus.

While these issues show how interest in the public roles of criminology gradually developed, the concept of *public criminology* was first coined by Carrabine, Lee, and South (2000) – thus prior to Burawoy's intervention – and increasingly emerged around 2007. Multiple calls have been launched since arguing that, as criminology flourished in the academy, its influence on policy development as well as on public knowledge about realities of crime and justice seemed to be decreasing (Garland & Sparks, 2000; Currie, 2007; Chancer & McLaughlin, 2007; Tonry, 2010; Loader & Sparks, 2011). In other words, "in times as ours when 'crime talk' flourishes, its voice seems – somehow, somewhere – to get lost" (Daems, 2008; p. 241). Loader & Sparks (2011) defined this situation as a *successful failure*. Some have argued that this marginalised role, in times when the need for criminological insight and understanding has become more and more urgent, is the result of both the diverse (pluralist) nature of the perspectives that criminologists have to offer and the lack of methodological rigour. In particular, a wide range of perspectives are represented in the field, as criminologists do not necessarily share a common language or theoretical perspective (Garland, 2011). This makes criminology rather vulnerable in a world of political scepticism (Dixon, 1995; Rock, 2010). Furthermore, Chancer and McLauglin (2007) argued that criminological issues are often linked with electoral themes and therefore mediated and contested by a range of actors. For instance, an atmosphere of 'penal populism' (Bottoms, 1995) and 'totemic toughness' (Stevens, 2011) has tended to pervade much public debate in this area. Here, a 'tough on crime' rhetoric trumps other kinds of argument and persuasion. In such an atmosphere, as various scholars have noted, it is very difficult for rational debate to occur (MacGregor, 2011, 2013; Monaghan, 2011; Stevens, 2011). In addition, findings that are contradictory or out of touch with the needs of policy-makers may lead to confusion or so-called *endarkenment* (as opposed to *enlightenment*) (Weiss, 1986). From the perspective of the scientific community, Currie (2007) pointed to the increasing pressure to publish in peer-reviewed journals at the expense of efforts to disseminate findings towards a non-academic public. Thus, in many ways, it is understandable that criminological research has struggled to impact on criminal justice policy.

Types of Public Engagement in the Policy-Making Process

Taking these issues into account, numerous debates have taken place exploring, defining, and addressing the varying roles criminologists may choose or have chosen to play in public work (Daems, 2008; Uggen & Inderbitzin, 2010; Tonry, 2010; Monaghan, 2014). Criminologists strongly differ in their opinions on public engagement, which range from a total absence from the public domain, the recognition of a dual role (being a participant in public and political debates as well as an independent producer of scientific knowledge), to positions as public intellectuals (Deflem, 2005; Chancer & McLaughlin, 2007; De Haan, 2008; Bauwens et al., 2013). In other words, some supporters of *public criminology* say that criminologists, with an independent, academic agenda (i.e. not influenced by political statements or election programmes), must become better at communicating findings to external audiences to overcome false representations in public and policy (Currie, 2007; Carrabine, Iganski, Lee, Plummer, & South, 2009), whereas others advocate a strategic call for action which involves, for example, building up networks with policy-makers or journalists.

The latter school of thought is strongly criticised by those who believe that public criminology can be considered as an implicit call for a stronger embedded criminology, in which social scientists tend to conform to the realities of power and generally accept the definitions of politicians as to what constitutes the most serious social problems (rather than a focus on independent scientific progress). For instance, Allen (2007), De Haan (2008), and Van Swaaningen (2009) warned that, in recent decades, criminologists have become increasingly bound to the state as a result of restructuring of research funding. They argued that, from the early 1980s onwards, most social research has been conducted under contract to government departments and moulded to the needs or priorities of the funders to focus on facts (rather than theoretical insights) and questions about *what works* (instead of *how it works*). Likewise, Walgrave (2008) stated that:

> Criminologists must be aware that governments use criminology as a menu. They choose what best satisfies their political hunger. They select out, or manipulate through selective financing, what they can use to support political options chosen beforehand. Very often, it is not criminology that is orienting policy, but policy that is orienting and canalizing criminology.
>
> (p. 3)

The most outspoken critic of public sociology (and thus public criminology) is Prof. Dr. Mathieu Deflem. He criticised the idea heavily by means of comparing it with a Marxist sociology oriented towards politics rather than science. The danger, as he stated, is sociology turning into political activism (Deflem, 2005).

This debate has further been animated by the publication of a book entitled *Public Criminology?* (Loader & Sparks, 2011) and its reviews (Wacquant, 2011; Daems, 2011; Hammersley, 2013). Loader and Sparks (2011) avoided the debate between advocates or opponents by means of reflecting on the *sociology of criminological engagement*. They offered a subjective typology of modes of engagement (Table 2.3) comprising three *cool* types (the *scientific expert*, the *policy advisor*, and the *observer-turned-player*) and two *hot* types (*the social movement theorist/activist* and the *lonely prophet*) (Wacquant, 2011). Daems (2011) classified this as a distinction between *airco-criminologists* and *pyro-criminologists*.

Loader and Sparks (2011) further argued that each of these types of engagement allows simultaneous memberships of both groups: policy-makers and scientists. At the same time, it is acknowledged that one researcher may adopt different roles through his/her career. Their thinking about criminological engagement ended with the introduction of the concept of *democratic underlabouring*. This refers to an acknowledgement that in a democracy, criminological knowledge should compete with other discourses (as a participant in the policy-making process) but does not

Table 2.3 Typology of Modes of Criminological Engagement

Types	*Description*
Scientific expert	The scientific expert focuses on production and dissemination of scientific knowledge and does not go beyond infrequent participation in formal advisory structures. The scientific expert uses knowledge and methodological skills to answer questions of policy-makers in a nuanced and well-considered way
Policy advisor	The policy advisor does a great part of their research on (short-term) contracts for the government, and perceives it as a responsibility to bring scientific knowledge to policy-makers through formal advisory structures or even informal contacts (behind the public scenes)
Observer-turned-player	The observer-turned player takes up the opportunity to participate directly in development of policy (e.g. as a representative of a Minister). This type is colloquially described as an expert who is getting his or her hands 'dirty'
Social movement theorist	The social movement theorist colloquially supports a critical/alternative discourse placing knowledge and skills at the service of those who are marginalised. This type does not go beyond infrequent participation in formal advisory structures
Lonely prophet	The lonely prophet focuses on theoretical engagement and the big picture while philosophising about social changes and movements. This type also does not go beyond infrequent participation in formal advisory structures

Source: adapted from Loader and Sparks (2011).

have the automatic right to guide policy. A more modest view with respect to the rules of politics and competition is supported. *Public criminology*, then, provides an articulation of the idea that criminology's purpose is to contribute to a 'better' politics of crime and its regulation (Loader & Sparks, 2011; Tonry, 2010).

Notwithstanding the reference to criminology in their title, Loader and Sparks (2011) provided a useful account of the general engagements between (social) science and the policy-making process, especially in relation to this book. However, as a general comment on their work, even though Loader and Sparks acknowledged that scientific knowledge may be just one of many elements in the policy-making process, they focus on individual actors while ignoring the more fundamental institutional issues of the policy-making process (e.g. how policy is made) and scientific community (e.g. managerial make-up of the university, and the overt and covert intrusion of the concerns of politicians) (Wacquant, 2011). Furthermore, they lacked any reflection on how academics perceive and manage the relationship between their academic activities and policy-making. Academics also often seem to rely on extra-scientific means of persuasion which can jeopardise their credibility (Daems, 2008). According to Uggen and Inderbitzin (2010), it is important to be aware of *airport criminologists*. These scientists, public scholars in particular, fly around as consultants and experts while losing sight of their scientific knowledge base (e.g. by means of misrepresenting their expertise). As such, providing accurate information may prove to be a challenge (Lackey, 2007). Finally, it also has been argued that Loader and Sparks omit, for reasons that are not clear, the position of the uninterested academic who is not willing to be involved in politics (Downes, Rock, & McLaughlin, 2016).

While the literature on 'public criminology' continues to grow, numerous commentaries have explored, defined, and addressed the varying roles criminologists may choose or have chosen to play when translating their work to significant publics. Yet the fruits of these labours is often under analysed. Whether and how public engagement meaningfully impacts upon and shapes knowledge utilisation in policy-making and whether it stands any chance of producing 'better' politics, has rarely been empirically tested (for an exception, see Drake & Walters, 2015). This book takes up the first challenge here.

International Perspectives on the Research-Policy Relationship: Knowledge Utilisation and its Barriers and Facilitators

Understanding knowledge utilisation is difficult: it is a complex task to demonstrate how outputs such as scientific knowledge affect outcomes and policy impacts (Rich, 1997). Assessments are difficult because of the multiplicity of actors and the dynamics of policy processes (Ritter and Lancaster, 2013). Empirical studies also often use different terms to refer to similar concepts (e.g. the notions knowledge/policy, science/policy, or research/policy are used as interchangeable concepts) (Berridge & Stanton, 1999; Bekkers, Fenger, Homburg, & Putters, 2004) or a distinction between basic[4] and applied research is often not made (Weiss, 2001; Smith, 2010). Methodologically, the measurement and specification of use (e.g. utilisation as outcome versus utilisation as process) and the checklists of variables (e.g. research products, policy contextual factors, dissemination and links between researchers and policy-makers) are diffuse. At the same time, some studies focus on particular research or research programmes while others take a policy on a particular topic or a particular policy measure to assess knowledge utilisation. Finally, there is a predominance of Anglo-Saxon examples (e.g. USA, Canada, Australia, and the UK), which suggests that extrapolation of these results to another country or policy domain is limited (e.g. because of the differences in political system or the sensitivities of the matter) (Tonry, 2010; Hyder et al., 2011; El-Jardall et al., 2012; Hantrais, Lenihan, & MacGregor, 2015).

Knowledge Utilisation

Empirical studies measuring the use of knowledge in policy-making in a particular policy domain at the local or national level operationalised Weiss' knowledge utilisation typology by developing a three-fold classification system distinguishing the *instrumental model*, the *political/symbolic model*, and the *enlightenment model* (Lester, 1993; Chan, 1995; Brereton, 1996; Rich, 1997; Oh, 1997; Sorian & Baugh, 2002; Hanney et al., 2003; Amara et al., 2004; Smet, 2013; Stevens, 2011; Monaghan, 2008a; Head, 2010; Freiberg & Carson, 2010).

Most empirical studies conclude that *conceptual* use is more common than *political/symbolic* utilisation, with instrumental use found less frequently (Chan, 1995; Brereton, 1996; Weiss et al., 2008; Bak Jørgensen, 2011). For instance, Chan (1995) pointed to Braithwaite's 'reintegrative shaming theory' which has been adopted in pre-trial programmes aimed at diverting juvenile offenders as an example of the enlightenment function. Furthermore, Marston and Watts (2003), analysing the use of research evidence in criminal (juvenile) justice policy, pointed to the risk that *evidence-based* policy becomes a means for policy elites to increase their strategic control (*political/symbolic* model). They concluded that the (often causal) assumptions of juvenile justice research preclude what might be considered a reasonable *evidence-based* approach to policy-making.

An overview of the existing literature on knowledge utilisation in the drug field indicates that the science-policy nexus is at least as complicated as in other domains – for example other studies regarding the environment, the family, and education point to equally contested matters. Given that debate in the drug policy field is often contested, part of a heated controversy or subject to rapid change, the notion of *evidence-based* policy was soon labelled as having less relevance (MacGregor, 2013). Except from a limited number of examples of direct use of knowledge (e.g. an epidemiological study, published in 1950, that demonstrated the connection between the rise in lung cancer and the habit of smoking eventually led to a new policy agenda for smoking almost 50 years later; Edwards, Strang, & Jaffe, 1993) and conceptual knowledge utilisation (e.g. Hall (2008) argued that evidence has produced slow changes over three decades in conceptual understandings of cannabis use in Australia), international studies showed that *political/symbolic* use of scientific knowledge appears highly prevalent in this policy area (Griffiths & McKetin, 2005; Room, 2005; Fitzgerald, 2005; Stevens, 2007b; Hall, 2008; Monaghan, 2009; Bennett and Holloway, 2010; MacGregor, 2013). Instead of a strictly rational relationship between research and policy, it is assumed that *evidence-based* arguments are more likely to be used as weapons in emotive debates (Head, 2010). In particular, drug policy carries great symbolic value as research findings may become elements in value-based arguments (Ritter, 2009; Room, 2005; Fitzgerald, 2005). In this context, Wodak (2008) stated that "in drug policy, what is effective is often unpopular while what is popular is often ineffective" (p. 227). For instance, research by Hughes (2007, 2009), assessing the role of evidence in the development and implementation of the Illicit Drug Diversion Initiative (IDDI) in Australia, showed that while policy-makers were supportive of the IDDI as a pragmatic response to drug users, they contend that implementation has suffered through a selective and variable emphasis on scientific knowledge. Wood, Kerr, Tyndall, and Montaner (2008) also concluded that ideology triumphed over evidence: the Federal Government disregarded the recommendations derived from a scientific evaluation about injecting facilities. Storbjörk (2014) argued that scientific knowledge was selectively used to support arguments both in favour of and opposing the reform of the Swedish substance abuse treatment system, in line with the findings above.

The *misuse of data* also came through. For instance, Rossi (2002) critically analysed a drug report of the United Nations Drug Control Programme. Apparently, the data taken from several publications was misinterpreted (Rossi, 2002). Similarly, Olsson (2009) critically reviewed an UNODC report by evaluating the empirical facts referred to and the main conclusions drawn about the success of the Swedish drug policy. He concluded that the scientific basis behind the report was flimsy, if it existed at all. For instance, prevalence data were presented without distinguishing among medical, experimental, occasional, and problematic use. The UNODC report also claimed that the Swedish drug policy caused a decrease in drug use. Other alternative explanations, such as employment rates and health consciousness, were not even analysed. Serving as another example, Griffiths and McKetin (2005) described some common misuses of epidemiological research about drug use. Two of the most common misuses reported were generalising from a non-representative sample (e.g. when researchers generalise from clinical or jail samples) and measuring one thing and generalising to another (e.g. when researchers confuse the epidemiology of drug use with the epidemiology of drug abuse). Equally, Hughes and Stevens (2012) highlighted the misuse of evidence in the case of the Portuguese decriminalisation. They concluded that divergent policy conclusions were derived from selective use of epidemiological data, which belied the largely positive implications of the Portuguese decriminalisation of illicit drugs.

In light of the *political/symbolic* model, one study also revealed another challenger of knowledge utilisation (and *evidence-based* policy-making) in the drug policy field. Reflecting on the debate about the classification of ecstasy in the UK, Monaghan, Pawson, and Wicker (2012) illustrated that scientific knowledge is sometimes side-stepped by policy-makers playing the *card of precaution* to postpone action. The precautionary principle, a complex question, particularly for politics in 'risk societies', entails that no full scientific knowledge is needed to make policy decisions; scientific indications (in the absence of scientific consensus) are considered sufficient (Franklin, 1998; Gelev, 2009). When a policy-maker is faced with a multiplicity of information and finds it difficult to identify the appropriate options for their particular situation, there is a tendency to invoke the precautionary principle (Singleton, Stevens, Ochoa, & Feilding, 2014).

Accordingly, rational frameworks of policy-making (*evidence-based* policy-making) were devalued in favour of assumptions on the power relationships and interactions/networks between various players in the policy-making process (*evolutionary* model–*processual* model; Stevens, 2007a; Monaghan, 2011). In a similar vein, in the drug policy field, discussion arose over the definition of scientific knowledge. How policy-makers perceive scientific knowledge may itself be politically loaded (Monaghan, 2011; Stevens, 2011). As a result, points of view, whereby the policy-making process is considered an *un-evidenced-based mess*, are often adopted in the drug policy domain (Monaghan, 2008b).

Barriers and Facilitators Regarding the Science-Policy Nexus

Following along the lines of the earliest paradigm concerning the science-policy nexus, the *two communities* thesis (Caplan, 1979), thoughts have been raised about how to bridge the gap between both (Lomas, 2000). In underpinning the several challenges of the rhetoric of *evidence-based* (drug) policies, the obstacles to interactions between research and policy in the field of drugs and elsewhere are often classified into three categories:

facilitators/barriers related to policy-makers or the policy-making context; facilitators/barriers related to research(ers); and facilitators/barriers in the links between those two.

Facilitators/Barriers for Policy-makers

Several systematic reviews highlight barriers for policy-makers to the use of scientific knowledge, such as limited budgets (e.g. economic context); timing mismatch (i.e. scientific research can take years to complete whereas policy issues often rise rapidly to the top of the political agenda); and the level and complexity of the policy-making process (Oliver, Innvar, Lorenc, Woodman, & Thomas, 2014; Embrett & Randall, 2014). From the perspective of the policy-makers, research findings are but one contributory source that is filtered into policy-making (Weiss & Bucuvalas, 1980; Ritter, 2009). Policy-makers take into account the rules of the game of which they are at least partially aware (Stevens, 2011).

Other powerful, legitimate elements are at the table too. For instance, policy-makers need to deal with the values and opinions of political parties (e.g. some parties, especially liberal and socio-democratic, seem to be more devoted to the value of scientific knowledge than others (Devroe, 2002)); the characteristics of the policy system (e.g. single-party system, two-party system, or multi-party system; government party versus opposition); political climate (e.g. moral panic and *windows of opportunity*); elections; affected stakeholders; and the general public (Wagner, Weiss, Wittrock, & Wollmann, 1991; Kingdon, 2002; Lenton, 2004; Bowen & Zwi, 2005; Mitton, Adair, McKenzie, Patten, & Perry, 2007; Ritter, Bammer, Hamilton, & Mazerolle, 2007; Huston, 2008; Klein Haarhuis, Hagen, & Scheepmaker, 2009). Each of these elements may determine how a social problem is constructed, how questions are asked, what answers are expected, and if or how scientific knowledge plays a role (Berridge, 2002; Hartnoll, 2004). For instance, a multi-party system seems to stimulate more knowledge utilisation than a single or two-party system (Weiss, 1999) and findings that fit with ideology and party interests are more likely to be used (Nutley et al., 2007). The same barriers can be applied to the drug field (Berridge & Thom, 1996; Muscat, 2008). For instance, in the case of treatment of heroin dependence (1990–2001) in Australia, Hall (2004) noted that research had a mixed impact on policy as the interface between research and policy depended on policy-maker interest and the availability of funding.

Next to *organisational* and *political factors*, the preparedness of the *individual policy-maker* to use research results, his/her prior knowledge, experience and beliefs are also crucial (Lavis, Robertson, Woodside, McLeod, & Abelson, 2003). This so-called *tacit* knowledge is knowledge acquired by individuals implicitly, through performing personal and professional activities (Smet, 2013; Richardson, 2013). For instance, policy-makers with more education and experience of research will be more in favour of using research.

Facilitators/Barriers for Researchers

Research contexts also shape the uptake of research. From the researcher's perspective, a barrier is the dissonance between what is rewarded within the academic community and what is valued by policy-makers (Nutley et al., 2007; Ritter, 2009). As writing policy-oriented briefings is not recognised as valuable work within the academic world, many academics argue that dissemination and engagement with policy-makers is not their role. For instance, a study by Landry, Amara, and Lamari (1999) found that nearly 50 per cent of the Canadian scholars in social science reported that they usually or always transmit their research findings to policy-makers and practitioners. However, because of increased research funding, there is a growing pressure to produce policy-relevant research. Stronger attachment to the commissioning authorities may diminish the independent capacity of academia to provide a space in which innovative ideas can be developed (Smith, 2010).

Next to the *systemic characteristics in which researchers work*, most common complaints are related to the *characteristics of scientific knowledge*: unresponsiveness to policy-makers' needs (e.g. research findings may not be relevant enough for practice-based issues and policy-makers prefer to use findings from the accepted body of knowledge over new, recent findings (Weiss et al., 2008)); fragmented data; the academic format of communication (e.g. concise and jargon-free communication is preferred; actionable messages are preferable to long research reports); and evidence that fails to cumulate or yields contradictory findings (an ongoing source of frustration for some policy-makers) (Lavis et al., 2003; Weiss et al., 2008; Wood et al., 2008; Bennett and Holloway, 2010). For instance, in the study by Sorian and Baugh (2002), policy-makers estimated that 49 per cent of the information they receive is not relevant to their current work. Furthermore, in his commentary from a drug policy-maker's perspective, Gregrich (2003), in his position as Chief of the Treatment Branch (Office of National Drug Control Policy) pointed to a number of issues that limit the usefulness of researchers' work. One of the issues relates to format. Format issues include the manner in which research reports are presented (e.g. language) and their often equivocal nature.

The presence of each of these barriers also depends on the social science discipline and research approach. According to Landry et al. (2001) the professional social sciences (social work, health, and employment) lend themselves to higher levels of utilisation than the disciplinary social sciences (economics, political science, sociology, criminology, and anthropology). The research approach (quantitative versus qualitative methodology) also plays a role (Rist, 1981). Even though qualitative research may contribute by means of determining the problem definition or identifying unintended consequences of decisions (Rist, 1981), politicians usually ask questions about the size of the problem and whether this is growing or not, so that prevalence and incidence values are the order of the day (Moore, 2008; Muscat, 2008). Reuter (1993) has pointed out that "for conscientious policy-makers dealing with drug problems at the national and local levels, prevalence estimation ought to be a fundamental element of sensible decision-making" (p. 167). The role of qualitative research in relation to drug policy is much more uncertain. Berridge and Stanton (1999) highlighted that policy interests may package a message from qualitative research but that qualitative research, by its very nature, is rarely so specific about guiding policy (Fountain, 2000; Denzin & Giardina, 2008). In accordance with what has been discussed above, within the *evidence-based* framework many believe that qualitative research does not count as research unless it is embedded in a randomised clinical trial (RCT) (Denzin & Giardina, 2008). In a similar vein, many authors have emphasised that systematic reviews of relevant evidence must be designed to ensure that policies and practices are informed by rigorous, transparent, up-to-date evaluations of relevant empirical evidence (Sorrell, 2007; Devroe, 2002).

Links between Researchers and Policy-makers

The links between researchers and policy-makers concern the way in which knowledge is disseminated and transmitted (*linking mechanisms*). Knowledge must be distributed from the producer to the policy-maker so that it can be used in making policy decisions (Webber, 1991; Elliott & Popay, 2000; Gregrich, 2003; Jacobson, Butteril, & Goering, 2003). A first element is to take into account the timeframes of both researchers and policy-makers. Research findings are not often presented to policy-makers at the times of greatest receptivity; the beginning of a legislature, budget development cycle, etc. Another critical element is the existence and power of effective linkage or boundary arrangements among researchers and policy-makers (Van Eijk & Hartkamp, 1992; Landry et al., 1999, 2001), in which strong (e.g. personal, long-term connection, and policy networks) and weak (e.g. media, working groups, conferences, and interest groups) links are distinguished (Wagner et al., 1991; Lampinen, 1992; Nutley et al., 2007; Weiss et al., 2008; Head, 2010). Referring to the latter (weaker) links, media or interest groups may be actively involved in underpinning future policy options with studies that criticise existing policy or suggest alternative policies. Strong factors related to the links between researchers and policy-makers include relationships of scientists with potential users of their research and the scientists' credibility (National Center for the Dissemination of Disability Research, 1996; Haynes et al., 2012). Policy-makers do not always have ready access to research results and they tend to accept guidance, information, and ideas from sources they know and trust. Accordingly, Hird (2009) and Haynes et al. (2012) emphasised the importance of a personal connection (i.e. to talk with each other) rather than focusing on written research. Duke (2001) and MacGregor (2013) also agreed that drug researchers should become more active agents in all stages of the policy process to stimulate the interplay between research and (drug) policy. Having long-standing relationships with key players inside and outside the policy-making process as well as participating in fora or committees are considered to be of great importance (Lenton, 2007; Lenton & Allsop, 2010). This is in accordance with the few studies that focus on how drug policy-makers get access to sources of research evidence in their drug policy-making, instead of on how policy is actually made in terms of interactions between evidence and policy (Bickford & Kothari, 2008; Ritter, 2009). The most popular way through which evidence accesses the policy-making process is by means of policy-makers seeking advice from an expert and consulting technical reports. It has been reported that the advantages of consulting an external expert include the speed with which the information can be obtained and the ability of an expert to synthesis the (often contrary) evidence. Consulting academic literature or relying on internal expertise or policy documents are the least commonly found approaches.

Policy-Making Processes: Government vs. Governance

While knowledge about the role of evidence in policy-making has increased in recent years with the rhetoric about *evidence-based* policies, theories on policy-making are by no means new. Policy-making is a complex undertaking with constituent parts and a variety of actors involved that must be examined. Numerous definitions attempt to cover the concept of *policy-making*. For instance, Howlett and Ramesh (1995) pointed to

> a complex phenomenon consisting of numerous decisions made by numerous individuals and organizations in government. These decisions are often shaped by earlier policies and frequently are linked closely with other seemingly unrelated decisions.
>
> (p. 3)

Kingdon (1995) defines this as a "set of processes, including at least the setting of an agenda, the specification of alternatives from which a choice is to be made, an authoritative choice among those specified alternatives and the implementation of a decision" (pp. 2–3). Although authors adopted different perspectives when defining policy-making, these definitions include the idea of a set of complex political processes or interactions of which the most crucial and final is the choice of a programme or solution to realise goals (Neilson, 2001). The complexity of the policy-making process refers to the different interests and diverse range of powerful players coming from different perspectives.

In the literature, some models conceptualise how the policy process works as well as the role that scientific knowledge might then play (Hanney et al., 2003). These models of policy-making may be useful for understanding how science and policy may connect (e.g. use may differ on how the policy-making process is structured) and are thus largely linked with the knowledge utilisation typologies (Nutley et al., 2007). Generally, these frameworks or narratives are grouped into three (overlapping) accounts (Neilson, 2001; Carden, 2004; Stone & Maxwell, 2005; Nutley et al., 2007; Monaghan, 2009; Stevens & Ritter, 2013) (Table 2.4).

The *rational or vertical approach* outlines policy-making as a problem-solving process which is rational, balanced, objective, and analytical. It assumes that policy-makers go through each logical stage of the process (agenda – alternatives – implementation – evaluation), and carefully consider all relevant knowledge (Sutton, 1999). It is also assumed that the authoritative policy *elites* (i.e. government officials) are the only actors involved, neglecting actors external to the policy-making process (e.g. media, interest groups). The role of the researcher is to research and present all of the policy options for policy-makers to encourage them to examine each of the options (Neilson, 2001). This common understanding of the way in which the policy-making process works is consistent with *evidence-based* policy thinking. However, this *speaking truth to power* approach is subject to substantive critique: it is perceived as too simplistic, mechanistic, and sequential for the process of both knowledge utilisation and policy-making which is, in reality, much more arbitrary and complex. In other words, *truth* is contingent and *power* is dispersed and mediated by a wider set of actors (Hird, 2009). Additionally, some authors characterise this belief in technocracy as naïve in its assumption that objective knowledge can be produced (Fraser & Moore, 2011).

Perceiving *policy-making as a narrative* directs attention towards processes of problematisation (e.g. how the problem was defined and understood? by whom?). Policy-making is seen as an arena where a variety of actors contest meaning, and scientific knowledge may contribute to the construction of the problem (Hajer, 1995; Bacchi, 2009; Fraser & Moore, 2011; Stevens & Ritter, 2013; Lancaster, 2014). Within this framework, it is considered that evidence itself is constituted in policy practice and the telling of policy stories (Lancaster, 2016). This model emphasises how language or discourse shapes the policy agenda (Roe, 1991). Centrality is not given to external events that cause policy

Table 2.4 Overview of Models of Policy-Making

Models of policy-making	*Description*
Authoritative choice (rational/vertical)	• Policy-makers as single actors confronting a problem ('government') • Scientific knowledge as instrumental • *Evidence-based* policy-making
Structured interaction (horizontal/pluralist/political)	• Multiple participants and diffuse authority in the policy-making process ('governance') • Focus on relationships and interactions • Influence scientific knowledge through participation in commissions or informal contacts
Narrative	• Processes of problematisation and social construction • Scientific knowledge is part of problem construction and framing

Source: adapted from Stevens and Ritter (2013).

change, but rather how these events are perceived. Using a policy narrative model may help to gain a deeper understanding of how policy is made and which discourses arise, compete, and emerge, but is less informative about the perceptions of policy-makers and/or scientists as to whether or not scientific knowledge is (not) used in the policy-making process, which is focus of this book (Neilson, 2001; Bak Jørgensen, 2011).

The *political/horizontal/pluralist* accounts offer another approach for exploring and explaining the science-policy nexus. These approaches perceive the policy-making process as more diffuse as it involves bargaining, conflicts, and negotiation, and the *dispersal of authority/power* through various spheres and levels of the political arena (e.g. in a country, policy-making is not restricted to the national level; regional and local government are also involved) (Monaghan, 2009). For instance, policy-making is not an authoritative process but a theatre in which a variety of actors interact with each other (Stevens & Ritter, 2013). Accordingly, decisions can be seen as the outcome of the interplay between diverse participants. Scientific knowledge is just one of the sources used by these multiple stakeholders. Focusing on interaction and allowing the input of a range of (internal and external) actors in the policy-making process, this approach has also been termed *governance*. A significant body of work on *drug policy governance* emerged from Australian researchers (e.g. Hughes, Ritter, & Mabbitt, 2013; Lancaster & Ritter, 2014), the UK Drug Policy Commission (UKDPC), and ALICE RAP research (Hughes et al., 2010; UKDPC, 2012; MacGregor et al., 2014; Duke & Thom, 2014). In contrast with the accepted view that drug policy-making is the prerogative of governments, the concept of 'governance' points, at the simplest level of distinction, to the growing influence of non-state actors in the policy-making process linking policy-makers to wider networks in a pluralistic and diverse civic society (Weiss, 2000; Sanderson, 2009; MacGregor et al., 2014). A framework of 'good governance' in the context of drug policy was outlined by UKDPC (2012) covering the following eight key elements: clearly articulated goals and objectives; *evidence-imbued* leadership; coordination of policy efforts; policy design that balances scientific evidence with other types of evidence and incorporates evaluation/feedback; development and use of an evidence base; attention to implementation based on sufficient financial resources; processes for accountability and scrutiny; and processes for stakeholder engagement. These issues may be critical to policy development or change including but not limited to the extent to which a policy is *evidence-informed* or not (Hughes, Ritter, & Cowdery, 2014). In this context, drug policy seems to be an area where particular challenges abound, not least because the polarised, mediatised debate around drug policy often prevents any open discussion (UKDPC, 2012).

The political/horizontal/pluralist approach can be seen as an umbrella term covering various views on the nature of policy-making (and knowledge utilisation): the incremental models which describe policy-making as a step-by-step, piecemeal, through trial-and-error process (Lindblom, 1959; Baumgartner & Jones, 1993); policy network models like the Advocacy Coalition Framework (Sabatier, 1998); and the Multiple Streams model (Kingdon, 2002) which seek to explain policy changes by means of, respectively, the presence of powerful and competing policy networks or the importance of context like political-climate, timing (e.g. when a policy *window of opportunity* opens). Inevitably, only a selection of the many theories of policy-making that scholars have advanced can be examined here. The pluralist theories that are discussed were selected because they are among the most prominent frameworks in the general literature. They also have the greatest potential for explaining drug-related policy decisions as evidenced by their application in drug-related studies (MacGregor, 2016).

Incremental Changes and Punctuated Equilibrium

Lindblom's *incrementalist model* (or the model of *mudding through*) is an early example of an alternative approach to the policy-making process (and knowledge utilisation) (Lindblom, 1959). Policy-making is seen as an interactive process as this approach compels actors to share their interests and views with each other. In an attempt to reduce uncertainty, conflict, and complexity, policy-makers take small incremental steps towards policy change (instead of fundamental, instrumental changes) (Neilson, 2001). In this respect, they tend to choose options that differ only marginally from existing policy (Sutton, 1999). Within this model, a greater role for (political) interest or values is acknowledged; scientific knowledge can be one of the many sources that influence policy-makers. As the conceptual as well as political/tactical uses of knowledge fit with this *muddling through* process, this interpretation of policy-making contrasts sharply with the EBP movement. There are, however, some limitations to this model (Monaghan, 2009). For instance, the incrementalist model does not explain how ideas are selected to be put on the agenda ('agenda setting'). As this model only focuses on small changes to policy, another critique is that it leaves researchers on the side-lines of the policy-making process ignoring any intense involvement of scientists in the policy-making process.

Lindblom's incrementalist model where decisions occur only in small increments, has a direct connection to the *punctuated equilibrium* theory of Baumgartner and Jones (1993). Consistent with the incrementalist argument, it is argued that large change is rare in a punctuated equilibrium process; policies spend most of the time in a period of stasis. However, consistent with the critics of incrementalism, the punctuated equilibrium model assumes that policies can also experience periods of dramatic change interrupting the periods of inattention and stasis. As such, Baumgartner and Jones (1993) put forward a way to resolve the dispute between incrementalists and their critics. The punctuated equilibrium theory predicts the incrementalist observation that large changes are rare while also predicting the existence of large changes in rare periods of punctuation.

Problems, Policy, and Politics

Kingdon presented the multiple streams or agenda setting model[5] (Kingdon, 2002; Bekkers et al., 2004; Devos, Rommel, Lannoo, Van Liefferinge, & De Wilde, 2010). While Kingdon's model has been criticised as lacking testability (Sabatier, 1999), it remains one of the most often cited and influential works in the policy field internationally, and provides one of the most accurate descriptions of the policy process. Kingdon's model focuses on the flow and timing of policy action. The strength of this approach is that it helps to analyse why and how some subjects and/or alternatives are considered for the policy agenda (Kingdon, 2002; Nilunger Mannheimer, Lehto, & Östlin, 2007). In particular, the stream model defines policy-making as the connection between three streams: the problem stream, the policy stream, and the political stream (Neilson, 2001; Brans et al., 2004).

The *problem stream* includes the process of problem recognition. Various factors may focus attention on a problem or issue of concern and its importance. In other words, it focuses on the political recognition of policy problems where problems come to the attention of policy-makers (Radaelli, 1995). The *political stream* comprises elements such as the national mood, organised political interests, and government through the influence by people, political parties, and political ideologies, and can either include or exclude certain issues from the agenda. The *policy stream* refers to the process of the presentation of ideas, generated by a policy community, and the development of alternatives. Proposals may be selected on the basis of criteria such as feasibility, harmonisation with dominant norms, and susceptibility of politicians. Participants such as scientists are not directly involved in just one of the three streams but can be involved in each of them. Thus, research must be completed for policy-makers to pay attention to their ideas, proposals, and solutions. Knowledge utilisation is rather unpredictable and may enter into policy-making from a variety of different sources.

The key to understanding agenda setting lies in the connection of the three streams. When this connection occurs, Kingdon spoke of the opening of a *window of opportunity* (Bekkers et al., 2004; Nilunger Mannheimer et al., 2007). Policy windows pass quickly and are missed if policy proposals have not already gone through a long process of '*softening up*' the system. At such moments, *policy entrepreneurs* (e.g. individuals championing a particular solution or intervention) may play a particular role in forging the connection. Sometimes a window closes when the problem is assessed as solved, or when there is a change in government. Because of its dynamic, unpredictable view of the policy-making process and knowledge utilisation, this model fits with the *enlightenment* model, in which scientific knowledge may gradually influence shifts in thinking or ideas (Nutley et al., 2007). A general drawback of this model is that little account is given to the actual minutiae of the policy-making process and, in particular, the conflict that occurs in the political arena (Monaghan, 2009). Additionally, as *windows of opportunities* for policy change open infrequently and briefly, the impact of research on policy needs to be evaluated over a long time period (Lenton, 2004).

Competing Interests – Ideology – Information

As one of the most accessible examples of the power, ideology, interest groups models,[6] Weiss (1999, 2001) developed an iterative model of policy-making about the influence of Ideology, Interests, and Information in policy-making. She acknowledged that as research findings move into the policy-making process, they are shaped by, and have to contend with competing beliefs and values (Lindquist, 2001). The distribution of power determines whose ideology, interests and information will be dominant. By *ideology* Weiss meant policy-makers' basic values, political orientation, or principles that underlie their approach. Policy-makers are expected to act in accordance with their political ideology, taking into account the organisation and context where policy-makers function. *Interests* reflect for the most part self-interests such as re-election and budget increases. *Information* may include research evidence, personal experiences, anecdotes, and media reportage. Scientific knowledge is just one type of information, competing with other types of information as well as ideology and interests (Weiss, 2001). The ways in which groups (including politicians, practitioners, and researchers) represent their membership, their relative power and influence are key to understanding the policy-making process. In sum, ideology and interests often stand in the way of scientific knowledge being influential (Weiss, 1999; Ritter & Bammer, 2010).

Policy Networks

Networks are considered an important means for enabling and encouraging knowledge and information sharing. Analysis of policy networks may be particularly useful as it illustrates how groups both influence the policy process and reflect the relative status and power of the various interests (Duke, 2003). In terms of knowledge utilisation, this model suggests that scientific involvement is important for knowledge utilisation as they may feed more directly into the policy-making process (Hanney et al., 2003).

The concept of a policy network is used as a label for the different types of involvement (see e.g. Heclo, 1978; Haas, 1992; Kingdon, 1995; Sabatier, 1998). They may be conceived as lying on a continuum differing in terms of level of integration, type of membership, and the role that scientists may play (Sutton, 1999; Neilson, 2001; Nutley et al., 2007). Nevertheless, a network approach fails to provide an account of why these networks form, how they change and how power is exercised, which is essential to advocacy and promoting evidence (Duke, 2003).

The Advocacy Coalition Framework (Sabatier, 1998) is one of the most widely discussed policy network theories. *Advocacy coalitions*, a concept based on the advocacy coalition framework (ACF) of Sabatier and Jenkins-Smith, consist of people (elected and agency officials, interest group leaders, researchers, and media) who share a set of basic values, causal assumptions, and problem perceptions (Sabatier, 1998). Looking at the cognitive biases of the different coalitions, coalitions are characterised by three belief systems: deep core, policy core, and secondary aspects. The *deep core* system comprises basic ontological and normative beliefs, the *policy core* is basic commitments and causal perceptions across the entire policy domain, and *secondary aspects* concerns narrowly held beliefs concerning the seriousness of the problem. Deep core beliefs are very resistant to change while secondary beliefs are most conducive to change. This model assumes that coalitions, presupposing an amount of coordinated activity from actors, seek power to translate their core beliefs into policy. Usually, two or four coalitions are part of the political system at any given time. According to this approach, policy change occurs through the interaction between wide external changes or shocks to the political system and the success of the ideas in the coalitions, which may cause actors in the advocacy coalitions to shift allegiances (John, 2003). Here, the goal of science may not be to directly influence policy but rather to improve the quality of the debate or evidence and introduce a shift in beliefs (which is partly linked with the *enlightenment* model) (Sabatier, 1998). The ACF is one of the most widely discussed policy theories, not least by those interested in the science-policy nexus (e.g. Kübler, 2001; Stevens, 2007b; Monaghan, 2011). While the model recognises scientists as players in the policy process and brings to the fore a consideration of the role of conflict and power, the model is mainly criticised because of its neglect of the social and historical context in which policy development or change occurs (Monaghan, 2011).

Roles of the Media and Interest Groups

The shared concepts found in the theoretical literature on policy processes help to clarify and explain why policy shifts do or do not occur. In a media sensitive and politically charged area, the policy process and knowledge utilisation within these processes are further complicated by means of the roles played by the media and interest groups (Lenton, 2004; Lancaster et al., 2011; Ritter & Lancaster, 2013). Given the central role of the media and interest groups in drug policy debates, this issue is of considerable importance for those who aim to better understand the complexity of the nexus.

Media and the Science-Policy Nexus

Debates on drug policies are never far from the media gaze, including newspapers, television, radio, as well as internet (McCombs & Reynolds, 2009; Lancaster et al., 2011). Existing studies on the influence of the media on the drug policy-making process have already highlighted a number of roles.

First, according to key media theories, the media can be perceived as a powerful player because of its ability to present issues through selection and salience, so called *framing*, and the ability to indirectly shape individual and community attitudes towards risk, known as *priming* (McCombs & Shaw, 1972; Lancaster et al., 2011). Thus the media can unintentionally, as a result of the characteristics of news production (e.g. limited space, driven by publicity and economic concerns), or strategically, make a significant contribution to how people think by influencing what they think about (Entman, 1989; Lancaster et al., 2011). For instance, several researchers have already argued that the media may fuel drug scares as well as increase curiosity about a new drug or stigmatise particular drug users (Goode & Ben-Yehuda, 1994; Lenton, 2007; Mosher & Akins, 2007; Taylor, 2008). The emergence of methamphetamine use and production in Canadian media provides one such example. Media coverage was found to have fuelled public fear and speculation by using terms such as *epidemic* and *plague* to describe the prevalence of this drug (Boyd & Carter, 2010).

Second, as policy-makers aim to understand what the public values and considers important, the media may also feed into political debate and policy-making (Scheufele & Tewksbury, 2007; McCombs & Reynolds, 2009). However, studies about the precise role of the media in *setting the political agenda* often yield contradictory results, as the influence of the media in political agenda-setting strongly depends on the type of issue covered, the specific media outlet, the kind of coverage, and the features of the political system at stake (Kingdon, 2002; Walgrave & Van Aelst, 2006). The role of the media in *shaping policy* is even more disputable (Chan, 1995). Nevertheless, some examples suggested that media may play a key role in precipitating policy change. They suggest that the media creates the news and provides images which can lead to widespread public panic (Goode & Ben-Yehuda, 1994). For instance, following media-generated panic, newly emerging psychoactive substances (such as mephedrone and so-called *legal highs*) shot to prominence in the political agenda in a matter of months, demanding action from the government. Eventually, this resulted in a change in the legal status of these substances in some countries (Bright, Bishop, Kane, Marsh, & Barratt, 2013; Lancaster, Hughes, Spicer, Matthew-Simmons, & Dillon, 2010; Van Hout & Brennan, 2011; Dabrowska & Bujalski, 2013).

Scientific knowledge is just one of the elements at work in the media. Although researchers have long been interested in the media's coverage of their field and individual work, the question of if and how *scientific knowledge* is really used in the media has received less attention, even more so in the field of drugs (McQuillan & Tse, 1996; Reed, 2001; Hijmans, Pleijter, & Wester, 2003; Smith, 2015). In a similar vein, the issue of whether and how the media actually affects the science-policy nexus remains empirically understudied. Some studies (Weiss & Singer, 1988; Wagner et al., 1991; Lampinen, 1992; McArthur, 1999, Lenton, 2004; Lancaster et al., 2011; Haynes et al., 2011; Ritter & Lancaster, 2013; Smet, 2013) only generally suggest that the media may act as a *linking or facilitating mechanism* between those who wish to influence policy (e.g. scientists and interest groups) and the actual policymakers. In this context, it is acknowledged that disseminating scientific knowledge through the media might entail risk as the media often provides misinformation or unbalanced stories, leading to a distortion of perception and the construction of dominant overarching narratives (Carvalho, 2007; MacGregor, 2012a). For example, the media's distorted attention on the crack cocaine epidemic in the late 1980s led to concern about drug abuse nationwide and generated support for the radical right-wing political agenda (Hartman & Golub, 1999). While scientific knowledge debunked the various myths arising from this media scare and presented a rather different picture, media stories did not correct any mistaken claims which led to governments stepping up their *war on drugs*, especially towards dangerous groups living in ghettos (Reinarman & Levine, 1997).

This particular contribution of the media can be explained by drawing on Brossard's (2009) analysis of the selection mechanisms employed by the media. These issues appear to be equally true of drugs policy (e.g. Coomber, Morris, & Dunn, 2000; Monaghan, 2011; MacGregor, 2013). First, geography may be a factor in media coverage of a topic. In particular, local, regional, or national pride may explain why some international studies or other regional studies are not mentioned. Second, the chance of scientific research being covered depends on the degree of actual interest in the topic. The researcher's individual reputation plays a decisive role too. Selection is often based on the nature of the understanding between the scientist and journalist. Fourth, journalism's focus on sensationalism and drama and the direction of its editorial agenda (e.g. driven by publicity and economic concerns) also influences the selection of scientific research. The starting point for journalists is what makes a 'good story' that fits in with their particular framework and narrative. Additionally, it is often considered that journalism and science are two communities separated by the academic style of research articles which make them inaccessible for journalists; the lack of rigor among journalists; the different time frames in the media and the scientific world; and so on (McQuillan & Tse, 1996; Maillé, Saint-Charles, & Lucotte, 2010).

The Role of Interest Groups

The idea that interest groups (civil society associations, NGOs or third sector organisations, alliances, coalitions, and networks of existing organisations, professional associations of lawyers or law enforcement officers, or user groups) can play a role in drug policy-making is widely recognised (Tops, 2001; Hall, 2004; Bergin, 2013; Lancaster et al., 2013; EMCDDA, 2013). Ritter (2011) explicitly argued that "drug policy is a perfect example of a complex social problem, without obvious solutions, driven by highly emotional arguments and strong interest groups" (p. 3). Likewise, Lenton (2004) considered the support by cannabis users to be one of the many conditions that could be seen necessary for the cannabis law reform in Western Australia.

Central to the challenge of interest groups is the introduction of their real-life experiences into the policy debate. Of particular relevance is a recent EMCDDA report on drug policy advocacy organisations in Europe (EMCDDA, 2013; O'Gorman, Quigley, Zobel, & Moore, 2014). This report described the tools used by these groups to influence drug discourse: participation in media debates, policy forums or conferences were reported as the most useful mechanisms while activist strategies, such as demonstrations and marches, were employed less frequently. Through different mechanisms (e.g. participation in hearings, media involvement, and demonstrations), interest groups may directly or indirectly seek to affect the policy-making process (Leiden, 1995; Chari, Hogan & Murphy, 2010). For instance, by means of the media, interest groups may aim for power, public support, or opposition, public awareness of the issue, and finally the formulation and acceptation of a solution to a problem (Becker, 1967; Goode & Ben-Yehuda, 1994). If they are part of a policy network (e.g. issue network model; see also above, 'Policy Networks'), members of interest groups can be particularly powerful by providing the network with valuable insights (Hanney et al., 2003). For instance, Epstein (1996) reported the successful participation of activists in construction of scientific knowledge about AIDS. By setting up partnerships with scientists, professionals, and policy-makers and learning the language of these experts, activists succeeded in presenting themselves as credible advocates. As a result, Members of Parliament may sometimes turn to interest groups for assistance in analysing or evaluating bills or resolutions. In this way, interest groups may influence the language or direction of bills and subsequent discussions (Leiden, 1995). Nevertheless, it is generally assumed that they have a rather limited ability to influence the policy-making process, especially as they tend to be less organised, have fewer resources, and may be less familiar with engagement in policy advocacy (Porter & Hicks, 1995).

However, as with the role of the media, details about their particular influence on the science-policy nexus have been largely missing in the literature. How the activities of interest groups may, or may not, have an impact on the contribution of scientific knowledge to the policy-making process is still unclear and is an avenue for further investigation in this book. One general statement on their role in the science-policy nexus was made by Weiss (1986) who speculated that interest groups may be a key channel for the flow of scientific knowledge, and so may provide an important route for research entering into the policy-making process.

Summary

A wide range of research on the relationship between evidence and policy exists, much of which dates back to the 1970s. Exemplary is Weiss' three-fold knowledge utilisation typology (1979), distinguishing rational/instrumental use, conceptual/enlightenment use, and political/symbolic use which has since proven to be very influential in the knowledge utilisation literature. Likewise, the roots of the different policy theories, offering some important insights into the potential role of evidence in policy-making, can be traced back to work undertaken around the 1970s-1980s. Growing political commitment to the *evidence-based* concept from the late twentieth century onwards then stimulated a renewed academic interest in public scholarship and the science-policy nexus in general. Clearly, debates about the actual and desirable relationship between evidence and policy are still ongoing. Several authors recently made useful additions to Weiss' three-fold typology. Stevens' evolutionary model (2007a, 2011) and Monaghan's processual model (2011), particularly relevant in the domain of drug policy, focus on the powerful selection mechanisms which are used by policy-makers and how scientific knowledge itself is conceptualised in the policy-making process. In addition, the early view of the policy-making process as an authoritative choice, focusing on the outcome of policy-making ('government'), has now been rejected in favour of the examination of policy-making as a structured interaction between several internal and external actors ('governance').

Understandings of the key barriers to and enablers of knowledge utilisation does not seem to have progressed significantly, despite numerous recent studies. It is clear that policy-makers need to deal with *institutional* barriers such as budgets, timing (e.g. *windows of opportunity*), values and opinions of political parties, type of policy system (multi versus single party system), elections, affected stakeholders, and the general public. The *individual* policy-maker's basic values, political orientation, and *tacit* knowledge are also observed to play an impeding role. Furthermore, the complexity of the knowledge utilisation process is found to be related to the *nature of scientific knowledge* and the *engagement of the scientific community*. However, how scientists themselves perceive and handle public engagements and the particular roles of potential linking mechanisms between science and policy such as media and interest groups are still unclear (Monaghan, 2011; MacGregor, 2013; Sznitman et al., 2014).

Clearly, the overall conclusion that can be drawn from this overview is the incredible variety of perspectives that scholars have developed to explain knowledge utilisation and policy-making. The shared concepts found in the theoretical literature may help to clarify and explain why policy shifts and knowledge utilisation do or do not occur. The question of which of these offers the most insight into drug policy-making is probed through the case-study presented throughout the rest of this book.

Notes

1 Created in 2002, it is an international research network that helps policy-makers and practitioners to make well-informed decisions by preparing, maintaining, and disseminating systematic reviews on education, crime and justice, and social welfare (Devroe et al., 2008).
2 The work of Michel Foucault developed from the early text on madness (*Madness and Civilization*) over the studies *The Order of Things* and *Discipline and Punish* to the final study of sexuality (*The History of Sexuality*). The first period has been described as a period of *archaeological* investigations, while the later studies have been seen as *genealogical* analyses. This evolution considered a transformation from a descriptive/historical perspective on discourses towards a greater critical consideration of the interface between discursive and non-discursive practices and the power-knowledge nexus (e.g. why and how discourses occur).
3 With the publication of *The Culture of Control*, Garland (2001) pointed to some important currents of change in crime policy over the previous 30 years: the decline of the rehabilitative ideal; the re-emergence of punitive sanctions and intensive control mechanisms; an increase in the emotional tone of crime policy as the fear of crime became a prominent cultural theme; the return of the victim; a focus on the protection of the public; the reinvention of the prison, etc. A focus on repression and punishment may therefore be considered as a resistance to the curtailment of their decision-making power by the power of the scientists, lobbyists, or advisors. Populist language and a simplification or distortion of problems may influence the fear of crime and may raise expectations that the government is able to secure the citizens (Garland, 2001; Nelen, 2010b).
4 Basic (or fundamental, bottom-up) research is driven by a scientist's curiosity or interest in a scientific question. Applied (or top-down) research, on the other hand, is designed to solve practical problems of, for example, policy-makers, rather than to acquire knowledge for the scientific community (Devroe, 2002).
5 This model is based on the garbage can model developed by Cohen, March, and Olsen (1972). The garbage can model assumes that decision-making is neither rational nor incremental and supposes rather coincidental congruence among problems, solutions, and choice opportunities.
6 Other models in this domain include the work of Foucault (1972) on the relationship between knowledge and power and the struggle of ideas and contested values in particular.

Chapter 3

Analysing Drug Policy

Documents, Elites, and Related Challenges

Chapter 2 outlined how, since the late twentieth century, *evidence-based* policy has become the benchmark by which policies are made and assessed. There is a stated desire by and for governments to formulate policies based on the best available scientific evidence (Nutley et al., 2007). With this in mind, there has also been growing academic dialogue about 'news-making' or 'public' criminology discussing the need for criminologists to shape the representation of 'newsworthy' items and to engage with a well-informed public and policy debates (Loader & Sparks, 2011). However, some criticisms of those appeals have become apparent, including questions regarding the role of 'scientific' evidence in the policy process and the variety of stakeholders (practitioners, media, and interest groups) which may frame their views, claims, and interests too and as such, influence the policy-making process (MacGregor et al., 2014). Drug policy is considered to be a particularly contentious area in which particular challenges abound (Lancaster et al., 2011; MacGregor et al., 2014). Therefore, examining what factors actually drive drug policy is important. So, too, is the role 'evidence' does or does not play in shaping policy decisions about drugs.

This chapter turns its attention to how the science-policy nexus in the field of drug policy can be explored and explained. In doing so, the chapter highlights the selection of the case of the development of Belgian drug policy between 1996 and 2003. Furthermore, it considers some methodological tools that can be used to explore these issues. Discourse analysis of either policy documents or newspaper articles, appears to be very useful for analysing historical material and may become an even more powerful tool when combined with other research methods such as interviews with key players. Also, a description is presented of the limitations and the challenges the researcher was faced with during data-collection and data-analysis.

The Case of the Development of Belgian Drug Policy Between 1996 and 2003

An interesting feature of the research interest in the science-policy nexus in the field of drugs is that of the methods employed. Previous studies mainly adopted a qualitative approach including interviews (Duke, 2001; Hughes, 2007, 2009; Monaghan, 2011; Ritter & Lancaster, 2013; MacGregor, 2013; Singleton & Rubin, 2014) and, to a lesser extent, participant observations (Stevens, 2011; Edwards & Galla, 2014). It has also been common to review key documents and analyse these in terms of the role of policy actors, scientific knowledge, and framings of problems (Lenton, 2004, 2007; Wood et al., 2008; Bennett & Holloway, 2010). In this field, the use of quantitative methods is rather rare. It has been argued that quantitative methods would reduce knowledge utilisation to variables and causal relationships, without providing insight into the experiences, beliefs, and values that actors and networks attribute to the science-policy nexus (Landry, Lamari, & Amara, 2003). Then, the object of study would be quantified: the focus would be on the frequency and extent of knowledge utilisation and the phenomenon would be cast into categories (assuming that it is a homogenous, unchanging, or static concept). Furthermore, answers to questions in a quantitative questionnaire may be expected to be unreliable because the firm structuring of questions may influence the answers received (Huber & Power, 1985). Respondents may tend to reply in a manner that will be viewed favourably by others (e.g. about political utilisation of scientific knowledge; *social desirability bias*). Statements about (indirect) knowledge utilisation cannot be studied adequately as each respondent has his/her own definitions of use (Rich, 1997; Landry et al., 2001; Klein Haarhuis et al., 2009). However, qualitative methods have their disadvantages as well: it is more difficult to determine the validity and reliability of data (e.g. it is problematic for qualitative researchers to make generalisations from a sample to a population; researchers' bias (e.g. subjectivity) are unavoidable) and qualitative research methods often require a lot of time and/or money while a rather small number of respondents is reached (Hammersley & Gomm, 2008; Decorte & Zaitch, 2016).

Following the call for a qualitative methodological approach to understand the reality and dynamics of the interaction between science and policy, it has also been argued that it is difficult to adequately trace the flow of information from the time it enters the policy-making process to the time that some action/decision is taken, unless the policy domain is monitored for at least a *long period* (Sabatier, 1998; Lindquist, 2001; Kingdon, 2002). Therefore, previous research mostly analysed knowledge utilisation in one or more cases (*case-study design*) using a *process design*. Here, a case is, for example, the historical development of a policy (Duke, 2001; MacGregor, 2013), the policy process at a given time (Stevens, 2011), or the implementation of a new policy measure (e.g. new legislation, the implementation of safe injecting rooms, or treatment of heroin dependence) (Erickson, 1998; Lenton, 2004, 2007; Hall, 2004, 2008; Hughes, 2007; Monaghan, 2009; Hughes & Stevens, 2010; Zampini, 2014). Selecting a *policy area*, *policy debate*, or *policy measure* may facilitate thorough assessment of the science-policy nexus because it may identify how far the policy-making process has been informed by scientific knowledge taking into account particular contextual issues (Swanborn, 2003; Bloor & Wood, 2006; Gerring, 2007). As research projects generate several effects, it is impossible to distinguish the impact of a particular research project from that of other influences with which the findings get mixed (Hanney et al., 2003; Ritter & Lancaster, 2013). Whereas the multiple-case-study design may allow the researcher to explore the phenomena under study following a replication logic, much research focuses on a single case, often chosen because of its unique characteristics (Bak Jørgensen, 2011; Zampini, 2014). Thus, case-studies, by providing a depth and richness indispensable to social sciences, have a general relevance and are able to generate ideas and theoretical conclusions about the science-policy nexus.

The development of Belgian drug policy between 1996 and 2003 provides an interesting case for looking at and discussing the relationship between science and policy. When there is a favourable political climate for policy change or development, Kingdon (2002) speaks of the opening of a *window of opportunity*. In the Belgian context, a particular *window* opened in 1996 and closed in 2003 (see Table 1.1, Chapter 1). Unlike most countries in Europe and elsewhere, drugs in Belgium did not raise any serious concerns until the 1990s (EMCDDA, 1995). The actual focus of policy-makers was to control drug-related criminality, the prevalence of which at that time might have been exaggerated by the rise of the Flemish and Walloon extreme-right parties (Vlaams Blok and Front National) in the large cities. Then, around the mid-1990s, the increase of the supply of both legal and illegal drugs (in quantity as well as variety) and the perceived rise in drug-related property crimes led to an increasing need for a comprehensive drug policy (EMCDDA, 1997; Cartuyvels & Hebberecht, 2002). Between 1996 and 2003, the drugs issue was brought into the public arena. Wider groups were drawn into the policy-making process: drug policy became the subject of contested debates among policy-makers, professionals, scientists, journalists, and the public. Another important element in the period was the influence of the international framework, especially via involvement in the European Monitoring Centre for Drugs and Drug Addiction (EMCDDA), and of other international alliances such as the International Narcotics Control Board (INCB) (Kenis, 1997; Hartnoll, 2004). Eventually, it took a Parliamentary Working Group on drugs (PWG) in 1996, appointed to investigate all aspects of the drug phenomenon by means of several national and international expert hearings, and a change of government for the first national drug strategy to be approved.

In 1999, Belgian voters rejected the long-standing Coalition Government of Christian Democrats and Socialists and voted into power a new six-party Coalition among the Flemish and French-speaking Liberals, Socialists, and Greens led by Flemish Liberal Leader Guy Verhofstadt (1999–2003). The new Coalition wrote a fairly extensive and specific Coalition Agreement that was seen to be "breaking with the past" (Verhofstadt, 1999). The will to take a clear and different direction opposed to that of the previous government produced a kind of consensus view on the right way forward. In 2001, the Verhofstadt I Government approved the first national drug strategy: the Federal Drug Policy Note (Federal Government, 2001). The central principle of the first national drug strategy was that drug use is a matter of public health, reflecting the emphasis placed on the broader social context and common aims such as drug prevention, reduction of drug-related harm, and crime deterrence (Guillain, 2003). Similar to national drug strategies implemented in, for example, Spain, France, Portugal, and the UK (EMCDDA, 2000), accurate scientific evidence, clear objectives, measurable performance targets, and evaluation were also considered key to the first national drug strategy in Belgium. Implementing one of the action points of the Federal Drug Policy Note, the Federal Government reformed the Belgian Narcotic Drug Law of 1921 and developed a new Ministerial Circular Letter in 2003. In doing so, Belgium de facto *depenalised*[1] cannabis possession for personal use – involving maintenance of criminal penalties in the criminal law without any application in practice (Guillain, 2003). As soon as the policy priorities and thus the legislative and prosecution framework had been redefined, the political issue in question faded from the political and public agenda by the end of 2003. Drug policy, and its *evidence-based* rhetoric in particular, has not been a political concern in Belgium since. This makes the development of Belgian drug policy between 1996 and 2003 a unique event.

Critical Discourse Analysis of Policy and Media Documents

Discourse is a complex term, and is not defined consistently.[2] Generally speaking, it is assumed that discourse is not a neutral communicative resource which reflects reality in transparent ways. The concept of discourse implies that *truth* is socially constructed through talk (McLaughlin & Muncie, 2013). The focus of discourse analysis is any form of written or spoken language, such as a conversation (e.g. interview), a newspaper article, or policy document. A discourse analysis is suitable for looking at *what is said* but also at *how something is expressed* (emic perspective or insider's view).[3] The emergence of meaning is always considered a matter of interaction processes between people and texts (*intertextuality*; see also below, Table 3.1). These interaction processes may in some cases focus on the micro-level of conversations (e.g. *Discursive Psychology* (*DP*),[4] *Conversational Analysis* (*CA*)) but sometimes also on the broader social or historical context (e.g. Critical Discourse Analysis (CDA), Foucauldian discourse analysis) (Wetherell, Taylor, & Yates, 2001b; Wodak & Meyer, 2001). Analysing and understanding the science-policy nexus not only requires textual analysis of what an individual says or writes (e.g. Are references to scientific knowledge made? How is scientific knowledge used?). It is also useful to explore how scientific knowledge itself has been conceptualised in the policy-making process (e.g. Which scientific research is considered useful? Who is considered to be a knowledgeable expert?). As argumentation and persuasion are involved, scientific knowledge may (or may not) find its way into policy through power struggles (Szarka, 2004).

The Critical Discourse Analysis Framework of Norman Fairclough

In this book, the Critical Discourse Analysis framework of Norman Fairclough has been applied. This approach oscillates between a textually oriented analysis (content) and a focus on macro-sociological analysis (context) (Fairclough, 2003). In particular, with the aid of the approach of Fairclough (2003), discourse is seen as *the use of language as a form of social practice*, meaning that discourse is inherent in every social action and interaction. The *dialectical* relationship between different levels of social practices (e.g. media coverage, parliamentary/governmental decisions, and academic discourse) and between discourse and other elements of social life (e.g. relations of power) are two of his main points (Fairclough & Fairclough, 2012). For Fairclough, a textual analysis alone is not sufficient for discourse analysis as it does not shed light on the links between texts and societal and cultural processes (Jørgensen & Phillips, 2002). Discourse is seen as the product of power because it embodies what is understood to *make sense*, to be *true* or to yield *authority* (Burchell & Foucault, 1991; Fraser, Hopwood, Treloar, & Brener, 2004). In this sense, the work of Foucault had a significant influence on the general framework of Critical Discourse Analysis. "Power does not belong to particular agents such as individuals or the state or groups with particular interests; rather, power is spread across different social practices" (Jørgensen & Phillips, 2002, p. 13). While policy-makers dominate or control political discourse, the same can also be said for other discourses, for example journalists control media discourse and academics control scientific discourse. Each powerful position presupposes privileged access to a particular resource such as money, status, or knowledge/information. In relation to the science-policy nexus, this may work in two ways: on the one hand, deciding who is trustworthy or qualified to advise in the policy-making process involves acts of power (Van Dijk, 2003; Acevedo, 2007). For instance, a medical policy discourse may come to constitute particular objects as distinct and factual as well as to qualify a doctor as a particular trustworthy individual with knowledge and authority (*processual model*; Monaghan, 2011). On the other hand, within the struggle between different knowledge claims, it is assumed that scientific knowledge that is structured and institutionalised through policy discourse is likely to attract the support of powerful groups (*evolutionary model*; Stevens, 2007b). In this context, Fairclough's focus on *intertextuality* (i.e. the use of text in other texts such as a newspaper article referring to a scientific report) may allow one to identify which texts and voices are included (and excluded) in a given text (Fairclough, 2003). Such an approach systematically describes the various strategies of a text, and relates these to the social or political context (Hajer, 1995; Vianello, 2011). Therefore, in the literature, this approach is identified as a suitable means for analysing policy as well as media discourses (Fairclough, 1998; Mautner, 2008; Thomas, 2009).

Fairclough's approach also represents the most developed methodological framework for CDA (Jørgensen & Phillips, 2002). Few Critical Discourse Analysts have developed clear methodological tools for empirical research of specific texts (Jørgensen & Phillips, 2002; Bacchi, 2009). Critical Discourse Analysts generally agree that a discourse analysis consists of detailed and repeated reading of the text in an attempt to identify categories, themes, ideas, views, roles, and so on, within the text itself (Wetherell, Taylor, & Yates, 2001a). However, a clear methodological framework can be perceived as a fruitful starting point, especially because interpretations of the data are always subjective: another researcher may interpret the same documented data differently (Wetherell et al., 2001b; Fairclough, 2003).

Fairclough's method of CDA consists of a three-dimensional framework: (1) textual analysis (e.g. description of the content, sentence structure and text structure, vocabulary, and social actors (who speaks?)); (2) discursive practices (e.g. production and interpretation of the meaning of the text, context of the author, and intertextuality); and (3) social practices (e.g. relation between the text and discursive practices and the wider society). Some refer to this framework as exercises in description, interpretation, and explanation where the last phase refers to the dialectical relationship between discourse and society, for which Fairclough claims affinity with Foucault (Fairclough, 2003).

Fairclough (2003) developed a checklist of analytical tools reflecting a dichotomy of *internal* and *external* relations to text, with the former focusing on the linguistic aspects of the text such as the semantic, grammatical, vocabulary, phonological relations, and the latter paying attention to the relationship between text and context. The approach applied in this book has been to examine the external relations, or in other words, the content of the text and the general discursive patterns and social context (i.e. the role of scientific knowledge in argumentative structures as well as the practices through which these utterances were made; Burchell & Foucault, 1991; Hajer, 1995). In particular, this analysis focused on: the textual elements that characterise (differences between) discourses (e.g. the terminology and definition(s) of drug use or drug policy options used and the use of existential, propositional, and value assumptions); how players are represented in the text and from which perspective or viewpoint; how scientific knowledge was represented; the relationship of scientific knowledge to other forms of information available; the players/networks referring to or discussing these scientific results and their motivations; and the various types of knowledge utilisation. The *external tools* are discussed in more detail in Table 3.1.

Documents are of particular importance for qualitative research because access can (sometimes) be easy and at low cost, because the information provided may not be available in oral form and because documents may give historical insight (Hodder, 2003). Documents are always written with a specific purpose and for a particular audience in a specific setting. In this book, policy and media documents are used as crucial material through which to analyse the links between science and policy in the development of the Belgian drug policy between 1996 and 2003. The analysis of the documents used traditional manual methods of examining the data. Practicalities apart (e.g. while some files were secured from editing, others were too large to import into a qualitative data analysis programme), qualitative data analysis programmes (e.g. NVivo, MAXQDA) are only considered useful in the early stages of a discourse analysis (e.g. to structure texts, to search them and to assist in rudimentary coding). It is assumed that software cannot assist enough to get to the deep level of analysis that is required for a discourse analysis (MacMillan, 2005). Thus, the analysis consisted of a detailed (re)reading of the documents. Relevant fragments were highlighted and given one or more corresponding codes. Subsequently, patterns and explanations in these codes were derived. Data were then organised chronologically (from 1996 to 2003) and thematically according to the central (theoretical) concepts of the study. The work in collecting and analysing the policy and media documents was completed by one researcher over a 13-month period (between July 2011 and October 2012).

Parliamentary/Governmental Discourse (Phase I)

Policy documents included formal, publicly available expressions of strategy and statements of intent made by the Federal Government, as well as parliamentary discussions. Given the selected case, the databases of the Federal Government and Parliament were searched, first using general keywords such as *drugs*, *drug use*, *substance use*, but eventually refined keywords such as *drug policy*, *Parliamentary Working Group on Drugs*, *Federal Drug Policy Note*, and *drug/cannabis law reform*. A strategy used to ensure that all relevant documents were retrieved for analysis, to prevent the exclusion

Table 3.1 External Relations to Text

External Tools	*Description*
Social events	Which contextual elements (e.g. political context, international discussions), related to the social events under study, are represented in the texts? To which social event or chronology of social events does the particular text belong? For example, in this case, a distinction can be made between parliamentary and governmental actions where texts are considered as elements of these social events
Genre	How does the text or interaction fit within and contribute to social action and interactions in social events? For instance, the genre of media texts may recontextualise the arguments which policy-makers have put forward
Discourse	Which (alternative or competing) discourses are represented by different social groups? For example, biomedical/clinical discourse, public health discourse, sociological discourse, legalistic/repressive perspectives
Assumptions	Which (implicit) assumptions are reflected in a discourse (i.e. assumptions about what exists)? Propositional assumptions (i.e. assumptions about what is or may be), value assumptions (i.e. assumptions about what is good and/or bad), and ideological assumptions
Difference	Which differences exist regarding terminology or discourse (e.g. about drug use/cannabis)? Within the policy-making process, the orientation of difference in the text may vary too: an openness to difference, an accentuation of difference and conflict or power, etc.
Intertextuality	How do texts draw on, incorporate, (re)contextualise, and dialogue with other texts? The meaning and content of any text or statement is shaped by what has happened before, as well as in anticipation of future responses. For instance, newspaper articles may refer to a scientific report, which then could be included in a parliamentary interpellation
Styles	Which persons are represented in the text and from which perspective or viewpoint? Do they perceive themselves as experts or as having authority? Are they part of a network? Which position do they take (e.g. dual roles: a policy-maker may use his role as a parent to support some arguments; a public role ranging from scientific experts to policy advisors, observer-turned-players, lonely prophets, or social movement theorists/activists)?
Modality	How do texts assess scientific knowledge in terms of truth and necessity? Is more power and authority attributed to scientists than to other actors? Which voices are included and excluded? For instance, a particular discourse may come to constitute particular experts or type of experts with authority
Evaluation	What are the choices made in describing, quoting, and portraying scientists, scientific knowledge and the interpretation of scientific research? For instance, statements concerning good/bad or (un)desirable, affective attributes of scientific knowledge (e.g. qualitative – quantitative data; theme/topic; terminology; quality judgements)

Source: adapted from Fairclough (2003).

of documents that might be marginally important, and to balance the narratives selected included an additional search with the keywords *legalisation*, *decriminalisation*, *depenalisation*, as these words were included in most of the initially selected documents. This search resulted in a total of 164 policy documents. Governmental documents involved were rather scarce because of their unpublished character, although a limited number of government papers and internal communications such as those of the Ministerial Cabinet could be accessed successfully through my interviewees.

Media Discourse (Phase 2)

Print media are rich sources of data for social scientists (Mautner, 2008). Print offers real practical advantages (e.g. it is easier to collect than audio-visual data, and more permanent than web material) as well as benefits related to the method (e.g. if you are interested in the content and sources of discourses, the major newspapers and magazines are obvious sources). Media analysis examined Belgian (including Flemish as well as Walloon) newspaper articles. In particular, the analysis covered the main Belgian newspapers and magazines: *Gazet Van Antwerpen*, *De Morgen*, *De Standaard*, *De Tijd*, *Het Belang van Limburg*, *Het Laatste Nieuws*, *Het Nieuwsblad*, *Het Volk*, *Knack – Le Vif/L'express*, *Trends – Tendances*, *L'Avenir*, *La Dernière Heure*, *L'Echo*, *Les Echos*, *Grenz Echo*, *La Libre Belgique*, *Libération*, *La Meuse*, *La Tribune*, *Le Soir*.

Most of the articles published in the Flemish or Walloon newspapers were collected from online media databases. In particular, the articles published in the Flemish newspapers were collected from the Mediargus database and articles published in the Walloon newspapers were collected from the Pressbanking database. However, as these databases have only been available since the end of the 1990s, the search was completed by examining archives. A total number of 1,067 articles were selected (using the same search strategy as with policy documents) and analysed.

Semi-Structured Interviews with 'Elites'

Retrospectively exploring experiences of policy-makers, scientists, journalists, and members of interest groups by means of semi-structured interviews further enhanced the understanding of the processes of knowledge utilisation, (informal) interactions between the multiplicity of actors, informal initiatives, networks, conflicts, and contextual issues in particular.

Definition of Elites

Elites have been the focus of definitional squabbles that vary across a range of domains and, as a result, there is much confusion and debate surrounding this concept (Littig, 2009). In economics, elites are sometimes regarded as occupying positions at the top of the employment and income pyramid (Woods, 1998; Harvey, 2010). Others define elites as persons who hold strategic positions within a social network such as, for example, senior management positions or leading consultants (Welch, Marschari-Piekkari, Penttinen, & Tahvanainen, 2002), or people occupying positions of influence within policy and political networks (Neal & McLaughlin, 2009). Common elements comprise having direct or indirect decisional power, having great insight in specific knowledge, and/or holding information difficult to explore by other methods. However, in this way, a different range of people may be perceived as elites: policy-makers, scientists, and professionals. In other words, what constitutes an elite is socially and, in case of elite interviewing, scientifically constructed (Bygnes, 2008).

Previous studies on the science-policy nexus mostly engaged policy-makers from different levels and hierarchies while the thoughts and experiences of researchers or other relevant persons (i.e. media and interest groups) were involved less often (Carden, 2004; Lindquist, 2001). In this book, the term elites is used to describe those people who are in positions of power in relation to the processes of drug policy-making. This rather broad definition, adopted from Duke (2002), acknowledges that in addition to overt indicators of power (e.g. policy-makers) there are also more hidden sites/actors of power and influence (e.g. police officers, judges, prevention workers, journalists, scientists, or interest groups).

Sampling

The discourse analysis identified which actors played an important role in the development of Belgian drug policy. Respondents were selected on the basis of what they might know to help the researcher fit in pieces of a puzzle which is called 'theoretical sampling' or 'purposive sampling' in the methodological literature (Aberbach & Rockman, 2002). Initially, 62 actors were identified and selected by means of the analysis of policy and media documents. However, eight respondents[5] explicitly refused to cooperate, three respondents had already passed away, and the contact details of one respondent (who was part of an interest group) were not found. Most refusing respondents felt they were not sufficiently knowledgeable about the subject (anymore), while two respondents refused because of medical health conditions. In case a respondent refused to cooperate or at the end of each interview, interviewees were asked to provide names and contact details of others they thought were important. Using the *snowball* technique (Farquharson, 2005), five additional respondents who worked on a lower level (e.g. ministerial cabinets/employees of MPs) were selected. This simple question supported the *snowball* process but also generated interesting data on who knew whom, who valued whom, and who networked with whom (which is important when studying the science-policy nexus).

Eventually, a total of 55 individuals were interviewed (face-to-face; one telephone interview was organised as the respondent was working abroad) over an eight-month period between January and December 2013, including 15 members of Parliament, two employees of members of Parliament, eight members of the Federal (and Regional) Government, eight employees of members of the Federal (and Regional) Government (including six employees of the Ministerial Cabinets and two civil servants), six scientists, six journalists, four members of interest groups, and six professionals working with drug users. Taking the selection of individuals based on documents into account, a clear limitation of this sample (and a recommendation for further research) is the underrepresentation of civil servants of the Federal Administration (Federal Public Services (FPS)). Policy-makers were broadly defined to include all stakeholders with responsibility for shaping policy, or in a position to influence its direction. However, it has been very difficult to access the historical policy process even where a number of interviews with retired policy actors were possible and where some internal documents were accessible. Even though Welch et al. (2002) warn researchers not to go only for the 'top shots', the discourse analysis revealed only the most visible (and most powerful) respondents whose names were included in the documents, for example ministers or MPs. Gaining access to these 'top shots' was the starting point of the fieldwork and already involved multiple levels of barriers (see below). As a result, there is an unfortunate lack of material on the role of civil servants, and as such, the book derives its evidence largely from the more visible aspects of the policy process within the Parliament and Government. As civil servants of the FPS do not come and go with the Minister but have a permanent tenure regardless of the political colour of the Minister, their perceptions would have been interesting to get a better sense of the *routine day-to-day* policy-making (e.g. detail on issues such as intra-political relations, civil service career management, the role of in-house research, etc.) in addition to *strategic* policy-making in terms of strategic/policy documents (see also Stevens, 2011).

Theoretical saturation, the point when no new data is emerging from the data collection tools but rather confirms previous ideas (Bloor & Wood, 2006), occurred after about 50 interviews (which was more or less consistent with my sample of 55 interviews). At the same time, it gradually became clear that the most important (and visible) actors involved in my case had been interviewed. The request to provide names and contact details of others they thought were important to interview directed the interviewer more and more to the same individuals already included in the sample.

Topic List

According to Conti and O'Neil (2007), semi-structured interviews seem the most appropriate approach in studying elites, as this may focus their responses on the specific topics of interest and accommodate the short amount of time offered for the interview. These semi-structured interviews were guided by a topic list which was prepared beforehand, and which provided a framework for the interview. The topic list or interview guide was based on the topic list used in the studies by Monaghan (2008a) and Duke (2002), and augmented by themes raised during the analysis of the policy and media documents. The interview schedule covered key themes such as the particular role of the interviewee in the debate, the content of the debate, the role played by scientific knowledge, ideological/political motives, media and interest groups in the parliamentary and governmental debates, and their perception of the *evidence-based/evidence-informed* characteristic of the development of Belgian drug policy. Following a cyclic-iterative process, the topic list was sometimes slightly adapted based on new information from previous interviews. The topic list was available in both languages (Dutch or French) and tailored (but still comparable) for each type of actor.

Data Analysis

The digital recording from each interview was transcribed in full. While the full transcription of all interviews was a time-consuming process, it engaged the researcher in the process of deep listening, analysis, and interpretation right from the beginning. In contrast with the discourse analysis, qualitative data analysis software NVivo was used to analyse these interview data. When an interview was transcribed, the transcript was immediately imported into NVivo to start with the coding. Adopting an open or exploratory perspective, none of the codes retrieved from the manual discourse analysis were imported into NVivo in advance. Data were subsequently coded and categorised to eventually find links with the theoretical concepts (e.g. types of scientific knowledge utilisation, representation of scientific knowledge and experts, other types of information, barriers, and facilitating mechanisms, media, and interest groups). Thoughts on how fragments or codes were linked with the theoretical concepts, methodological issues, or results of the discourse analysis were written down in memos. Analysis of the interview data followed a cyclic process in which an accumulation of interview data and of codes was supported. Data were eventually also organised chronologically (from 1996 to 2003) and thematically according to the central (theoretical) concepts of the study.

The findings from the interviews, included in the following chapters, are supported by narrative statements (i.e. quotes) to allow transferability of the findings to other studies (case-to-case transferability). No details were presented of the institution in which respondents were working, or the particular topics on which they were working, where that could lead easily to their identification. A number and a general typology (policy-maker, journalist, scientist, or member of interest group) was assigned to each respondent as a means of protecting identities in line with relevant ethical obligations in conducting social research (Decorte & Zaitch, 2016).

Challenges of Access, Knowledge, and Power in Interviewing Elites

Although 'elite interviews' are conducted regularly, there is little methodological work setting them apart from other interview techniques (Denzin & Lincoln, 1994; Decorte & Zaitch, 2016). At first, interviewing 'elites' appeared not that different from interviewing 'non-elites'. The process of question design, the importance of flexibility of the interviewer, the usefulness of keeping abreast of current events as well as avoiding a 'conventional' interview setting are equally applicable for both 'elites' and 'non-elites'. However, there seemed to be some particular dissimilarities which made interviewing 'elites' both an art and a craft.

Powerful groups or 'elites' have the power to create barriers, shield themselves from and resist the intrusiveness of social research (Aberbach & Rockman, 2002). Even though it is often described that 'elites' may be just as difficult to locate and identify as, for example, marginalised drug users (Smith, 2006), it became clear that the process of gaining access to 'elites' was far less time-consuming than previously anticipated. A mix of 'personalisation' of the research and the use of existing gatekeepers was successful in gaining access. The use of the snowball technique was then effective to get beyond spokespersons and high-level respondents and to obtain data on who knew whom and who networked with whom.

One of the other specific challenges encountered is when interviewees resist giving accurate or straight answers to questions (Borer, 2012). It was indeed observed that 'elites' are influenced by direct or indirect decisional power and getting them to tell something on a personal level was sometimes a difficult task. The interviewer had to be aware not to become hostage to different agendas and struggles in the course of fieldwork. The role of a well-informed 'outsider' who is willing to listen appeared to be a helpful strategy: the researcher has the insight of a knowledgeable 'insider' but applies the neutrality (sometimes naivety) of an 'outsider'. Therefore, elite interviewing seems to be more productive in the interpretative (why?) and procedural (how?) stages of a research project than in the explorative phase (Bogner, Littig, & Menz, 2009).

Additionally, in qualitative methodological discussions it is often said that there is an imbalance of power between the researcher and the participants (Aguiar, 2012). Usually in the relationship between researcher and interviewee, the researcher is the one with the higher status. In contrast, 'elites', more than other groups, seem to try to dictate the conditions and progress of an interview. For example, 'elites', being used to speaking in public and defending their views, tried to take control over the conversation by starting to pose the researcher tricky questions about the findings or by making remarks about the research or researcher. To cope with the power asymmetry, it became clear that effective strategies are to move away from an 'organisationally' or 'politically' oriented dialogue and to create a set of priorities as to what to focus on if unexpected situations emerge where 'time is up'.

Finally, it is important for qualitative studies, not at least for elite interviews, to emulate reliability and validity (Berry, 2002). Achieving reliability was challenging because each interview was unique given that the topic list was tailored. Furthermore, elite interviewees' accounts are more likely to be affected by bias because they may have many other (self-serving) concerns and background assumptions. Gaining valid and reliable data from elite interviews therefore required making a good first impression (i.e. way of contact, guarantee of anonymity, justification of the research, and selection of the expert) and to have made proper preparation. Establishing trustworthiness and reliability in interviewing 'elites' also encouraged a triangulation of data from multiple sources.

Summary

This chapter examined how the science-policy nexus in the drug field can be explored and explained. Consistent with the knowledge utilisation literature in the drug field, a case-study appears to be an appropriate technique for intensively studying complex processes and interactions among several actors within a particular setting and time period. In this book, the case of the development of Belgian drug policy between 1996 and 2003 has been selected because it covers a *window of opportunity* (Kingdon, 2002) where a major policy development came about in the way the drugs issue was, and still is, perceived in Belgium.

The Belgian case has been investigated by means of the discourse analytical approach of Fairclough (2003) in combination with semi-structured interviews to understand the complex, changeable social processes involving a variety of actors. In particular, the discourse analysis consisted of a detailed and systematic reading of 164 policy documents including formal, publicly available expressions of strategy and statements of intent made by the Federal Government, as well as parliamentary discussions. Media analysis examined a total number of 1,067 Belgian (including Flemish as well as Walloon) newspaper articles. Additionally, despite its particular challenges, a total number of 55 elite interviews helped to better understand the interactions among multiple actors, contextual developments, informal initiatives, networks, conflicts, and strategies. Reflexivity and sensitivity towards the individual research processes was shown, reporting methodological choices, analytical processes, and researcher's bias as completely and truthfully as possible.

Notes

1 *Depenalisation* involves maintenance of criminal penalties in criminal law, yet removing or shortening the periods of incarceration, or reducing fine amounts, as possible sanctions. An important distinction between different types of alternatives is the differentiation between de facto and *de jure*, or in other words, between changing the law that applies (*de jure*), or by modifying the way the law is used or applied in the various stages of the criminal justice system (de facto) (Room et al., 2010).

2 While some authors understand discourse as the "language that is structured according to different patterns that people's utterances follow when they take part in different domains of social life" (Jørgensen & Phillips, 2002, p. 2), others offer a critical approach considering causes and consequences of broader, historical, contexts and changes (Wodak & Krzyzanowski, 2008). According to Michel Foucault (1972):

> we shall call discourse a group of statements in so far as they belong to the same discursive formation [...]. Discourse is made up of a limited number of statements for which a group of conditions of existence can be defined. Discourse in this sense is not an ideal, timeless form [...] it is, beginning to end, historical – a fragment of history [...] posing its own limits, its divisions, its transformations, the specific mode of its temporality.
>
> (p. 117)

3 The general label of *discourse analysis* is mostly applied to both formal linguistic techniques as well as theoretical propositions of, for example, Laclau and Mouffe or Foucault (Torfing, 1999). However, a distinction is sometimes made between *discourse analysis* and *discourse theory*, with the latter notion particularly referring to the theoretical propositions. Herein, the general label *discourse analysis* will be used.

4 Discursive psychology (DP) considers that human thinking (e.g. reasoning and emotions) is an inherently social activity ingrained in one's use of language. For instance, reasons are seen as mental constructions made within the context of a person's larger social and cultural world view and his or her need to convey a particular image of the self (Bagozi & Dabholkar, 2000). In other words, DP studies the identities, minds, and selves within naturally occurring discourse. As discursive psychology also analyses talk between people, it has similar assumptions to Conversation Analysis (CA) (Wetherell et al., 2001a).

5 These eight respondents comprised one practitioner and seven policy-makers. Four were French-speaking and four were Dutch-speaking actors.

Chapter 4

Incremental Steps in the Opening of a Policy Window

There often tend to be long periods of stability punctuated by brief periods of major policy change or development (Lindblom, 1959). The Belgian case is no different. Until the 1990s, there was a period of stability whereby the dominant paradigm was framed by the international control conventions and the basic Belgian law of 1921 in particular. Drugs occasionally came up on the public agenda and, as such, remained a relatively small and specialist issue. From the late 1980s and early 1990s onwards, some smaller incremental changes occurred, paving the way for the opening of a *window of opportunity* (Kingdon, 2002) for policy development in 1996. This chapter provides an overview of incremental developments prior to the 1996–2003 period, showing the influence of international pressures, the developments in neighbouring countries, especially in the Netherlands, and the increasing visibility of the drug problem in Belgium.

The Inception and Expansion of the International Framework

As mentioned above, drug policies may differ among nations in both appearance and substance. Some nations treat drugs primarily as a problem for law enforcement; others focus their efforts primarily on prevention and education. However, what they have in common is that drug policy is not only a matter of government policy but also something which is developed by networks of players and institutions, not least by the international framework (Ghodse, 2008).

During the twentieth century, the politically accepted and correct norm was to use harsh anti-drug language and the rhetoric of a *drug-free* world (Boekhout van Solinge, 2004). In Belgium, as in many other European countries, a drug law was in force. The basic Belgian law concerning the traffic in toxic substances, hypnotics, narcotics, disinfectants, and antiseptics dates back to 24 February 1921. This law was passed to fulfil Belgium's international obligations under the International Opium

Convention of The Hague of 1912 (De Ruyver, 1988; Cesoni, 2008; Fijnaut & De Ruyver, 2014). Like several other countries, Belgium ratified the International Opium Convention in 1912 because of the moral value inherent in this international commitment and the importance of being associated with it (De Ruyver, Vermeulen, & Vander Beken, 2002). Generally, at that time, in Belgium and elsewhere, there was little anxiety about a drug use problem and accordingly there was not a great deal of media hype about the topic of drugs, showing how ignorant many politicians were about drugs (MacCoun & Reuter, 2001). As an exception, some minor concerns were raised in Belgium at the time of the ratification (De Ruyver, 1988; Todts, 2004). For instance, some registrations showed that 2–3 per cent of Belgian prisoners (in some prisons: 6 per cent) were addicted to cocaine. As a result, for the first time emotions ran high in the parliamentary debate: "The Government is almost completely disarmed by the fatal drug abuse that occurs in all classes of our population" (*Hand.* Kamer 1920–1921, 21 December 1920, 108/1).

The internationalisation of the production of drugs continued to grow and there was increasing mobility on the demand side (Hartnoll, 1998). Under enormous pressure from the US government and some powerful allies, law enforcement became practically the only means through which governments attempted to control drug use and trafficking (Levine, 2003). Medical treatment of those experiencing problems as result of addiction remained limited. Political leaders and governments throughout the world supported drug prohibition and constructed a global drug prohibition system, regulated by UN conventions (1961, 1971, and 1988). The United Nations Single Convention on Narcotic Drugs (New York, 1961) was the first important consolidation of the prohibitionist international drug control system. This UN convention streamlined and tightened controls on production, use, and distribution of illicit narcotics (Hartnoll, 1998). The possession of cannabis was placed under the strictest control regime in the Convention (similar to cocaine and heroin), on the basis that it was widely abused. The 1961 treaty also created the International Narcotics Control Board (INCB) to collate the parties' legal drug requirements and to monitor legitimate trade.

In the 1960s, drug use exploded around the world, most notably in developed Western nations (Chatwin, 2011). As the increase was closely related to the pervasive use and availability of synthetic, psychotropic substances such as amphetamines, barbiturates, and LSD, the United Nations Convention on Psychotropic Substances (Vienna, 1971) was established. Dealing with psychotropic substances next to narcotics, it formed a companion instrument of the 1961 UN Convention. It was also at that time that President Nixon declared a *War on Drugs* and the rest of the world fell into line. For instance, in the UK, the key act of drug legislation, the 1971 Misuse of Drugs Act, came into force (Pryce, 2012). In

Belgium, the basic Belgian law of 1921 was amended by the law of 1975, again partly to fulfil the international obligations (namely the United Nations Single Convention of 1961 and the UN Drug Convention of Vienna of 1971). The prohibitionist philosophy of the UN treaties was endorsed. Possession of drugs remained prohibited; the concept of aggravating circumstances (i.e. drug use by minors; drug use in group) was implemented; a denunciation clause was integrated; cannabis was classified like other illicit drugs; and a strong enforcement of drug trafficking was the main focus (De Ruyver, 1988). On the upside, the 1975 amendment did expand the options for probation measures for drug users, enabling faster diversion into drug treatment, although the prevention and treatment offer remained scarce (De Ruyver et al., 2012). Meanwhile, the Netherlands took the first step in the opposite direction. The debate on Dutch drug policy sparked off and resulted in the Opium Act (1976) making a distinction between cannabis and other drugs, in that the possession of small quantities of cannabis is considered to be a minor offence. The reservation to the 1971 treaty led the way to further development of the appeasement policy (*gedoogbeleid*) on the use and sale of cannabis, ultimately resulting in the *coffee-shop* model (Boekhout van Solinge, 2004; Fijnaut & De Ruyver, 2008).

In the late 1980s, the international control system was further elaborated. The 1988 United Nations Convention against illegal traffic in narcotic drugs and psychotropic substances (Vienna, 1988) was primarily concerned with how control should be enforced and with international cooperation against international drug trafficking. Given the proximity of the Netherlands with its distinctive drug policy, another important international instrument created in this climate is the 1990 Schengen Convention. In 1985, the Schengen Agreement, which was directed towards the free movement of persons, goods, and services, was established. One of the goals of this Agreement was to improve the cooperation between judicial and police services in the EU. Some elements focused specifically on the drug issue (Guillain & Marchand, 1998). In particular, the 1985 Schengen Agreement stipulated that the five original Schengen countries (Belgium, Luxembourg, the Netherlands, Germany, and France) had to target illegal drug traffic vigorously as well as coordinate their actions efficiently. In this context, the Schengen Agreement also aimed to harmonise the legislation on drugs among the Schengen countries. However, this original compromise proved to be inadequate: the harmonisation of legislation on drugs appeared to be a stumbling block as it was not clear which national legislation or practice should be adopted as the standard (e.g. a liberal policy of the Netherlands or a stricter policy of France). Ongoing debate, with France taking the lead, speculated on the negative consequences of Dutch drug policy (Fijnaut & De Ruyver, 2008; De Ruyver, Ponsaers, Vermeulen, & Vander Beken, 2010). As a compromise, the 1990 Schengen Convention, applying the 1985 Schengen Agreement, adopted some new stipulations (Articles 70–76). For instance, a permanent working group was set up to monitor the situation in the Schengen area. Furthermore, a political solution to the harmonisation issue was found by invoking the former UN drugs conventions. In particular, member states were expected to take criminal and/or administrative measures to tackle illegal production and trafficking of drugs (including cannabis) as well as possession for the purpose of illegal sale or export. At the same time, a general agreement was included stating that if a country's drugs policy deviates from that of others (thus including an implicit link to the *coffee-shop* model of the Netherlands), all parties must take measures to limit the impact of this discrepancy on those other countries. Nevertheless, until the Schengen Convention was formally ratified in 1995, the discussions continued, especially regarding the (negative consequences of the) divergent policy of the Netherlands and its formal recognition by the other Schengen countries. Accordingly, the possible (negative) impact of the liberal policy of the Netherlands on the drug policy in Belgium was a commonly heard argument in the debate about the drug policy in Belgium during the 1990s. For example, it was argued that an explosion in the *coffee-shop* market and a Europe without borders (according to the Schengen Convention) has led to an increasing amount of foreign (Belgian) drug tourism to the Netherlands (Fijnaut & De Ruyver, 2014).

Despite international and national efforts, drug problems seemed to increase all over the world during the (late) 1980s. In particular, there was a rise of the heroin epidemic all around the world, with many new heroin users tending to be young and unemployed (Parker, 2001; Edwards, 2004). Parallel to this development, recreational drug use (especially cannabis but also ecstasy, LSD or amphetamines) was increasing and changing in youth cultures. Some commentators even suggested that drug use had become *normalised* among certain youth groups (Parker et al., 1998; Shapiro, 1999). The drug situation no longer being restricted to problematic drug users raised more questions about the effectiveness of the strict prohibitive *War on Drugs* (Tonry, 1995; MacCoun & Reuter, 2001). A new way of dealing with drug use emerged as well as the recognition that drug use was most probably 'here to stay'. It is in this context that the European Monitoring Centre for Drugs and Drug Addiction (EMCDDA) was established, next to international bodies such as the United Nations (UN) through its office on drugs and crime (UNODC) and the World Health Organization (WHO), which are both involved in coordinating the UN response to the drug problem and in monitoring the international drug situation and the formation of international drug policy or law enforcement organisations concerned with drug-related crime control (Kleiman & Hawdon, 2011). Its main aim was to provide the European Union and its member states with information on Europe's drug problem, including data needed to draw up informed drug laws and to identify the most efficient and effective practices for various drug control operations (Stimson, 1997; EMCDDA, 2008).

The changing situation led to shifts in policy in a growing number of countries by the end of the 1980s and the beginning of the 1990s (EMCDDA, 2004; UNODC, 2008; Muscat & Pike, 2012). The focus was diverted away from zero-tolerance towards a better balance between suppression and protection of public health (Jelsma, 2008). Hence, a harm reduction approach, with the installation of methadone substitution programmes, needle exchange projects, etc., was incorporated in Australia (Lenton & Single, 1998; O'Malley, 2002; Webster, 2007; Reuter, 2011; Courtwright & Hickman, 2011) and most European nations (e.g. first in the UK, Switzerland, and the Netherlands in the late 1980s, and around the early 1990s in more resistant countries such as France and Sweden). The USA proved much more resistant to public health and harm reduction approaches. The introduction of harm reduction measures and shifts in national drug strategies in general appeared to be a good example of an *incremental* event building up to policy development in Belgium. While, at first, higher priority was given to the unsolved killings by the criminal Gang of Nijvel[1] and the poor and chaotic communication between police and justice, the topic of drugs eventually raised some awareness among Belgian policy-makers at the beginning of the 1990s (Todts, 2004).

The Beginning of the 1990s: Awareness of and Ideas about Drugs are Changing in Belgium

Since the beginning of the 1990s, drug use (especially new drugs such as XTC) became more visible in certain (youth) cultures in Belgium (BIRN, 2000), not least because media attention increasingly focused on drug use in mega-clubs (Vercaigne & Walgrave, 1995). In a similar vein, some large cities (especially in the French-speaking part of Belgium: Liege, Charleroi, Mons) were confronted with a steep increase of frequently occurring crime which seriously affected the quality of life in a number of neighbourhoods (Guillain, 2003). Even though this was not backed up by scientific data, police officers supported the idea that problematic drug users were responsible for the increase in crime and in public nuisance. With the increased visibility of the drug problem in Belgian society from the beginning of the 1990s onwards, politicians gradually made it a political issue (Todts, 2004).

First of all, in the 1992 Government Agreement, put forward by the new Prime Minister Jean-Luc Dehaene (CVP, Flemish Christian Democrats), it was stated that

> Drug use causes an increasing amount of criminality. The struggle against drug traffic must be oriented towards the supply and demand

of drugs and must contain a better prevention, a more efficient repression and a better medical treatment in prisons.

(Federal Government, 1992, p. 8)

Within this framework, the Federal Minister for Internal Affairs, Louis Tobback (SP, Flemish Socialists), outlined a prevention policy under which the local administrative authorities were held responsible for the expansion and implementation of an integrated, local prevention policy (Beyens et al., 2001; Cartuyvels & Hebberecht, 2002). Then, in 1992, the government set up *safety and prevention contracts* to sustain local authorities in their response to crime and nuisance. In particular, the municipalities were allowed to install projects with regard to drug prevention, drug treatment, and local drug coordination (Verslag namens de Parlementaire Werkgroep belast met het bestuderen van de drugproblematiek, *Parl.St.* Kamer, 1996–1997, 1062/1-3; De Ruyver et al., 2004). For instance, the emergence of local medical-social treatment centres for drug users (MSOC), ambulant drug treatment centres, and outreach projects were financed through contracts with the Ministries of Interior and Social Affairs. Also, (smaller) municipalities without a security (or prevention) contract had the opportunity to implement projects related to drug prevention or drug treatment and to recruit staff such as outreach workers or prevention workers (these contracts were called 'drug plans' or 'drug plan contracts') (Hebberecht, 2009). Thus, in accordance with the international attention for the harm reduction approach, Belgian political interest was raised in low threshold harm reduction initiatives such as medical-social treatment centres for drug users (MSOC) (BIRN, 2002; Todts, 2004), needle exchange projects (e.g. a pilot project was set up in 1993 in Antwerp; Kinable, Casselman, Todts, & Van Deun, 1994),[2] and maintenance therapy for drug addicts (i.e. methadone) (De Ruyver, Van Bouchautte, & Reisinger, 1993).[3] Exemplary too is the conference that was set up in 1994 by the Minister of Public Health, Jacques Santkin (PS, French-speaking Socialists). An 'epistemic community', defined by Haas (1992) as a network of professionals with recognised expertise in a particular domain or issue area, shaped the drug debate at this time, composed of addiction psychiatrists, doctors, pharmacists, etc., from various countries. This conference played an important role in opening up discussion on organisation of legal substitution treatments. The actors involved turned progressively towards a more positive approach of this kind of treatment, but it was only in 2002–2003, with the Law of 22 August 2002 and a Royal Decree of 28 March 2003, that a definition and practice of substitution treatments as well as the goals they should pursue were formalised.

Second, although at odds with the initiatives aimed at applying a preventive health approach to experimental users, Minister of Justice Melchior Wathelet (PSC, French-speaking Christian Democrats) issued guidelines pertaining to a common prosecution policy with regard to narcotic substances (De Ruyver et al., 2004). He took a severe approach, pointing to increasing drug use, fear of the escalation of *soft* drugs to *hard* drugs (Guillain, 2003) and feelings of insecurity. By means of the Ministerial Circular Letter of 26 May 1993, the Minister of Justice instructed Public Prosecutors to respond to every instance of (problematic) use regardless of type of drugs. Although Belgian law had not penalised the *use* of drugs as such, the Public Prosecutors had to proceed on the assumption that *possession* is the prerequisite for use, and possession of drugs (irrespective of type and quantity) is in itself an offence constituting valid grounds for prosecuting the user (Vander Laenen, 2001).[4]

Third, a clear example that an awareness for political action (in terms of the development of a comprehensive Belgian drug policy) was developing through the 1990s was the establishment of the Federal Action Plan Toxicomania-Drugs (10-point plan)[5] by the Federal Government. This 10-point plan was intended to define action priorities on drugs, which could then serve as a starting point for the establishment of concrete initiatives (Cabinet of the Prime Minister, 1995). The 10 action points of the Federal Action Plan Toxicomania-Drugs were (1) to allocate to social security the material benefits that were confiscated in the fight against drug trafficking, (2) to improve the training of prison personnel with regard to the problem of drug addiction, (3) to develop needle exchange programmes, (4) to extend the power to close down establishments where drug crimes are committed, (5) to establish medical-social treatment centres for drug users (MSOCs),[6] (6) to combat recreational drug use, (7) to extend scientific research (e.g. epidemiological research and the scientific evaluation of the medical-social treatment centres for drug users), (8) to optimise the treatment of drug users, (9) to extend the measures to reduce the supply of drugs, and (10) to establish research into the consequences of drug use for road safety. Despite a clear lack of a univocal approach to the drug phenomenon, importantly, an increased credence was given to scientific knowledge as an instrument for developing drug policy. The 10-point plan was strongly appreciated by those working in the field (De Ruyver et al., 2012). One must remember that at the time there was no Belgian drug policy, and policy-makers hardly had any experience of the drug phenomenon.

A key actor in this period was Prof. Dr. Brice De Ruyver. His position seems to be similar to the concept of *policy entrepreneur*, as articulated by Kingdon (2002), or *policy advisor* as put forward by Loader and Sparks (2011). While maintaining a firm distinction between scientific research and giving advice to policy-makers, *policy advisors* engage in providing evidence to formal advisory structures, advising MPs or Ministers informally and establishing contacts with professionals (e.g. police, outreach workers) to influence the policy-making process rather indirectly (Loader

& Sparks, 2011). In particular, perceiving it as his responsibility to bring scientific knowledge to policy-makers through formal advisory structures or even informal contacts, Brice De Ruyver picked up the growing need to establish a comprehensive national drug policy in Belgium. From 1993, an annual conference 'Drug policy 2000' was organised to develop and stimulate the interaction among practice, science and policy (De Ruyver, Vermeulen, De Leenheer, & Van Der Straten Waillet, 1995). The scientific organisation committee was composed of several scientists, practitioners and a representative of the government. During these national conferences several drug-related topics were discussed. The topics addressed clearly followed the main interests of the media and policy-makers. These conferences encouraged a greater role of scientific knowledge in the policy-making process and stimulated debate about (different) ideas as well as cooperation among (Dutch-speaking and French-speaking) practitioners, scientists, policy-makers, and journalists. These important and highly attended conferences were other incremental steps to the opening of a policy window by setting and keeping this particular issue high on the political and public/media agenda. In other words, they led to the widespread attention and shared concern that some type of action was required.

Summary

Policy shifts and developments are often precipitated by events that simply cannot be ignored, such as the arrival of the heroin epidemic and HIV in the 1980s. However, in Belgium, while the basic Belgian law relating to the traffic in toxic substances, hypnotics, narcotics, disinfectants, and antiseptics dates from 24 February 1921, the first *incremental* steps towards the development of a comprehensive Belgian drug policy were laid rather late. The supposed increase in drug-related property crimes together with the availability of government funds led to the creation of *drug prevention and security contracts* between the Federal Government and the cities at the beginning of the 1990s. Even though projects initially were set up from a crime prevention perspective, these contracts gradually broadened the discourse on drug problems. For the first time, the need for a comprehensive drug policy was stressed and a harm reduction perspective was explored, which was in accordance with the emerging trend in many countries at that time.

Simultaneously, several initiatives actually opened the door to the rationale for an *evidence-based* policy. Increased attention to scientific knowledge as an instrument for developing drug policy was evident in the *Federal Action Plan Toxicomania-Drugs* (Cabinet of the Prime Minister, 1995). This initiative can be seen as one of the first explicit steps in the development of an interest in (and influence of) policy-funded research and evaluation research about drugs in particular. At the same time, Prof. Dr. Brice De Ruyver took up a role as a *policy entrepreneur* (Kingdon, 2002), also called a *policy advisor* (Loader & Sparks, 2011), in highlighting drug policy issues and bringing them to public attention. Through the annual national conferences 'Drug Policy 2000', he engaged in the debate among scientists, practitioners, and policy-makers with their criticism and enthusiasm for knowledge about the drug phenomenon and possible policy solutions. Those conferences can be seen as one of the initiatives improving the acknowledgement of scientific knowledge in the policy-making process.

Clearly, several events provided the opportunity for a period of contention (or policy window) to ignite as a response to evidence on and perceptions of a changing problem. In Chapter 5, the first milestone in Belgian drug policy development between 1996 and 2003 is discussed.

Notes

1 During the 1980s, the Gang of Nijvel carried out a number of very violent and bloody raids on supermarkets in which a total of 28 people were killed. The unsolved killings by this criminal gang together with the poor and chaotic communication between police and justice, threatened the legitimacy of the entire police and justice system and caused a moral panic (Todts, 2004).

2 The results of this pilot project were very positive, but the legal context and the political climate at that time impeded implementation of the project in Flanders. In 2000, needle exchange projects were formalised by a Royal Decree (5 July 2000) and finally operationalised in 2001.

3 At that time, there were large differences between the more liberal practices in Brussels and the French-speaking part on the one hand, and the more cautious Flemish region, where maintenance treatment was still exceptional and where therapeutic communities were still influential, on the other hand.

4 Increasing workloads and creating an increasing number of conscientious objectors (i.e. social workers and prosecutors), the implementation of these guidelines appeared unsuccessful (Dienst Strafrechtelijk Beleid, 1996). Additionally, many cannabis users ended up in prison, and there was a lack of uniformity in the application of the prosecution policy.

5 The concept toxicomania refers to the security discourse that was common at that time (Guillain, 2009).

6 The installation of medical-social treatment centres for drug users (MSOCs) was largely inspired by the network of low-threshold (methadone) programmes in Amsterdam. Mr. Johan Vande Lanotte is considered to be the driving force of the 10-point plan and the installation of medical-social treatment centres for drug users (MSOCs) in particular (Fijnaut & De Ruyver, 2014).

Chapter 5

The Parliamentary Working Group on Drugs

1996–1997

Chapter 4 outlined how, with the increased visibility of the drug problem, not least in Belgian society, Belgian drug policy-makers gradually 'discovered' the drug phenomenon. Until the mid-1990s, there was no coherent Belgian drug policy, and policy-makers hardly had any experience of the drug phenomenon (De Ruyver et al., 2012). This situation changed with the establishment of the Parliamentary Working Group on drugs (PWG) in 1996. The drugs issue was brought into the political and public arena and became the subject of contested debates among policy-makers, professionals, scientists, journalists, and the public.

The PWG can be perceived as the first milestone in the development of Belgian drug policy. It was the first time the drug phenomenon was studied seriously by policy-makers and priority was given to a systematic approach with a proper assessment of evidence. After almost two years of expert hearings and some working visits, the opinions and statements of various experts in the PWG were compiled into a draft document, after which the members of the PWG discussed it and agreed on a final report. In general, the final report of the PWG marked a trend towards the emergence of a multidisciplinary and coherent approach to the multidimensional drug phenomenon that covers various aspects of life (*Parl.St.* Kamer, 1996–1997, 1062/1–3). Prevention had to be the first goal and a criminal approach towards drug users was supported by a so-called *ultimum remedium* ('last resort') philosophy. In particular, as one of its main conclusions and recommendations, the PWG recommended developing an *integrated and integral drug policy*, with both vertical policy coordination between different policy levels (federal, regional, provincial, and local) in the domains of prevention, treatment, and social policy, and horizontal coordination among the various policy domains and at the various levels. Concerning *epidemiology and evaluation*, the need for quantitative and qualitative studies among the general population and among special and at-risk populations was re-emphasised.[1] Epidemiology would provide the facts and figures for drug policy. Structural and person-orientated *prevention* was to become the priority. The recommendations emphasised the need for a professional statute for prevention workers and paid special attention to youth, psychoactive medicines, smart drugs, and the consequences of drug use for road safety. For drug users experiencing problems, a wide variety of (drug-)treatment services and general *treatment* services (from low-threshold facilities to therapeutic programmes) had to be established. As for highly problematic drug users, a harm reduction approach was chosen and the stimulation of harm reduction initiatives other than substitution treatment was advised. Finally, the main issue of *repression* was the fight against illegal drug production and traffic. Supported by the so-called 'last resort' philosophy, problematic drug users in the criminal justice system had to be oriented more towards treatment. Measures to combat the use of drugs in prison also had to be instituted. The PWG further supported the distinction between cannabis and other illegal drugs by giving the *lowest prosecution priority* for the possession of cannabis for personal use, unless it causes public nuisance or in the case of a problematic user.

Having discussed specific topics such as drug epidemiology, criminalisation of drugs, prescription and substitution of methadone and/or heroin, international drug production, and methadone and/or heroin substitution, the advice of the PWG was to develop a *normalisation policy*,[2] a so-called *third way* between prohibition and anti-prohibition (*Parl.St.* Kamer, 1996–1997, 1062/3, p. 992), which can be seen as an outcome of a powerful struggle between a social and public health framework and a legalistic/repressive framework. The final conclusions and recommendations of the PWG reflected how the thinking about the drug phenomenon had developed. The focus on drug use as an issue of public health rather than of criminal justice (based on the repressive drug law) included an important formalisation of the change in discourse first raised by the 1995 Federal Action Plan Toxicomania-Drugs earlier on.

This chapter reviews how the PWG has obtained and used scientific knowledge, and whether the final recommendations and conclusions of the PWG have been enacted upon this evidence, taking into account the policy environment which contains many actors and pressures.

The *Bottom-Up Approach*: Processes of Non-Government Stakeholder Involvement

Each of the previously mentioned events in Belgium and elsewhere provided the background for some (even though rather isolated) *incremental steps* gradually opening a *policy window* (Kingdon, 2002). However, timing and opportunity are crucial, presupposing that an issue may never appear on the policy agenda without a campaign, crisis, or focusing event (Cairney, 2016). In this case-study, the event actually igniting the opening of the policy window was a threat in the French-speaking newspaper *Le Soir*

(17 November 1995) by MP Patrick Moriau (French-speaking Socialist party, PS) to submit a proposal to *depenalise* (and in a later stage *legalise*) cannabis possession (in contrast with the repressive Belgian law). Several newspapers picked up the decisive article and published the core of it the day after. With headlines like "PS wants to legalise cannabis" (18 November 1995, Flemish newspaper *Gazet van Antwerpen*), they immediately created a climate in which concepts such as 'danger', 'death', or 'disease' were linked with the concept of legalisation of cannabis (instead of depenalisation which was argued by MP Moriau). Several interest groups advocating for drug users' rights (*Belgian Cannabis Consumers' Organisation, A citizen just like any other, Association against the prohibition*) also took advantage of media attention in an attempt to publicise their ideas and to persuade the public and policy-makers to share their point of view. Their initiatives ranged from media coverage to the organisation of demonstrations, which is in accordance with the main mechanisms employed by interest groups to influence drug discourse (EMCDDA, 2013; O'Gorman et al., 2014).

In accordance with Lenton (2004), it seemed that once the topic was highly covered in the media, it was harder to ignore for policy-makers. Media coverage trickled down into the parliamentary debate by means of questions and interpellations (*Hand.* Kamer 1995–1996, 13 November 1995, 230/1) and eventually made the Federal Parliament decide to establish a PWG to inform itself about the complexity of the drug phenomenon. In doing so, the media (and interest groups) thus played a significant role in empowering the *enlightenment* function of scientific knowledge in this case: media coverage not only shaped political action but also generated a widespread consultation of non-government stakeholders, including scientists. In particular, the PWG, formally composed of one or more representatives of each political party seated in the Commissions of Justice, Internal Affairs and Public Health in Belgian Parliament, aimed to study the complexity and multidisciplinary nature of the drug phenomenon to determine the future orientation of Belgian drug policy.

> Even though the working method may be time-consuming and ambitious, it is valuable to ask international, national and local experts to make an inventory of the multidimensional aspects of the phenomenon, such as: health risks; implications for security and public order; judicial elements, such as (inter)national drug trafficking and drug-related criminality, and social and economic factors.
>
> (Verslag namens de Parlementaire Werkgroep belast met het bestuderen van de drugproblematiek, *Parl.St.* Kamer, 1996–1997, 1062/1–3)

The amount of time allowed for in-depth deliberation was critical as well as the clear, multidisciplinary focus. Members of the PWG relied on a wide range of experts (59 over a period of two years) to get an idea of good practices as well as of scientific findings regarding the drug phenomenon. In addition, a specialist advisor – a criminologist (Prof. Dr. Brice De Ruyver) – was appointed to attend the hearings, report on them and explore possible ways of thinking about the drug phenomenon.

There was a broad representation of publics (i.e. professionals, interest groups, and scientists – toxicologists, pharmacologists, epidemiologists, criminologists, and sociologists), as several MPs had to compromise on competing ideologies in selecting experts. The selection and non-selection of expert advice can be seen as an integral part of the policy process (McCann, 2008; Miller, 1999). A lot of care was given to political (i.e. party policy and majority vs. opposition) and cultural/linguistic (e.g. Flemish MPs preferred the selection of Flemish experts) issues. At the same time, in line with literature on policy networks (Sutton, 1999; Neilson, 2001; Nutley et al., 2007), it appeared that personal contacts/networks were at least as important as the expertise and competence of experts. Therefore, it comes as no surprise that a certain degree of overlap was observed between the scientific organisation committee of the conference 'Drug Policy 2000' and the pool of university professors[3] appointed to conduct the research projects which were commissioned and funded by the Government in the 1990s on the one hand, and the stakeholders involved in the PWG on the other.

> Every member of the PWG made a list of experts and those who were mentioned on several lists are invited automatically. Yes ... mostly one knows one or more experts personally [...]. It is not only about the expertise of an expert but, yes, the access to policy or the contacts with policy-makers, both elements I think.
>
> (Respondent 35, policy-maker)

> These conferences did build up a strong network [...] Policy-makers had a good idea of who, in the French-speaking part as well as in the Dutch-speaking part, was involved in several domains.
>
> (Respondent 50, scientist)

In particular, the experts can be divided into three categories: 12 scientists, 44 practitioners, and three representatives of interest groups of ex-users. The first category included national and international scientists, selected from different countries (related to the importance given to the international framework) and different angles: pharmacology, epidemiology, and criminology. Reflecting the *evidence-based policy* account which is premised on the notion of an independent, truth-seeking scientist (Hartnoll, 2004; Nutley et al., 2007), policy-makers clearly assessed scientific knowledge as the way to get at 'truth' and to understand a phenomenon satisfactorily. The PWG sought 'certainties' or 'facts' and scientific knowledge was assumed to reflect 'objectivity' and 'authoritative, truth-producing' data. But, at the same time, members of the PWG acknowledged that practitioners were considered to have a better sense of crucial real-world information building on their practical hands-on experience. Practitioners were selected from police (6), justice (9), treatment services (19), and prevention services (10).

> Scientific knowledge played a role in the PWG [...] Scientific knowledge represents authoritative, truth-producing data [...]. It is the only objective source which can provide data for policy-makers.
>
> (Respondent 51, policy-maker)

> Several experts were heard in the PWG [...] huge gaps in scientific knowledge remain and practitioners may have a better sense of practical day-to-day issues.
>
> (Respondent 29, policy-maker)

Furthermore, each of the activities of the interest groups, outlined above, had successfully provided an opportunity to press for the inclusion of lay knowledge as evidence in formal advisory structures. In the PWG, interest groups arrived at their own interpretation of evidence to steer decisions in one way or another and at the same time heating up and polarising the debates. For example, those supporting drug users' rights regularly pointed out that a conviction for cannabis possession can have significant adverse impacts and thus use should be legalised; an argument gratefully used in the political struggle especially by progressive political voices.

As well as these categories of experts, some members of the Federal Government and the Federate Government were also invited and heard in the PWG. Although it was the goal of the PWG to study the phenomenon thoroughly, this selection was still in accordance with the prevailing discourse of the period prior to the 1990s: both the Federal Minister of Social Affairs and the Federal Minister of Public Health were not heard in the PWG (*Hand.* Kamer 1996–1997, 24 juni 1997, 175).

This so-called *bottom-up approach*, characterised by public deliberation and participation which challenges the traditional *top-down approach* and also recognises the plurality of expert knowledge including informal expertise, has been one of the strong characteristics of the development of Belgian drug policy. Belgian policy-makers could learn from a wide range of (inter)national experiences or expertise, positive and negative. The final report of the PWG on drugs mainly mirrored the needs and expectations of the different domains in the professional field and in the academic world at that time (Verslag namens de Parlementaire Werkgroep belast met het bestuderen van de drugproblematiek, *Parl.St.* Kamer, 1996–1997, 1062/1–3). In particular, it can be pointed out that the recommendation to develop a comprehensive, public health policy in Belgium, taking into account the broader social context including drug prevention, reduction of drug-related harm, and crime deterrence, is a clear result of this approach (De Ruyver et al., 2012). Also, that this initiative was taken up by the Federal Parliament[4] (rather than the Federal Government[5]) allowed a more open and in-depth dialogue instead of what immediately would have been a polarised and contested debate in the Federal Government. While the Government must decide on policy goals, the work of a PWG is different in the sense of aiming to scrutinise and build up advice to be presented to the Government. Similar to the findings of MacGregor's (2012b) study of parliamentary committees in the UK in relation to drug policy governance, the PWG played an important role in regard to the creation of a cross-party political forum and the critical assessment of policy goals and objectives, development and use of evidence, and stakeholder engagement. In the next paragraph, following the scope of the book, the contribution of scientists in discussing and defining the recommendations for future Belgian drug policy in the PWG is outlined in more detail. Several examples showed how scientists took up the opportunity to participate directly to the PWG and how (un)successful this was in the light of knowledge utilisation.

Scientists in the PWG: 'Cooling Devices' vs. Mobilisation of 'Heating' Alternatives

For some scientists, the most fruitful way to cultivate a rational policy approach is to emphasise scientific credibility and methodological rigour. Their public engagement is restricted to passively disseminating what they know alongside rare participation in formal advisory structures. In particular, several *scientific experts*, as articulated in the typology of Loader and Sparks (2011), participated in the PWG in 1996. In doing so, they carefully replied to questions for information but were not proactively seeking engagement outside these formal advisory structures (they considered this a 'red line' not to be crossed):

> My contribution was for the most part illustrative, I gave some additional information. That's it [...] I was not searching for participation, I did not make an effort. I always try to formulate clear recommendations. Maybe this is not good enough and maybe I should participate in the policy-making process. The question is then, to what extent is your scientific research compromised or does one have the impression it is compromised?
>
> (Respondent 24, scientist)

> I just presented some facts, data and that is it [...]. They asked me as an expert. I do not take the initiative myself to get involved actively. That is not my goal as an academic.
>
> (Respondent 13, scientist)

Clearly, in this position most tensions remain between the public role and the academic position with often competing audiences and expectations. While this form of engagement entails minimal involvement in the policy-making process, those *scientific experts* have sought to influence the policy-making process in a light touch way through the dissemination of data and interpretations. This is in accordance with the *conceptual* or '*enlightenment*' model of knowledge utilisation where scientific knowledge can be conceived as part of the process of policy-making via the percolation of new ideas (Weiss, 1979; Nutley, 2003). For instance, in the PWG (1996–1997), *scientific experts* stimulated thorough discussion and reflection among policy-makers. By repeatedly referring to (foreign) epidemiological data, statistics (e.g. crime statistics, conviction statistics, emergency unit statistics, or number of alcohol and drug controls), and the policy-funded studies of De Ruyver, Vermeulen, Franck, and Van Daele (1992; Poverty, drug use, and criminality) and of Vercaigne and Walgrave (1995; Youth between (sub)cultures and business: a study focusing on discotheques, house music, and nuisance), their contributions served as strong scientific support for, respectively, the argument that (problematic) drug users in the criminal justice system had to be oriented more towards treatment, and the argument that prevention initiatives have to pay special attention to youth, smart drugs, and the consequences of drug use for road safety.

According to Loader and Sparks (2011), *social movement theorists/activists* take up a similar role as *scientific experts* as they primarily aim to produce scientific knowledge and do not go beyond infrequent participation in formal advisory structures. However, they seek to influence in a different manner by acting as a 'heating device' and injecting critical/alternative discourse into debates. *Social movement theorists/activists* align themselves with social groups whose interests are not served by policy-makers and aim to place knowledge and skills at the service of those who are marginalised or excluded (e.g. drug users). In the PWG, issues concerning the largely unproblematic characteristic of drug use, the role of self-control strategies, and the legitimacy of the criminalisation of drugs (cannabis in particular) have been put forward by these scientists.

> As scientists, we have to engage in the movement for the reduction of the harm for drug users by critically addressing the existing presuppositions about drugs in society [...]. For instance, most community based drug use is highly 'controlled' [...] and associated with low risk for the large majority of drug users [...] these insights are relevant for policy-makers who are looking for alternatives.
>
> (Peter Cohen, scientist; Report of the PWG, pp. 172–185)

Those struggling for alternative politics were, however, not successful in impacting knowledge utilisation in policy-making. Their insights only succeeded in heating up the political climate and were used as ammunition in the PWG (*political/symbolic* utilisation; Weiss, 1979). As suggested by Walters (2003), policy-makers may rationalise their position by choosing to neglect or dismiss findings which do not support their political agenda (or so-called *deviant* knowledge). For example, representatives of the government easily distorted these scientific arguments by criticising them as irrational or incorrect (a tactic of creating '*flak*'; *evolutionary* model; Stevens, 2007a). Accordingly, the Minister of Internal Affairs Johan Vande Lanotte (SP, Flemish Socialists) stated that "There is no rational argument to determine the line between innocent and dangerous drug use" (Report of the PWG, p. 827). Similarly, even though several scientists underlined the disproof of the stepping-stone theory in the hearings, the Minister of Justice Stefaan De Clerck (CVP, Flemish Christian Democrats) noted: "It is a real danger that youngsters would start with other illegal drugs, if cannabis became freely available..." (Report of the PWG, p. 795). Mr. Kris Van Limbergen, the advisor of the Cabinet of the Minister of Internal Affairs, also ignoring the scientific disproof of this theory, argued that "recreational drugs may be very tempting as so-called step-up drugs" (Report of the PWG, p. 668).

In addition, a specialist advisor – a criminologist – adopted an active engagement in the PWG. Prof. Dr. Brice De Ruyver can be seen as a privileged member of the PWG which is linked with the particular public role of an *observer-turned-player* (Loader & Sparks, 2011). Some of his position also seems to be similar to the concept of *policy entrepreneur* as articulated by Kingdon (2002). In particular, as a consequence of his expertise and networks (resulting from his organisation of the national conferences 'Drug Policy 2000'), he was appointed by the PWG to attend the hearings, to summarise them, and to explore possible ways of thinking about the drug phenomenon. His draft of the final report of the PWG served as a starting point in the political discussion about the future goals and objectives of Belgian drug policy among the members of the PWG. Altering the tone of the political discussion, the final report of the PWG eventually produced a clear expression of the changing discourse by the PWG, with the emergence of the public health approach instead of a strict repressive discourse: "the working group believes that it is neither useful nor effective to apply a criminal procedure in case of violations of the drug law" (Report of the PWG, p. 1004). At this point there is also accordance with the *conceptual* or *enlightenment* model of knowledge utilisation (Weiss, 1979; Nutley, 2003).

However, simultaneously, the *observer-turned-player* offered and tailored advice in accordance with the preferences of the policy-makers. In particular, the summary of the hearings displayed a lack of sensitivity to the views of *critical* contributors (*social movement theorists/activists*) focusing on the largely unproblematic characteristic of drug use, the usefulness of self-control strategies, or the *decriminalisation* of cannabis possession. As advocated by Loader and Sparks (2011), this type of public engagement can indeed be described as a role where the expert is getting his or her hands 'dirty', addressing the very thin line between being a neutral/external expert or a policy-advocating expert. While the draft of the final conclusions and recommendations was required to provide a sufficient base for policy debate, it is evident that a summary of the hearings had to retain autonomy/neutrality completely including the alternative, critical voices too. Several respondents explained these practices of selectivity as being related to the characteristics of the political context.

> It makes no sense to integrate findings that are supporting a totally different view than the view policy-makers want to end with [...]. The expert has to take a neutral point of view [...] but some issues indeed have been left out.
>
> (Respondent 4, policy-maker)

> Policy-makers have followed the debates, they know the sensitivities and possibilities and, within this framework, the expert has to write a summary [...]. If the expert does the proper thing by including critical voices too, the political discussion is certainly hampered. It is his task to elucidate the political debate [...]
>
> (Respondent 50, scientist)

Leaving aside the different levels of engagement, it also became clear that each of those scientists presented their knowledge in the PWG as 'speaking truth to power', as originally articulated by Wildavsky (1979) and later on discussed by e.g. Jasanoff (1990) and Boland (2008). In doing so, they acted as producers of privileged, authoritative knowledge claims by using propositional assumptions (i.e. assumptions about what is or can be or will be the case; 'truth') and active verbs without any bibliographic references. For instance, "cannabis use leads to ...", "it is determined that 90% of the drug addicts ...", "the prevalence of poly drug use has increased", "the war against drugs caused a lot of suffering", "50% of youth has experimented with drugs". However, in their efforts to possess and speak *truth*, it remains important to be cautious regarding the knowledge some scientists brought into policy debates. A nuanced account of the nature of scientific knowledge is necessary which is in accordance with the *processual* model of knowledge utilisation (Monaghan, 2011). Although scientists regularly expressed their awareness of the importance of a careful presentation and interpretation of scientific results (especially numbers),[6] some seem to jeopardise their credibility. Uggen and Inderbitzin (2010) called such scientists, flying around as consultants and experts while losing sight of their scientific research base, *airport scientists*. During the hearings in the PWG, some scientists neglected the main principles of scientific research by not taking into account, for example, accurate methodological designs or unambiguous terminologies. Terminological impurities (e.g. a comparison of percentage users of hashish and percentage of users of cannabis, a comparison of drug prevalence rates while neglecting that some rates only focused on cannabis use and others on the use of cannabis, ecstasy, and cocaine) and neglecting statistical significance in studying the relationship between cannabis use and truancy were two such problems. In another example, studies using different methodologies were compared. In particular, a scientist compared an opinion poll of a newspaper to a population survey among youth to get comparable and valuable results. He mentioned that "a school population survey can be compared to the opinion survey carried out by the newspaper *Le Soir* in 1980 as this research was set up in a similar method" (Report of the PWG, p. 57). Another scientist stated: "These numbers are the result of a methodological approach that is not really satisfactory from a scientific point of view. Nevertheless, they show that the use of multiple illicit substances has increased" (Report of the PWG, p. 57). Juggling numbers or scientific results was also found. Scientific results were distorted in several ways, which were often very subtle, for example making blunt interpretations, false generalisations, and causalities. For instance, one scientist made a false interpretation regarding poly drug use. In particular, he mentioned that "90% of drug addicts use several substances" (Report of the PWG, p. 189), while the original research concluded that "90% of the daily heroin users are poly drug users". Another scientist replied to the questions of the members of the PWG "We found that truant youth use twice as many illegal drugs" (Report of the PWG, p. 83), while he originally stated in the hearing that "non statistical significant numbers showed that 28.5% of truant youth ever used cannabis" (Report of the PWG, p. 59).

The Political Struggle over the Criminalisation of Drugs: Impact of Politics and the Media

Respect for a variety of expert evidence and the existence of a space for deliberative dialogue in the PWG were core mechanisms in allowing a cross-party and *evidence-informed* agreement in the PWG to be reached. One notable exception was the recommendation to apply the lowest prosecution priority for the possession of cannabis for personal use, which was not supported fully. While it is clear that the criminalisation of drugs, cannabis policy in particular, was the trigger for the emerging interest in the Belgian drug policy development, the political struggle on this issue sheds some light on the problematic nature of the *evidence-based* policy rhetoric. Here, the exercise of power and the desire of policy-makers for the maintenance and enhancement of their own position strongly impacted on the use of evidence. In particular, even though most scientists, practitioners, and representatives of the interest groups seemed to nuance the dangers and risks of cannabis use, proposals for decriminalisation of cannabis were resoundingly rejected by policy-makers. As noted in previous studies, processes of knowledge utilisation may be particularly bedevilled by reluctance by policy-makers when they touch on issues that concern law enforcement or the international prohibitive framework such as cannabis policy (Monaghan, 2014; Houborg & Asmussen, 2014).

First of all, as a signatory to the main international conventions, Belgium was bound to have a particular policy in place. Right from the start, several international drug-control treaties (e.g. the UN treaties of 1961–1971–1988 and the 1990 Schengen Convention), strongly supported by the international community, determined particular policy choices regarding the usefulness of the criminalisation of drugs. For instance, as described by the members of the PWG: it was important to take into account "the boundaries of the Belgian drug policy in regard to the international conventions and the attitude of the international community on drug policy" (Report of the PWG, p. 944). At the same time, in the Netherlands, by the mid-1990s it had become clear that the system of tolerated distribution of cannabis through *coffee shops* was not an entirely successful strategy. The Dutch Government acknowledged the adverse implications and changed direction in 1995 with the Drug Note '*The Dutch drug policy, continuity and change*' (Dutch Government, 1995). Priority was given to the control of and fight against these unforeseen effects of the tolerance policy (Fijnaut & De Ruyver, 2008). Accordingly, it was stated in the PWG that: "A solution like the Dutch coffee-shop model is not recommended as a part of the traffic and profits are not controlled by the Government (which is an opportunity for mafia)" (Mr. Philippe Bastin, practitioner; Report of the PWG, p. 466).

Second, another challenger of the *evidence-based* rhetoric, and linked with the *two communities thesis* (Caplan, 1979), can be attributed to the institutional characteristics of the political setting (e.g. political party instructions, majority versus minority issues, and individual experiences of policy-makers). For instance, the fact that members/representatives of the Government were heard in the PWG impacted on the opinions and the direction of the members of the PWG (who were of the same political colour). Exemplary, therefore, is discussion about the contribution of Mr. Lucien Nouwynck, the advisor of the Minister of Justice Stefaan De Clerck (CVP, Flemish Christian Democrats). Based on the findings of the French Commission Henrion,[7] Mr. Lucien Nouwynck provided a more moderate view and pleaded for a pilot project that would implement controlled regulation of illicit drugs for a short time period. His progressive perspective was remarkable, taking into account his membership of the rather conservative Christian Democrats. This position was not at all appreciated by the

Flemish Christian Democrats and hampered the relationship with the Minister completely.

Another example, illustrating the importance of politics, is the debate on terminology. While the draft of the final report by Prof. Dr. Brice De Ruyver initially recommended a de facto *depenalisation* of cannabis possession for personal use (Report of the PWG, p. 947) by means of issuing a new Ministerial Circular Letter (in substitution for the 1993 Ministerial Circular Letter of Minister of Justice Melchior Wathelet (PSC, French-speaking Christian Democrats)), members of the conservative parties took the lead to delete the phrasing "de facto depenalisation of cannabis possession for personal use" to avoid discussion about the (anti-)prohibition of drug use as well as any comparisons with the criticised Dutch drug policy of tolerance.

> The Flemish Christian Democrats (CVP) could not agree with certain elements [...]. The draft of Prof. Dr. De Ruyver created a lot of discussions. I know that Flemish Christian Democrat Vandeurzen rejected some paragraphs [...] CVP was apprehensive about a too liberal direction.
>
> (Respondent 42, policy-maker)

> The elimination of 'depenalisation' was supported by the CVP because of its connection with the concept of legalisation. Of course, both concepts mean different things but their demand was related to communication issues and public opinion.
>
> (Respondent 7, policy-maker)

For this purpose, policy-makers made use of several *political tactics* to attain greater authority or a higher position, or to favour their electorates. For instance, members of the Government (consciously) made incorrect interpretations to find support. Cannabis is not legalised in the Netherlands, in contrast to what was frequently stated. Minister of Internal Affairs Johan Vande Lanotte argued: "In the Netherlands, they make complaints about the consequences of hasty legalisation" (Report of the PWG, p. 853). The misuse of terminology has fuelled clear misconceptions about the reform. Eventually, the concept of de facto *depenalisation* was removed and the final conclusion only mentioned the *lowest prosecution priority for cannabis possession for personal use*, unless it causes public nuisance or in case of a problematic user (Report of the PWG, p. 1004).

Another recurring issue during the political struggle on the criminalisation of drugs was related to determination of a number of grams for personal cannabis use. At that time, Flemish and French-speaking Christian Democrats refused to determine a quantity for personal use (even though Prof. Dr. Brice De Ruyver initially argued that "obviously, it is necessary to determine what amount can be considered as quantity for personal use" (De Ruyver, 1997, p. 19)). A respondent clarified:

> The number of grams ... CVP refused to determine the number of grams. If one decided to limit the use to five grams, this should mean that four grams is not harmful. CVP rejected any quantification.
>
> (Respondent 42, policy-maker)

While the debate over the criminalisation of drugs was politicised, a similar mechanism was witnessed in the media coverage on Belgian drug policy over the two years of expert hearings. As an example of the *priming* effect of media (McCombs & Shaw, 1972), media coverage reduced the complexity of the discussion in the PWG to just one topic: cannabis policy. Headlines related to the PWG (1996–1997) refrained this focus. "Commission on drugs. White smoke on the legalisation of cannabis" (27 June 1996, Walloon newspaper *La Peuple*). Furthermore, the reporting of these debates in the press has tended not to focus on the scientific deliberation or evidence-base; instead media informed the public (and thus policy-makers) in a rather coloured way. Drugs were very often spoken about in terms of 'soft drugs' versus 'hard drugs', and often the general concept 'drugs' was used to refer to one drug like cannabis. In addition, concepts like 'legalisation', 'depenalisation', 'decriminalisation', and 'tolerance policy' were regularly used without differentiating between each of them. Equally, media did not make a distinction between the use and possession of cannabis, in spite of the important juridical difference: in Belgium, drug possession is prohibited while drug use is not. In creating a scenario where only certain facts are considered newsworthy, a journalist explained parts of the imperatives governing journalism:

> Newspapers, media, are more in favour of explicit opinions so, as a result, the debate is narrowed [...] I am a lawyer but the public debate has to be simple. In many newspapers, these concepts were used wrongly. A juridical nuance is not interesting. The bottom-line is: is it allowed or not? Can my son smoke joints? Can it be sold?
>
> (Respondent 45, journalist)

Describing Belgian cannabis policy as a tolerance policy (*gedoogbeleid*) and making incorrect comparisons with the Dutch cannabis policy (*coffeeshop* model), media coverage provoked the reactions of several politicians. Members of the Flemish Christian Democrats reacted furiously in the Flemish media against any tolerance policy and the use of the concept '*depenalisation*' as they were very concerned with how their electorate (and public opinion in general) would perceive and respond to this direction (even though there were no elections coming up).[8] Likewise, the power of the media can be blamed because of its assumption of a *five grams limit* in line with the Dutch policy. "In order to have some sort of policy alignment with the Dutch policy, the five grams limit could be used as a criterion. The last Dutch drug note of September 1995 allows the same amount" (19 February 1997, Flemish newspaper *De Morgen*). Narrowing down the focus to one single element and stimulating further confusion and conflicting interests, the media discourse on the development of the Belgian drug policy also appeared to feed into the PWG in supporting assumptions in this political struggle (and thus refuting scientific arguments). For instance, Federal Minister of Internal Affairs Johan Vande Lanotte (SP, Flemish Socialists) used a newspaper article from Mr. Pino Arlacchi (former Director-General of the United Nations Office, current member of the European Parliament) in the Italian newspaper *L'Espresso* as a support for his statements about the drug policy in the USA. Flemish Minister of Health Policy Wivina Demeester-De Meyer acted similarly.

> Drugs in the United States (the end of fatalism). The following data are to a large extent derived from the article of the rather famous 'Pino Arlacchi' in 'L'espresso' of 16 April 1996 [my emphasis].
>
> (Mr. Johan Vande Lanotte, Federal Minister of Internal Affairs, SP, Flemish Socialists; Report of the PWG, p. 815)

> Ms Demeester-De Meyer declares that the way the drug problem is shown in the media often goes together with a lot of sensation. For example, a daily newspaper recently published a brochure in which a direct plea was made for the legalisation of drugs [my emphasis].
>
> (Mrs. Wivina Demeester- De Meyer, Flemish Minister of Health Policy, CVP, Flemish Christian Democrats; Report of the PWG, p. 791)

Summary

The aim of this chapter has been to shed light on the first milestone in the development of Belgian drug policy between 1996 and 2003. The PWG played an important role in the drug policy-making process, scrutinising future policy goals and objectives. Scientific knowledge was significantly a tool used by policy actors to discuss and define the recommendations for future policy. The new frameworks for understanding of the drug phenomenon, provided by hearings of (inter)national experts, did '*enlighten*' the policy debate (*conceptual* or '*enlightenment*' model; Weiss, 1979) and clearly altered the discourse in the drug policy-making process. In the political struggle on the criminalisation of drugs, however, scientific knowledge was mainly used as ammunition for political sides (Weiss, 1979; Stevens, 2007a) or even side-stepped by political commitments. In this context, the influence of the

Dutch situation arose, along with references to the international conventions. These examples identified through the analysis of the PWG can be considered as illustrations of the institutional barriers to knowledge utilisation as documented by Caplan (1979) in his *two communities thesis*.

This snapshot further showed the various modus operandi of scientists, articulating the types of public engagement put forward by Loader and Sparks (2011), and how this role can be fuzzy, especially when participating actively in the context of policy-making. The role of the *observer-turned-player* is situated on the very thin line between being a neutral/external expert or a policy-advocating expert. His summary of the hearings tended to offer and tailor advice in accordance with the preferences of the policy-makers (cfr. *evolutionary model*; Stevens, 2007a) and, as such, displayed less sensitivity to the views of more critical accounts (of e.g. *social movement theorists/activists*). In a similar vein, in accordance with the *processual* model of knowledge utilisation (Monaghan, 2011), it seemed necessary to be cautious regarding the nature of scientific knowledge that scientists brought into policy debates. Several forms of misuse of science by scientists were distinguished during the hearings (e.g. using ambiguous terminologies or ignoring statistical significance). If scientists misrepresent their expertise they are involved in and become so-called *airport scientists* (Uggen & Inderbitzin, 2010), there is even less hope for well-informed coverage in the policy-making process.

In accordance with key media theories (McCombs & Shaw, 1972; Lancaster et al., 2011), the media can be perceived as a powerful player in defining public interest (*agenda-setting*) and in contextualising issues through selection and prominence (*framing*). For instance, it was media coverage, and not scientific knowledge, which initially shaped political action in Belgium in terms of the establishment of the PWG. As the PWG prioritised a systematic approach with a proper assessment of existing and new evidence, the media (and to a lesser extent interest groups) can be said to have played a significant role in empowering the *enlightenment* function of scientific knowledge. Unfortunately, right from the start, media framing has tended not to focus on the diversity of issues underpinning Belgian drug policy (e.g. international drug production and methadone and/or heroin substitution); instead, media attention, heating up the political climate, had come down to the legitimacy of the criminalisation of drugs, and cannabis policy in particular (*priming*).

By detailing the first milestone in the development of Belgian drug policy between 1996 and 2003, it became clear which *models of knowledge utilisation* (Weiss, 1979; Stevens, 2007a; Monaghan, 2011) were prevalent, as well as through which *types of public engagements* (Loader & Sparks, 2011) scientific knowledge contributed to the PWG and how (un)successful this was. Chapter 6 will illustrate how these issues apply during an era in which topics other than drugs became more central to the political agenda.

Notes

1 The need to extend scientific research such as epidemiological studies and evaluations (e.g. evaluation of the medical-social treatment centres for drug users) was already stressed in the Federal Action Plan Toxicomania-Drugs (10-point plan) (1995).

2 A policy where the drug phenomenon is considered to be a permanent social reality (*Parl.St.* Kamer, 1996–1997, 1062/3, p. 992).

3 For instance, the studies 'Poverty, drugs and criminality' (1992) and 'Desirability of methadone maintenance treatment' (1993) were allocated to Prof. Dr. Brice De Ruyver (UGent) and another study 'Inventory of epidemiological data in Belgium and in some neighbouring countries' (1996) to Prof. Dr. Brice De Ruyver (UGent), Prof. Dr. Joris Casselman (KULeuven), and Prof. Dr. Alfred Noirfalise (ULg). A study creating a manual for evaluation of the medical-social treatment centres for drug users (MSOCs) (1997) was also allocated to Prof. Dr. Brice De Ruyver (UGent) and Prof. Dr. Alfred Noirfalise (ULg). Evaluation of the MSOCs (1999) was allocated to Prof. Dr. I. Pelc (ULB), Prof. Dr. B. De Ruyver (UGent), Prof. Dr. J. Casselman (KULeuven), Prof. Dr. A. Noirfalise (ULg), and Prof. Dr. C. Macquet (ULg) (Bullens et al.,1999).

4 Belgium is a federal State with a bicameral Federal Parliament consisting of a House of Representatives and a Senate. The Federal Parliament has the power to control the executive branch and monitor its initiatives but, simultaneously, it holds legislative power.

5 The Federal Government holds the federal executive power: it has responsibility for developing and implementing policy and for drafting laws within particular domains such as public finances, the army, judicial system, social security, and foreign affairs, as well as substantial parts of public health and home affairs. The power to make decisions is not the exclusive preserve of the Federal Government and the Federal Parliament. The leadership of the country is also in the hands of various partners (Communities and Regions), who independently exercise their authority within their own domains.

6 They criticised official numbers as they tell us more about the activities of the service rather than any real increase/decrease. Population surveys (i.e. opinion polls and surveys among the general population and school populations) were criticised because of their limited methodological quality and/or comparability.

7 In 1994, the Minister of State for Social, Health, and Urban Affairs, Mrs. Simone Veil, appointed a Commission, headed by Robert Henrion, to examine and reconsider the French drug policy (Boekhout van Solinge, 1996; Nathanson, 2009).

8 The next elections were held in 1999.

Chapter 6

Turbulent Intermezzo

1997–2000

The Parliamentary Working Group on drugs (PWG), charged with studying the drug problem in Belgium, acted as a useful mechanism for agreeing on the concepts or perspectives for understanding of the drug phenomenon and for influencing Federal Government policy through clear recommendations. However, while the drug phenomenon received policy-makers' attention and viable policy solutions were available in terms of the final recommendations and conclusions of the PWG, it took some time to become accepted within government. Kingdon (2002) regards such a *period of 'softening up'* as vital because *windows of opportunity* are likely to close quickly and policy-makers are often resistant to major policy change. Policy actors often prefer to take one small step at a time to move in their preferred direction. The intermezzo between 1997 and 2000 can be considered as such an important period of '*softening up*': separate initiatives were supportive in getting the public and policy-makers used to the new ideas and in building acceptance for the recommendations and conclusions of the PWG. In addition, these initiatives did prevent the closing of the policy window, especially because the entire Belgian drug debate was overshadowed by the Dutroux paedophilia case.[1] A Parliamentary Inquiry Commission, also referred to as the Dutroux Inquiry Commission (October 1996–April 1997),[2] was created to investigate possible police and judiciary incompetence and corruption. From mid-1997 onwards, the focus of the political (and media) discussion shifted to reforms of the judicial authorities and the police (the so-called 'Octopus' negotiations).

In the literature it is also acknowledged that, during a *period of 'softening up'* (Kingdon, 2002), a change in government may be enough to eventually ignite a policy change or development (Cairney, 2016). In the Belgian case, it actually took a change of Belgian government in 1999 for the major policy development to occur. The fairly extensive and specific Coalition Agreement of the new *six-party* Coalition among the Flemish and French-speaking Liberals, Socialists, and Greens led by Flemish Liberal Leader Guy Verhofstadt (1999–2003) can be considered as "breaking with the past" (Verhofstadt, 1999), paving the way for the development of the first national drug strategy in 2001.

A Period of '*Softening Up*'

International Context

For a long time, drugs were scarcely discussed within the framework of the European Community.[3] It was not until the Treaty of Maastricht (1992) that drugs, along with many other new subject areas, were brought within the European Union's competence (Boekhout van Solinge, 2002). The European Union focused on consolidation of common measures for combating drug addiction and drug trafficking, for promoting international cooperation, and for supporting the efforts of the United Nations. The 1997 Amsterdam Treaty was a reconfirmation of the 1992 Maastricht Treaty but also determined for the first time that the highest priority should be given to the reduction of drug-related harm (De Ruyver et al., 2002). Article 152 aimed at cooperation to stress the objective to reduce drug-related health damage alongside the traditional cooperation in the prevention field. This article provided a judicial basis for the member states to implement *harm reduction* strategies. Following the UN conventions, these provisions also required the application of criminal sanctions on the supply side. On the demand side, there were no explicit requirements in relation to the criminalisation of the use and possession for personal use. The European Action Plan to Combat Drugs 2000–2004 was built on this framework by which drug problems increasingly came to be seen as public health problems (European Commission, 1999; De Ruyver et al., 2002; Chatwin, 2011).

Furthermore, following the implementation of the 1990 Schengen Convention, the Inter-parliamentary Advisory Council of the Benelux countries provided a report about drug policy in Benelux in November 1998. While describing the different drug policies, the recommendations of the Benelux report clearly showed agreement about the importance of a *normalisation policy*, as a third way between a prohibitionist and anti-prohibitionist policy (Inter-parliamentary Advisory Council of the Benelux countries, 1998; Fijnaut & De Ruyver, 2008). The notion of a 'normalisation policy' first appeared in the conclusions of the PWG (1996–1997), but its international acceptance has been decisive for further development of Belgian drug policy (see Chapter 7).

In addition to the Drug Note of 1995 ('*The Dutch drug policy, continuity and change*'), the Dutch Government published its official paper 'Pathways to the back door' in April 2000 which addressed publicly the problems of drug tourism, the professionalisation and commercialisation of home growers, and organised crime (and the problem of the supply side of the *coffee-shop* model) (Dutch Government, 2000). For the first time, it was also acknowledged that these side effects were not just a national issue but resulted in negative consequences for neighbouring countries (cfr. Article 71 Schengen Convention). Meanwhile, the international pressure on the Dutch liberal drug policy continued: illustrative is the United Nations General Assembly Special Session in 1998 which pursued the total elimination of drugs from the world by setting 2008 as the target to "eliminate or significantly reduce" the global illicit drugs market (UNGASS, 1998). This situation supported the rejection of the *coffee-shop* model by Belgian policy-makers once more (Fijnaut & De Ruyver, 2008; De Ruyver et al., 2010).

Ministerial Circular Letter of 8 May 1998: Answer to the Recommendations of the PWG

One of the most important initiatives that kept the drug issue on the political agenda in Belgium was the establishment of the new directive (of 8 May 1998). The new directive replaced the guidelines of the Ministerial Circular Letter of 5 May 1993 which did not distinguish between types of drugs and was based on the premise that every violation had to lead to a consequence (e.g. prosecution, praetorian probation, etc.). The negative evaluation of the 1993 Ministerial Circular Letter by the PWG did put some pressure on the Minister of Justice Stefaan De Clerck (CVP) to take action. Following the final conclusions and recommendations of the PWG, the new Ministerial Circular Letter of 8 May 1998 confirmed the 'acceptance' of the need for a more realistic and contemporary drug prosecution policy. For the first time a distinction was made between the prosecution policy with regard to cannabis and other illicit drugs. It was argued that "cannabis products are substances that cause fewer health problems" (Ministerial Circular Letter of 8 May 1998, nr. COL 5/98, p. 2). The Ministerial Circular Letter instructed Public Prosecutors to give the lowest priority to the prosecution of cannabis possession for personal use,[4] unless the use causes public nuisance (defined as environmental pollution, noise, verbal aggression, use or being under the influence of drugs in public space)[5] or in case of problematic use (defined as sustained regular use, dependence, addiction, lack of socio-economic integration or crises; in such a case, orientation towards treatment is recommended).[6] Provided there were no aggravating circumstances, the police officer (taking his subjective assessment into account) had to make a *simplified process-verbal*. A list of these records was then sent to the Public Prosecutor biweekly or monthly. The 1998 Ministerial Circular further asked the Public Prosecutors to be severe in the case of retail sale but to take into consideration (by reducing the punishment) cases in which the only purpose of the sale was to finance one's own use.

The 1998 Ministerial Circular followed the conclusions of the PWG by re-emphasising that the possession of illegal drugs remained punishable and that the lowest prosecution priority was given to the possession of cannabis for personal use. However, the details about the application of the Ministerial Circular Letter (e.g. a clear definition of concepts) remained unclear (De Ruyver, Casselman, Meuwissen, Bullens, & Van Impe, 2000). Consistent with the *political/symbolic utilisation* of scientific knowledge (Weiss, 1979), the new directive still ignored vague notions such as *public nuisance* and *problematic use* being heavily criticised by both the academic world and practitioners (Kaminski, 1998). At the same time, regular registrations by the Public Prosecutor formed the main criterion to determine persistent regular use of cannabis. Problematic use, therefore, was rather linked with the risk of being controlled by the police.

'Drugs Policy 2000' Conferences

During this intermezzo, three 'Drugs Policy 2000' conferences took place. Each of these conferences clearly included matters addressed by the Parliament and/or Government earlier on. For instance, in 1997, during the fifth conference, a lot of attention was given to the final report of the PWG which was submitted a few months before. Panel sessions concerned topics such as the professional statute of prevention workers, the controlled substitution of heroin, and the lowest prosecution policy for cannabis possession. Similarly, during the seventh conference (1999), the emphasis was on the development of an integrated and coordinated drug policy, implementation of prevention projects in schools and drug treatment in prison, and international enforcement of drug traffic. The programme of this conference clearly took into account the issues stipulated by the 1999 Federal Government Policy Statement as will be discussed below. The close link with the political agenda meant that these conferences provided an ideal forum to discuss particular issues among scientists, practitioners, and (sometimes) policy-makers as well as to build up a (new) network (i.e. in the 1999, a six-party Coalition led by Flemish Liberal Leader Guy Verhofstadt was voted into power. At the same time, policy-makers were allowed to test their ideas against the views and opinions of practitioners and scientists. According to some interviewees, these particular conferences influenced the acceptance of the evolving drug policy discourse and served as important precursors of the policy coordination structures (Drug Health Policy Cell and the General Drugs Policy Cell) introduced by the Federal Drug Policy Note (see also below).

> Those conferences [...] really exercised the minds and stimulated interaction. I think that the consciousness of shared responsibility eventually has led to more cooperation which, in the next phase, has expanded to the Drug Health Policy Cell and the General Drugs Policy Cell [...]. It also stands for the foundation and development of a broader discourse: it is not only justice but also treatment and public health.
>
> (Respondent 26, practitioner)

Taking the lead in organising these annual conferences, the position of Brice De Ruyver again calls to mind the role of a *policy entrepreneur*, which, according to Kingdon (2002), can be seen as a driver of the '*softening up*' processes, intended to prepare and educate both the public and the policy-makers.

Stakeholder Engagement: Policy Memorandum

The annual conferences 'Drug Policy 2000' not only helped to recurrently stimulate debate about (different) ideas among a variety of stakeholders, but also to engage cooperation between (Dutch-speaking and French-speaking) practitioners. An exemplary action was the initiative of practitioners on the eve of the 1999 federal elections. Dutch- and French-speaking practitioners united their concerns and interests related to policy options, budgets, or staff in a Policy Memorandum (Memorandum Group, 1999).

> This Memorandum is endorsed by almost every organisation. The drug issue is a public concern. There is need for a repressive as well as for a curative and preventive component. When establishing the latter, this Policy Memorandum can be an important policy instrument.
>
> (1999 Drug treatment and prevention Policy Memorandum)

In this document, obviously linked with the final conclusions and recommendations of the PWG, they pleaded for clarification of the 1998 Ministerial Circular Letter, development of a uniform registration system, improvement of the collaboration between justice and treatment, establishment of a prison policy, establishment of a forum for better cooperation and coordination between different policy actors, and so on. During the intermezzo, the distribution of the Policy Memorandum influenced some arguments of MPs in the parliamentary debates preceding and following the elections of May 1999 (e.g. *Vr. en Antw.* Senaat, 12 januari 1999, nr. 1–90, 4733 (Vr. nr. 1479 M. Olivier)). Later on, the distribution of the Policy Memorandum successfully resulted in an invitation to engage in a discussion about the Federal Drug Policy Note with the Ministers directly (see below). In this way, Belgian drug policy development was based on a framework on which a broad range of policy implementers agreed.

Media Coverage and Interest Groups

Internal conflicts and financial disputes rapidly decreased the power of interest groups. Thus, during the intermezzo, interest groups (e.g. *Belgian Cannabis Consumers' organisation*; *A citizen just like any other*; *Association against the prohibition*) were no longer as vigorous in promoting their ideas and persuading policy-makers through the media.

In contrast, the media continued to provide the context for (public and) political discussion about Belgian drug policy. The time and the space spent on the *cannabis issue* resulted in (the public and) policy-makers evaluating the PWG along the cannabis dimension (*priming*; McCombs & Shaw, 1972). For instance, MPs (and the public) believed that there was just one struggle: either cannabis use is harmless and should be decriminalised (if not legalised); or cannabis is harmful to health, and therefore its use should continue to be prohibited. In this context, the Flemish media paid far more attention to the drug phenomenon than the French-speaking media, and both parts of the country presented the debate rather differently. The Flemish media discourse was largely informed by a biomedical/clinical discourse inspired by articles focusing on health problems (e.g. the relationship between cannabis use and cancer or the risks of heart attack). For instance, the Flemish newspaper *De Morgen* reported "14.000 drug addicts end up in hospitals each year" (23 December 1998, *De Morgen*). Likewise, the Flemish newspaper *De Standaard* implied that "Cannabis also contains more carcinogens than tobacco. Three joints are equivalent to 20 cigarettes" (1 December 2000, Flemish newspaper *De Standaard*). On the other hand, the French-speaking media had a rather more nuanced but critical approach, largely focusing on the unproblematic nature of persistent (cannabis) use.

> The challenge is to speak the truth [...]. It was previously demonstrated that there are a lot of myths [...]. Overdose and the risks of a hepatitis C pandemic are often discussed but self-control strategies of drug use, proven to be successful, not.
>
> (21 November 2000, French-speaking newspaper *Le Soir*)

Thus, the media coverage of the debate depended on which part of the country one lived in or which newspaper one read.

Newspaper articles often included expert opinions, police statistics, prevalence rates, emergency cases, and international studies. On the one hand, newspapers included scientific knowledge as a 'response' to an event that had taken place or was brought to attention. For example the Flemish newspaper *De Morgen* reported: "... according to a study commissioned by the Ministerial Cabinet, which the newspaper could consult ..." (18 November 1998). On the other hand, scientific knowledge was presented as factual information by the media itself. "An American study has shown that 10% of the people who ever experimented with drugs get addicted" (14 May 1998, Flemish newspaper *Gazet van Antwerpen*).

Nevertheless, in accordance with Carvalho (2007) and MacGregor (2012a), analysis revealed that the presentation of scientific knowledge in the media was often inaccurate or distorted. First of all, newspapers commonly omitted methodological and contextual information. Prominence was given to very general and vague labels of scientific knowledge. "A recent publication of a French report argues that cannabis may be less harmful than tobacco" (17 July 1998, French-speaking newspaper *Le Vif*). Equally, any bibliographic information (e.g. the names of researchers and their institutional affiliations) was often left out, which makes it difficult to assess the credibility of the source quoted. At the same time, newspapers presented scientific knowledge in a rather simplistic and one-sided way. In particular, journalists seemed to not amend or qualify their story with potentially contradictory research or expert opinions. For instance, even though the 'stepping-stone theory' has proved to be unsustainable and lacking any real evidence base, this perspective still trickled down into the media discourse without any comment. "Studies in the U.S. have shown that one in 10 of 18-year-old youngsters gets addicted. In other words, the progression from soft to hard drugs is much easier than a few years ago" (27 February 1999, Flemish newspaper *Het Nieuwsblad*). In their drive for sensationalism, journalists at times provided additional information or included their own interpretations without taking the original scientific perspective into account. "It is clear, cannabis use is really harmful" (9 December 2000, Flemish newspaper *De Standaard*). Finally, in a moment of calm, some newspapers took the opportunity to '*recycle*' scientific knowledge that had been published previously. Although these results were 'old', newspapers presented them as 'new' (by using active verbs). Although it had been discussed before in Flemish newspapers *De Standaard* (July 1997) and *Gazet van Antwerpen* (October 1997), another Flemish newspaper presented the particular registration study (regarding the number of prosecutions in Flanders) as 'new' in April 1998. "While presenting the new Ministerial Directive [...] Antwerp researchers announced that the number of booked drug users has never been so high" (28 April 1998, Flemish newspaper *De Morgen*).

In the light of the findings above and by drawing on Brossard's (2009) analysis of the selection mechanisms employed by the media, it is clear that the media can unintentionally, as a result of the characteristics of news production (e.g. limited space, driven by publicity and economic concerns), or rather strategically, make a significant contribution to how people think by influencing what they think about (Entman, 1989; Lancaster et al., 2011).

> The editors were interested in the cannabis issue, not in the other drug policy issues. They argued that the public was only interested in the cannabis discussion.
>
> (Respondent 46, journalist)

> I search for experts who are knowledgeable about the topic. I also read other journals to find out what they write about the topic. That is often the way it works in journalism [...]. One time, I remember, my

> editorial chief forbade me to speak to someone because he was too much in favour of decriminalisation.
>
> (Respondent 54, journalist)

Attention to Drugs and Drug Policy in Parliamentary Activities

Although general attention to the drug issue decreased, each of the initiatives mentioned above grabbed the attention of the MPs. In keeping the issue of drugs on the parliamentary agenda, the MPs posed questions[7] or submitted interpellations, resolutions,[8] or bills.[9] As parliamentary debates are typically argumentative, MPs express, defend, and attack opinions and political positions and, therefore, use several resources (e.g. media reports, scientific research, personal experiences, etc.). As such, in accordance with the drug policy governance literature, parliamentary processes may link policy-makers to wider networks in a pluralistic and diverse civic society (MacGregor, 2012b).

It comes as no surprise that the parliamentary focus was on the most controversial topic too: cannabis policy. The media itself seemed to be a powerful player in *setting the policy agenda*. MPs often showed their care and concern about this public issue discussed in the media by asking parliamentary questions or addressing it in a speech. MPs also clearly acquired information about scientific knowledge as contextualised in newspaper articles. "On 18 December 1999, a newspaper reported that researchers discovered that cannabis smoke is much more carcinogenic than tobacco smoke" (Intervention by MP Vlaams Blok, extreme-right Flemish party). Thus, as articulated by previous studies (Weiss & Singer, 1988; McArthur, 1999; Lenton, 2004; Lancaster et al., 2011; Ritter & Lancaster, 2013), the media operated as *linking mechanism* or *knowledge distributor* between science and policy.

Furthermore, MPs often used data from policy-funded studies and epidemiological research, or even non-academic reports of international organisations (e.g. EMCDDA and WHO) or conclusions of international Commissions (e.g. British Wootton Commission (1969), Canadian LeDain Commission (1970), Dutch Baan Commission (1972), French Roques Commission (1997)). Two MPs introduced their bill as follows: "It is our intention to develop a coherent policy based on objective scientific research, independent of ideologies [...]. The claim that cannabis use causes a loss of motivation is disproven by recent scientific research" (Mr. Vincent Van Quickenborne & Mr. Patrik Vankrunkelsven, MPs VU&ID, Flemish Nationalists; *Parl.St.* Senaat 2000–2001, nr. 2–585/1). In this context, scientific knowledge was most often presented without naming the author or institution (e.g. 'research shows', 'research confirms', 'some authors mention', or 'the literature shows'). Footnote references and bibliographies were rarely included and often incomplete (wrong order, no author, no place of publication, no page numbers) or out-of-date. These footnotes also revealed that the reports of those studies were not consulted in detail and that the internet was an easy source in the search for supporting research. This finding is in accordance with Ritter (2009) who found that the third most commonly mentioned source used by policy-makers was the internet (notably Google and websites of national research centres).

> (Footnote): CONNER C., «Marijuana and alcohol use in pregnancy», Drug Intelligence and Clinical Pharmacy, 18(3): 233–234, Mars 1984; «Encyclopédie médicochirurgicale, Toxicologie, Pathologie professionnelle, Dépendance vis-à-vis des drogues illicites» 16–001-G-60, pp. 8, 9; ESCOHOTADO A., «Histoire élémentaire des drogues. Des origines à nos jours», Ed. Du Lézard, Paris, 1995; DEWEY W., «Cannabinoid pharmacology», Pharmacol. Rev., 1986, 38, pp. 151–178 [...]"
> (Mr. Patrick Moriau & Mr. Thierry Giet, MPs PS, Walloon socialists; *Parl.St.* Kamer 1999–2000, nr. 0727/001)

> Cannabis can be distributed by pharmacies (1) [...], Inhalation of marijuana smoke relaxes the muscles within the body (5) (Footnote): See www.maripharm.nl.
> (Mr. Vincent Van Quickenborne & Mr. Patrik Vankrunkelsven, MPs VU&ID, Flemish Nationalists; *Parl.St.* Senaat 2000–2001, nr. 2–585/1)

In terms of models of knowledge utilisation, the selection of scientific knowledge or scientific advice tended to depend on the political ideology of the MP and their personal preferences/networks/education. For instance, an MP with a medical background was more in favour of consulting and referring to doctors or psychiatrists, while former academics tended to consult scientific experts. Accordingly, there were also some examples of *cherry-picking* (or *trawling*; Stevens, 2007a) of scientific knowledge. For instance, although scientists, practitioners, and MPs agreed in the PWG that there was no scientific evidence in favour of the *stepping-stone theory*, this argument was ignored by some MPs. They assumed that there was a strong link between alcohol use and cannabis use and between cannabis use and the use of other illegal drugs. The existence of a connection between the use of cannabis and the use of other illegal drugs was one of the most cited arguments in favour of a repressive approach. "We are starting to find some indications, concerning alcohol, for possible genetic predisposition, but it is certainly not enough to claim that there is or isn't a stepping-stone theory. It is too early to say" (Mr. Jan Van Erps, MP CVP, Flemish Christian Democrats; *Hand.* Kamer 1996–1997, 24 juni 1997,

175). Furthermore, those who participated in the parliamentary debates often stressed their aim of taking into account scientific knowledge to please their electorates and gain authority. For instance, on the threshold of the Federal elections in 1999, some of them used a well-stocked portfolio of commissioned research to demonstrate that they attach importance to scientific knowledge. "I aim to take these numbers into account. I commissioned a survey among youngsters in secondary schools" (*Hand.* Kamer 1998–1999, 15 juli 1999, 003, 63). This is linked with the *status model* of Cross et al. (2000), which assumes that policy-makers may use examples of commissioned research as a kind of status symbol. As such, favouring *evidence-based* policy can be seen as a rather strategic stance. Given these kinds of references, it appears to be necessary to differentiate Weiss' *political/symbolic* model (Weiss, 1979).

Weiss' *political/symbolic* model (Weiss, 1979) also seems to be failing to distinguish between instances where research is truly being used as opposed to where research is being misused or misinterpreted. First of all, *juggling with numbers or scientific results* was a common practice. For instance, the prevalence rates of cannabis use among young people were used to argue about the prevalence of cannabis use among the Belgian national population. "Cannabis use in Belgium. The use of cannabis in Belgium is lower than the European average [...] one out of five European youngsters has experimented with cannabis" (Mr. Vincent Van Quickenborne & Mr. Patrik Vankrunkelsven, MPs VU&ID, Flemish Nationalists; *Parl.St.* Senaat 2000–2001, nr. 2–585/1). Additionally, conclusions from ongoing or finished studies in other countries were fully or partially *transposed* to the Belgian situation, without taking into account the different contextual elements. The only condition was that these studies have proven the particular point of view. "The conclusions of international studies, quoted by the respected Member, can be transposed completely or partly to the Belgian situation [...] the studies conducted abroad are useful and the side effects are acceptable" (Mr. Marcel Colla, Federal Minister of Public Health SP, Flemish Socialists; *Hand.* Kamer 1996–1997, 24 juni 1997, 175). Finally, it comes as no surprise that next to scientific knowledge *political tactics/strategies* were also often used to enhance or disprove the credibility of the opinions or sources offered. The parliamentary process is a political game between majority and opposition where party policies and internal party hierarchies play a role. For instance, MPs made use of rather *extravagant vocabulary* and *metaphors*. Members of the Flemish extreme right party Vlaams Blok were regularly termed as *preachers*, while members of the green parties (AGALEV/ECOLO) were called *drug prophets*. Similarly, some MPs used personal (ad hominem) insults.

> The drugs prophets played tactically very well. Something that would not have been thinkable one or two years ago [...] Mr Lozie, you are a

> very intelligent person and you have developed all your arguments in a very constructive, premeditated and sophisticated way. I can't cope with this level.
>
> (Mr. Filip De Man, MP Vlaams Blok, Flemish extreme right party; *Hand.* Kamer 1996–1997, 24 juni 1997, 175)

Also, since the concept de facto *depenalisation* was replaced by the *lowest prosecution priority for cannabis possession for personal use* in the final report of the PWG (see above), MPs confusingly (and often consciously) referred to the liberalisation of cannabis as a *de jure depenalisation*, a *decriminalisation*, and even a *legalisation*. For instance, MP Filip De Man (Vlaams Blok, Flemish extreme right party) argued that "Regarding soft drugs [...] the proposed legalisation of cannabis use is a bad solution" (*Hand.* Kamer 1996–1997, 24 juni 1997, 175). Accordingly, one of the primary talking-points of the Federal Minister of Justice in answering the questions and the interpellations involved clarifying that the Belgian Government was not talking about legalisation or decriminalisation (*Hand.* Kamer 1996–1997, 24 juni 1997, 175).

The strategy of projecting the effects of criminalisation or legalisation based on analogies of experiences of other places (e.g. the Dutch *coffee-shop model* versus the American *War on Drugs*), so-called *policy platonism* (MacCoun & Reuter, 1997), was also commonly used. For instance, it was stated by some MPs that the depenalisation of cannabis possession will increase the demand (*Hand.* Kamer 1999–2000, 13 juni 2000, 716/1). Arguments were supported by the 1997 Amsterdam Treaty, the report of the Inter-parliamentary Advisory Council of the Benelux countries as well as the 2000 Dutch policy paper 'Pathways to the back door'.

An appeal to *emotions* was another important strategy. It involved inciting emotions in people to persuade them that a particular statement or argument is true or false, independent of the scientific evidence. As in the example below, drug use was often linked with committing suicide, HIV, death, and criminal organisations. "Drugs are the direct cause of crimes and social or health problems (absenteeism, car accidents, HIV) [...]. Important enough to break the taboo and think about solutions" (Mr. Filip De Man & Mr. Gerolf Annemans, MPs Vlaams Blok, Flemish extreme right party; *Parl.St.* Kamer 1999–2000, nr. 0389/001).

As a final example, the use of *personal opinions or experiences* (so-called *tacit* knowledge) rather than rational arguments was common practice too. Many Members of Parliament complemented their role as MP with other roles (*dual role*). For instance, participants made references to their role as a doctor, as a parent, or as a practitioner (e.g. health worker). "As a physician, I also believe that..." (Mr. Jef Valkeniers, MP VLD, Flemish Liberals; *Hand.* Kamer 1996–1997, 24 juni 1997, 175).

Table 6.1 Composition of the Belgian Government and Parliament (1996–2003)

	Government Dehaene II	*Government Verhofstadt I*
Start date	23 June 1995	12 July 1999
End date	12 July 1999	12 July 2003
Number of parties	4	6
Composition Coalition	CVP	VLD
	PSC	PS
	PS	PRL-FDF-MCC
	SP	SP
		Ecolo
		AGALEV
MPs majority	82 MPs	94 MPs
MPs opposition	68 MPs	56 MPs

The First Verhofstadt Government (1999–2003): A Historical Switch

An important change was established on 13 June 1999. Although the Prime Minister had come from the Christian Democratic Party for many years, in the 1999 Federal elections, a Coalition led by Flemish Liberal Leader Guy Verhofstadt was voted into power. The first Verhofstadt Government (1999–2003) was a *six-party Coalition* among the Flemish and French-speaking Liberals, Socialists, and Greens (Table 6.1). The green parties moved to the majority for the first time. Conversely, Christian Democrats moved from a long-standing majority position towards the opposition.

The Verhofstadt I Government (1999–2003) expressed the intention to develop a coherent drug policy. Even though it has long been the exclusive domain of Justice, there was clear agreement to address the drug issue from a public health approach (Federal Government, 1999). Exemplary is the commotion raised by the *Federal Safety and Detention plan*, which summed up the priorities for Belgian integral security policy in 2000 (*Hand.* Kamer 1999–2000, 13 juni 2000, 716/1; Devroe, 2002). It included several measures and projects regarding drug-related nuisance and crime and solely reflected a *legalistic/repressive* discourse (Guillain, 2003). As the *Federal Safety and Detention plan* included no links with the balanced and public health approach, the government felt an increasing pressure to fulfil its commitment to develop a drug policy reflecting a public health discourse.

> The Minister of Justice wrote a Federal Safety and Detention plan and presented it to the Council of Ministers. However, this document did not follow the public health approach put forward by the PWG and the Federal Governmental Declaration. The Council of Ministers

did ask Minister of Public Health to write another one [...]. They blew the whistle on the Minister of Justice.

(Respondent 20, policy-maker)

Interestingly, the new Verhofstadt I Government (1999–2003) also recognised the importance of evidence as a valuable resource in policy-making and in the evaluation of policy choices. Scientific knowledge regarding the drug phenomenon in Belgium increased slowly during the intermezzo (De Ruyver et al., 2004; Devroe, 2010)[10] and in the 1999 Federal Government Policy Statement, it was emphasised that science was an important resource in policy-making (as an answer to the lack of scientific research in Belgium, highlighted in the PWG). These elements seem to demonstrate leadership imbued with a high interest in scientific knowledge or, in other words, *evidence-imbued leadership* as articulated by previous research on drug policy governance (MacGregor et al., 2014).

Within this framework, the Verhofstadt I Government stressed that the Federal Government had the task of presenting an *evaluation report* to the Parliament regarding the current drug policy within six months. The evaluation study *Belgian drug policy in the year 2000: state of the art three years after the recommendations of the PWG* (De Ruyver et al., 2000) detailed the actual state of the drug problem and captured recommendations of the PWG that had already been implemented by the time the policy was created. This review process provided the fundamental framework for action: it kept the drug issue on the political agenda and increased the likelihood that the Federal Government would meet the *evidence-based* goals that were set out in the 1999 Federal Government Policy Statement (Federal Government, 1999). "Related to the drug issue, the Government will provide an evaluation study within 6 months [...]. Based on the results of this study, the Government will, in close cooperation with the parliament, develop a coherent drug policy" (Federal Government, 1999, p. 36). Thus, the evaluation did not just build the evidence base about what works, it also improved the process of policy development by holding to account those responsible for its development.

The report of the PWG and the evaluation study [...]. The Federal Drug Policy Note had to be in accordance with these documents [...] They did not have to start 'from scratch' [...]. At least, the study did put some pressure on the Government to develop a Federal Drug Policy Note [...] Members of Government have their responsibilities.

(Respondent 50, scientist)

As another example illustrating the *evidence-imbued* leadership, Prof. Dr. Brice De Ruyver became the security advisor to Prime Minister Guy Verhofstadt in April 2000. Assistance in the development of an *evidence-based* coherent Belgian drug policy was one of his main assignments.

Following the typology on public engagement by Loader and Sparks (2011), there are elements of this role which are closely linked with the public engagement of an *observer-turned-player*. His prominent role in the policy-making process (at the governmental level in particular) is quite unique in the Belgian (drug policy) context and confirms the intention of the new Government to allocate a larger role to scientific knowledge in the policy-making process.

Summary

This chapter detailed the intermezzo period from 1997 to 2000 when, because of exogenous factors (the Dutroux Affair and the reorganisation of the entire police and justice system), debates over drug policy slipped slightly off the agenda. From Kingdon's (2002) perspective there were elements of this period that could be seen as a '*softening up*' phase. The international context, the launch of a new Ministerial Circular Letter in April 1998, the engagement of non-government stakeholders in terms of a Policy Memorandum, the attention to drugs and drug policy in parliamentary debates, the extent and nature of media coverage, and the annual conferences 'Drugs Policy 2000', all helped to create a general climate that affected policy-makers' thinking and prevented the policy window from closing.

Eventually, in 1999, Belgian voters rejected the long-standing Coalition Government of Christian Democrats and Socialists and voted into power a Coalition led by Flemish Liberal Leader Verhofstadt. This change turned out to be an important facilitator of the development of a public health drug policy. The will to take a clear and different direction as opposed to the previous government produced a kind of consensus view on the right way forward. It occurred parallel with an emergence of the rhetoric of *evidence-based* policy in drug policy debates: the credence given to scientific knowledge as an instrument of developing drug policy increased. In other words, *evidence-imbued* leadership was introduced.

Another key issue to emerge out of this chapter was the difficulty in capturing how some examples could be classified according to Weiss' three-fold typology. First of all, through the observation of several instances of making blunt interpretations or false generalisations and causalities in the parliamentary debates, it became clear that Weiss' *political/symbolic* model (Weiss, 1979) fails to distinguish between instances where research is being used appropriately as opposed to research being misused (see also Stevens, 2007a). Second, Weiss' *political/symbolic* model does not cover the occasions where scientific knowledge is cited simply to justify the government's commitment to knowledge utilisation or *evidence-based* policy-making. For example, in accordance with what Cross et al. (2000) termed the *status model* in the literature, policy-makers aim to gain credibility (and status) by referring to studies that they (or their predecessor) commissioned. Given these references, Weiss' *political/symbolic* model (Weiss, 1979) seems too simplistic.

This chapter also provided the platform for a set of empirical findings demonstrating how the distinction between science and the media is a false dichotomy: the latter were a key force in the promotion of the former – albeit in a distorted way. Although media appeared to be a valuable *linking mechanism* between science and policy (see also Weiss & Singer, 1988; McArthur, 1999, Lenton, 2004; Lancaster et al., 2011; Ritter & Lancaster, 2013), by no means did it provide scientists with a guarantee of a more *evidence-based* drug policy, not least because media contextualisation also largely depended on which part of the country one lived in.

In a response to all this, in 2000, the drug issue gradually re-entered the political agenda in Belgium. The Belgian Government proceeded to translate the final conclusions and recommendations of the PWG into an official policy document, the Federal Drug Policy Note. Its development in 2001, the second milestone in Belgian drug policy between 1996 and 2003, will be discussed in the Chapter 7.

Notes

1 Marc Dutroux kidnapped, tortured, and sexually abused 6 girls aged between 8 and 19. He was arrested in August 1996: two girls were rescued from an underground dungeon and four were found buried in his garden. This case led to intense criticism of the Belgian police and justice system. Causing anguish among the Belgian people, a protest march was held through Brussels by 300,000 people. In 2004, Marc Dutroux was convicted and imprisoned for life (Cartuyvels, Delpérée, & Delwit, 1997).

2 In a Parliamentary Commission of Inquiry (e.g. Dutroux Inquiry Commission, Parliamentary Inquiry Commission on the *Gang of Nijvel*), witnesses, as well as interpreters and experts, take an oath and are subject to the same obligations as when questioned by a so-called investigation judge. A Parliamentary Committee of Inquiry can also conduct searches and seize documents. Commissions of Inquiry at which witnesses or experts are heard are public, unless the committee decides otherwise. Furthermore, the committee is obliged to report in a given time to the plenary meeting. The plenary meeting then votes on motions submitted in the report of the Commission of Inquiry (Fijnaut, Huyse, & Verstraeten, 1998; Devos, Rommel, Lannoo, & Van Liefferinge, 2009).

3 This is in spite of some interesting initiatives preceding the formal decision that drugs should indeed be an EU-issue (Treaty of Maastricht): the Stewart-Clark Committee (1985–1986) and the European Committee to Combat Drugs (CELAD) (1989) (Boekhout van Solinge,2002; Fijnaut & De Ruyver,2014).

4 Generally defined as the limited possession for personal (single or occasional) use (Ministerial Circular Letter nr. COL 5/98, p. 4).

5 Public nuisance is defined for the first time (no definition was integrated in the final conclusions and recommendations of the PWG).

6 Even though the final conclusions and recommendations of the PWG vaguely defined problematic use as "the problematic nature of use depends on the drug and the nature of use", the 1998 MC did not succeed in obtaining a more clear definition of problematic use.

7 In contrast with interpellations, questions are always directed to one Minister and cannot lead to the resignation of the Government or a particular Minister (Devos, 2006; Van der Hulst, 2010). In the plenary meetings as well as in the standing Commissions of the Chamber of Representatives (not in the Senate), members may intervene with a parliamentary interpellation. An interpellation requires one or more ministers or the government to explain some act or policy. Interpellations can be followed by a motion (Devos, 2006). *Hand.* Kamer 1996–1997, 24 juni 1997, 175; *Hand.* Kamer 1996–1997, 26 juni 1997, 178; *Hand.* Kamer 1996–1997, 22 september 1997, 393; *Hand.* Kamer 1997–1998, 22 maart 1999, 774, 1–2; *Hand.* Kamer 1998–1999, 15 juli 1999, 003, 63; *Hand.* Kamer 1998–1999, 16 juli 1999, 005, 135; *Hand.* Kamer 1999–2000, 15 december 1999, 0025/037; *Hand.* Kamer 1999–2000, 15 december 1999, COM 074, 9–13; *Hand.* Kamer 1999–2000, 25 januari 2000, COM 094, 5–9; *Hand.* Kamer 1999–2000, 15 juni 2000, 061, 16; *Hand.* Kamer 1999–2000, 4 juli 2000, COM 255, 18; *Hand.* Kamer 1999–2000, 9 november 2000, 081, 12; *Hand.* Senaat 1997–1998, 7 mei 1998, 1–183; *Vr. en Antw.* Kamer, 9 oktober 1998, nr. 49/B152 (Vr. nr. 951 F. Van den Eynde); *Vr. en Antw.* Senaat, 12 januari 1999, nr. 1–90, 4733 (Vr. nr. 1479 M. Olivier); *Vr. en Antw.* Senaat, 4 januari 2000, nr. 2–6, 201 (Vr. nr. 170 V. Van Quickenborne); *Vr. en Antw.* Senaat, 4 januari 2000, nr. 2–6, 203 (Vr. nr. 171 V. Staveaux-Van Steenberge); *Vr. en Antw.* Senaat, 18 januari 2000, nr. 2–7, 236 (Vr. nr. 191 V. Van Quickenborne); *Vr. en Antw.* Kamer, 4 februari 2000, nr. 50/22, 2415 (Vr. nr. 67 F. Van den Eynde); *Vr. en Antw.* Senaat, 20 juli 2000, nr. 2–67, 11 (Vr. nr. 2–333 V. Van Quickenborne); *Vr. en Antw.* Senaat, 20 juli 2000, nr. 2–67, 15 (Vr. nr. 2–334 L. Caluwé).

8 A resolution concerns a reaction regarding a foreign political situation or event (Devos, 2006; Van der Hulst, 2010). For instance, a resolution was submitted by members of the green parties: Mr. Vincent Decroly (Ecolo, French-speaking Greens), Mrs. Martine Schüttringer (Ecolo, French-speaking Greens), Mr. Frans Lozie (AGALEV, Flemish Greens), Mr. Olivier Deleuze (Ecolo, French-speaking Greens), and Mr. Jef Tavernier (AGALEV, Flemish Greens). They provided arguments in favour of a revision of the international conventions (Voorstel van resolutie waarbij de Belgische regering wordt verzocht op de Algemene Vergadering van de VN in juni 1998 te bevorderen dat de internationale verdragen op het gebied van drugs worden herzien (ingediend door Mr. Vincent Decroly, Mrs. Martine Schüttringer, Mr. Frans Lozie, Mr. Olivier Deleuze, and Mr. Jef Tavernier), *Parl.St.* Kamer 1997–1998, nr. 1571/1).

9 Voorstel van wet tot regeling van de teelt, de distributie en de verkoop van cannabis (ingediend door Mr. Vincent Decroly, Mrs. Martine Schüttringer, and Mr. Frans Lozie (Flemish and French-speaking Green party)), *Parl.St.* Kamer 1996–1997, nr. 1186/001; Voorstel van wet tot wijziging van de wet van 24 februari 1921 betreffende het verhandelen van de giftstoffen, slaapmiddelen en verdovende middelen, ontsmettingsstoffen en antiseptica, teneinde het gebruik van cannabis uit het strafrecht te halen (ingediend door Mr. Patrick Moriau and Mr. Thierry Giet (both PS, French-speaking socialists)), *Parl.St.* Kamer 1999–2000, nr. 0727/001; Voorstel van wet tot wijziging van de wet van 24 februari 1921 betreffende het verhandelen van de giftstoffen, slaapmiddelen en verdovende middelen, ontsmettingsmiddelen en antiseptica, ten einde het bezit van cannabis en derivaten ervan gedeeltelijk uit het strafrecht te halen (ingediend door Mr. Daniel Bacquelaine and Mr. Olivier Chastel (both PRL-FDF, French-speaking liberals)), *Parl.St.* Kamer 1999–2000, nr. 0461/001; Voorstel van wet tot verstrenging van de straffen zoals bepaald in de wet van 24 februari

1921 betreffende het verhandelen van de giftstoffen, slaapmiddelen en verdovende middelen, ontsmettingsstoffen en antiseptica (ingediend door Mr. Filip De Man and Mr. Gerolf Annemans (both Vlaams Blok, Flemish extreme right party)), *Parl.St.* Kamer 1999–2000, nr. 0389/001; Voorstel van wet tot regeling van de teelt, de distributie en de verkoop van cannabis (ingediend door Mr. Vincent Decroly, Mr. Paul Timmermans, Mrs. Zoé Genot, and Mrs. Simonne Leen (Flemish and French-speaking Green party)), *Parl.St.* Kamer 1999–2000, nr. 0780/001; Voorstel van wet tot wijziging van de wet van 24 februari 1921 betreffende het verhandelen van de giftstoffen, slaapmiddelen en verdovende middelen, ontsmettingsstoffen en antiseptica (ingediend door Mr. Vincent Van Quickenborne and Mr. Patrik Vankrunkelsven (both VU&ID, Flemish Nationalists)), *Parl.St.* Senaat 2000–2001, nr. 2–585/1.

10 First of all, the Belgian Federal Science Policy Office (previously known as the Federal Office for Scientific, Technical and Cultural Affairs (OSTC)) established research programmes in support of socio-economic (1995–2000) and judicial policy themes (1997–1998). In later years, a Social Cohesion research programme (2000–2004) was also established. These research projects, commissioned by the Belgian Federal Science Policy Office, included a study regarding drug use in prisons (1999–2000; social and economic research programme), an inventory of drug-related research (1995–1996; social and economic research programme) (De Ruyver, Hap, Marchandise, Schleiper, & Vermeulen, 1997; Verslag namens de Parlementaire Werkgroep belast met het bestuderen van de drugproblematiek, *Parl.St.* Kamer, 1996–1997, 1062/1–3; see also above), a study about the public expenditures of Belgian drug policy (2000–2004, Social Cohesion research programme), and so on.

Chapter 7

The First National Drug Strategy

Federal Drug Policy Note (2001)

In 2001, the first national drug strategy – the Federal Drug Policy Note – officially made an end to the period where drug policy measures were entirely incoherent and absolutely not embedded in a public health or social framework. Belgian drug policy formally became balanced[1] in approach, with great emphasis placed on the broader social context and common aims such as drug prevention, reduction of drug-related harm, and crime deterrence (Guillain, 2003). In this context, the Federal Drug Policy Note indicated that the drug phenomenon is considered to be a permanent social reality (i.e. *normalisation* policy). Both illicit and licit drugs were covered and different Federal Ministers were considered responsible for the implementation of the national drug strategy[2] (De Ruyver et al., 2004; De Ruyver et al., 2007). The main priorities of the Federal Government were to reduce the number of drug users, the physical and mental effects related to drug use, and the effects of the drug phenomenon on society. Accordingly, three pillars were put forward: (1) prevention of drug consumption; (2) harm reduction, treatment, and re-integration; and (3) law enforcement as the last resort (Federal Government, 2001, p. 7). This approach, supported by the first Verhofstadt Government (1999–2003), was in line with the final conclusions and recommendations of the PWG and the international trend by which drug problems came to be seen as public health problems (e.g. Inter-parliamentary Advisory Council of the Benelux countries, 1998; EMCDDA, 2000; European Commission, 1999). Similar to national drug strategies implemented in, for example, Spain, France, Portugal, and the UK, accurate scientific evidence, clear objectives, measurable performance targets, and evaluation were also considered key to the Federal Drug Policy Note in Belgium (EMCDDA, 2000).

The Federal Drug Policy Note consisted of three distinguishable parts. The *first part* captured the recommendations of the PWG (Federal Government, 2001; pp. 8–14). The *second part* described the actual state of the drug problem and captured recommendations of the PWG that had already been implemented by the time the policy was created (pp. 14–31). The *third part* contained five action points (based on the three pillars of the

Federal Drug Policy Note) and followed the same construction as the first two parts (pp. 31–68): (1) a global and integrated approach; (2) evaluation, epidemiology, and research; (3) prevention; (4) health care, harm reduction, and reintegration; and (5) repression. As far as the recurrent political struggle on the criminalisation of drugs was concerned, the Federal Drug Policy Note outlined the need for differentiation and individualisation of the criminal intervention towards drug users, taking into account the specific situation (cannabis versus other illegal drugs; experimenting; problematic use; personal use; dealing with profit, and so on). In accordance with this point of view, the Federal Government supported a reform of the Belgian Narcotic Drug Law of 1921 and the development of a new Ministerial Circular Letter (Federal Government, 2001; p. 58) – which is elaborated in Chapter 8. The execution of the several action points received a substantial budget input: €12.4 million was made available (De Ruyver et al., 2004). In accordance with the recommendations of the PWG, the Federal Drug Policy Note dictated the use of this budget in favour of domains other than repression (e.g. prevention and treatment). Nevertheless, some initiatives were still considered too expensive (e.g. the creation of residential time-out projects and the establishment of a controlled heroin maintenance project) (Internal communication Memorandum Group, 26 October 2000).

This chapter documents the run-up to, and the announcement of, the Federal Drug Policy Note in 2001 which constituted the second milestone in Belgian drugs policy. After elaborating the internal government decision-making within the lap of a multi-party government coalition, the (f)actors that played a role in these and following debates and, thus, in the development and acceptance of the Federal Drug Policy Note, are addressed.

An Inter-Cabinet Working Group (ICWG): The Development of the Federal Drug Policy Note

The Federal Government, under the coordination of Federal Minister of Public Health Magda Aelvoet[3] (following the public health approach), started working on a national drug strategy in 2000. An Inter-Cabinet Working Group (ICWG)[4] including (representatives of) the Federal Ministers of Justice, Internal Affairs, Social Affairs, Economic Affairs and Public Health was established on the request of the Council of Ministers. Thus, once the commitment 'to take action' had been made, the work developed largely behind the scenes within government. Many action points of the Federal Drug Policy Note were decided rather easily. This is unsurprising as the final conclusions and recommendations of the PWG and the period of '*softening up*' produced a kind of consensus view on the right way forward. However, three topics challenged the cohesion of the coalition partners (Internal communication Ministerial Cabinet, 17 January 2001).

First, in the 'drug plans' (or 'drug plan contracts' between the Federal Government and municipalities to implement projects related to drug prevention or drug treatment; see Chapter 4), the *funds* related to treatment were assigned to the Minister of Interior Affairs. In the ICWG, then, it was proposed to assign these funds to the Minister of Public Health instead, to be more in accordance with the public health approach. As became clear in the Federal Drug Policy Note, this particular assignment of funds eventually became the responsibility of the Minister of Public Health in close cooperation with the Minister of Interior Affairs (Federal Government, 2001, p. 36). Second, the *division of budgets among the action priorities* was also debated among the coalition partners in the Government. Consequently, as a (preliminary) solution, the Federal Drug Policy Note did not include any concrete budgets on most action points. Third, a political struggle developed between the coalition partners on the *direction of cannabis policy*. This struggle mainly covered the following three points.

First of all, policy-makers were very much concerned with the international aspects of their policy competences. An important feed was that the International Narcotics Control Board (INCB) contacted the representatives of the Minister of Public Health Magda Aelvoet to express their concern about the trend in some European countries, including Belgium, of policies becoming less rigorous. Therefore, accordance with the international framework (e.g. 1990 Schengen Convention, the 1995 Dutch Drug Note and the official report 'Pathways to the backdoor' (2000)) was one of the most compelling arguments in these debates. It is also within this framework that the input of the analysis of some drug policies in European countries was considered important (see also below, 'Observer-turned-player'). Afraid to be isolated internationally, a member of a Ministerial Cabinet argued in the preparation of the final discussion in the Inner Cabinet on 18 January 2001:

> Legalisation means resigning from the international conventions. Juridically, the reasoning is water-tight (several international experts support this argument). The Ministerial Cabinets of the Minister of Labour Onkelinx, the Minister of Mobility Isabelle Durant and the Minister of Public Health Magda Aelvoet are in favour of a broad interpretation [...]. The Government has to decide if they should resign from the conventions. Then, the Government runs the risk of feeling the heat at the European level. Such a decision will have consequences on other policy debates too. No other country has taken this step.
>
> (Internal communication Ministerial Cabinet, 17 January 2001)

Regardless of any individual disagreements among policy-makers, the French-speaking Socialists and the Flemish and French-speaking Green party were in favour of a more far-reaching liberalisation, including a reservation to the international obligations. The other coalition partners such as the Flemish Socialists (SP), the French-speaking Liberals (PRL-FDF-MCC), and the Flemish Liberals (VLD), were opposed to what they called 'a too liberal policy'. Eventually, the particular phrase in the Federal Drug Policy Note that "the Federal Government is an advocate of the need to rethink the international conventions in order to produce a realistic response to cannabis use as well as the establishment of harm reduction initiatives" (Federal Government, 2001, p. 46) reflects the political compromise. The phrase is comparatively radical internationally even though it can be seen as a compromise within Belgium.

Second, the determination of the maximum limit of the *number of grams* for personal use was also heavily debated. With the discussion of the final conclusions and recommendations of the PWG in 1997 in mind,[5] the Verhofstadt I Government also had difficulties in determining what amount had to be considered as for personal cannabis use. Some coalition partners (Flemish Socialists (SP), Flemish Liberals (VLD), and French-speaking Liberals (PRL-FDF-MCC)) did not want to determine a number of grams. Others (Flemish Greens (AGALEV), French-speaking Greens (Ecolo), and French-speaking Socialists (PS)) initially introduced a maximum of 15 grams of cannabis and a maximum of five female cannabis plants (Guillain, 2003). To reach an agreement, the Prime Minister suggested a '5 gram limit'.

> The option of a '5 gram limit' is developed by order of the Prime Minister to convince the French-speaking Socialists (PS). The Minister of Labour Mrs. Laurette Onkelinx is in favour of legalisation and this suggestion is rather persuasive.
>
> (Internal communication Ministerial Cabinet, 17 January 2001)

However, in a political context with a multi-party government coalition, parties were strongly competing for authority and for voters. Bargaining led to the following compromise (postponing direct action): instead of the determination of a number of grams, the Federal Drug Policy Note recommended a legislative change and the development of a new Ministerial Circular Letter to guide judicial, administrative authorities and the police in tackling (local) drug issues, drug-related crime, and nuisance (see also Chapter 8).

Evidence-Imbued Policy-Making and Non-Government Stakeholders' Involvement

Evidence-imbued leadership is imperative in facilitating a central role for evidence use throughout the various stages of the policy process. Much rests, therefore, on political leaders' attitudes towards evidence (Monaghan, 2014).

In 1999, the Verhofstadt I Government underlined that scientific knowledge was an important resource in policy-making. In other words, the Government displayed an awareness of the benefits of *evidence-imbued* policy-making. Indeed, between meetings of the ICWG, representatives of the Federal Ministers often consulted (inter)national scientists to get some background information, unravel a problem, determine clear definitions (e.g. of legalisation or depenalisation), or support or refute an argument in the discussion. Scientific knowledge was perceived as a necessary resource in the policy-making process, useful in the development of a policy and in the evaluation of policy choices.

> Scientists and practitioners were not invited into the Inter-Cabinet Working Group, but we always tried to prepare ourselves and to check which issues were of any importance, which decisions were supported or not, which initiatives worked or not [...]. Concepts like legalisation, depenalisation, decriminalisation ... it was the task of scientists to elucidate these concepts clearly.
>
> (Respondent 20, policy-maker)

Perceiving *use* as simply including references to scientists and scientific studies, some publications and conference contributions of (inter)national scientists were included in the Federal Drug Policy Note (Federal Government, 2001, p. 57). Equally, the Federal Drug Policy Note included references to the 1994 Consensus Conference and the national conferences 'Drug Policy 2000' (Federal Government, 2001, p. 53). However, as with the Parliament, most of the references to scientific knowledge or experts were labelled in a general manner. "Ethnic minorities who abuse illicit drugs are apparently underrepresented in some treatment services [...]. A lot of research on this topic exists" (Federal Drug Policy Note, p. 48). "Research, Belgian experiments and foreign experiences stressed the desirability of case management in substance abuse treatment" (Federal Drug Policy Note, p. 49). In spite of this, several characteristics of scientific knowledge were also said to impede the interaction between scientists and policy-makers and the use of scientific knowledge in the ICWG. This is in accordance with the *two communities thesis* referring to the idea that policy-makers and scientists operate in two different worlds and speak two different languages (Caplan, 1979). For instance, whereas scientific studies can take years to be completed, policy issues often rise rapidly to the top of the political agenda (e.g. one legislature only lasts for four years) (Weiss & Bucuvalas, 1980; Ritter, 2009). The consequence of scientists and policy-makers operating under very different time-frames was clearly illustrated in the preparation of the final discussion in the Council of Ministers on 18 January 2001. A member of the Ministerial cabinet argued: "A study of three ULB professors argued that legalisation is consistent with the international UN-conventions. They however acknowledged that their study only shows 'preliminary' results of a 'quick' study. [...] In other words, their study is worthless" (Internal communication Ministerial Cabinet, 17 January 2001).

Observer-Turned-Player

Within the *evidence-imbued* leadership, the example of Brice De Ruyver clearly illustrated the intention of the new Government to allocate a larger role to scientific knowledge in the policy-making process. As stated above, criminologist Brice De Ruyver was appointed as the security advisor to Prime Minister Guy Verhofstadt in April 2000. It became clear that this type of public engagement meaningfully impacted on and shaped policy. This position seems to be similar to the concept of 'policy entrepreneur' as articulated by Kingdon (2002) and of *observer-turned-player* as put forward by Loader and Sparks (2011). He was able to function equally well in both the academic and political world and speak both languages fluently. Such a role required a substantial transition by the scientist, who moved from a position of absolute 'outsider' to a knowledgeable 'outsider'.

> A scientist has to be aware that he is a technician, not a politician. A scientist presents his knowledge and expertise but he remains a technician. A scientist does not determine the direction of the policy [...]. Working at the governmental level is special: the aim is to unite the representatives of the Ministers and to decide.
>
> (Respondent 50, scientist)

Having a privileged position, he gradually discovered how policy was made and who or what exerted the most influence. In particular, this role enabled the *observer-turned-player* to promote the *instrumental* utilisation of his own scientific research and that of others in the political arena. The instrumental view assumes that scientific knowledge has a direct bearing on policy (Weiss, 1979; Nutley, 2003). As a clear example, the evaluation study *Belgian drug policy in the year 2000: state of the art three years after the recommendations of the PWG* (De Ruyver et al., 2000) inspired the Federal Drug Policy Note (Federal Government, 2001). On the one hand, the second part of the Federal Drug Policy Note (pp. 14–31) described the main conclusions of the evaluation study conducted by De Ruyver and colleagues (De Ruyver et al., 2000). This detailed the actual state of the drug problem and captured recommendations of the PWG that had already been implemented by the time the policy was created. On the other hand, the recommendations of the evaluation study were influential in determining the specific policy actions by the Federal Government (third part Federal Drug Policy Note, pp. 31–68). For instance, the *evaluation report* stressed that, to finally realise an integral and integrated drug policy with a vertical and a horizontal policy coordination, "the establishment of a General Drugs Policy Cell must be considered as necessary and crucial" (De Ruyver et al., 2000, p. 8). Accordingly, the establishment of a General Drugs Policy Cell was one of the most important action points of the Federal Drug Policy Note in pursuing a global and integrated approach (Federal Government, 2001, p. 31). As a second example, inspired by the particular recommendations of the evaluation study regarding the problem of driving under the influence of illegal drugs and medication (De Ruyver et al., 2000, pp. 13–15, 23), the Federal Drug Policy Note included a number of actions (e.g. prevention campaigns, implementation of drug tests, etc.) (Federal Government, 2001, p. 43). Also, the persistent concern about the lack of reliable numbers or registrations and the lack of (funding for) epidemiological studies on drug use was re-emphasised in the evaluation study (De Ruyver et al., 2000, pp. 20–21). In the Federal Drug Policy Note, the Federal Government eventually demonstrated commitment and responsiveness: for example by means of establishing a research programme supporting decision-making in the field of illegal drugs (Federal Government, 2001, pp. 37–41). As this evaluation study gave direction to Belgian drug policy, and finally led to action/implementation by the Federal Government, this is an example of *instrumental knowledge utilisation*. An evaluation study fulfilling this particular role fits with the literature on *evidence-based* policies (Devroe et al., 2008). As stated by Devroe (2002), "evaluation studies lead to direct measurable and usable results for policy-makers" (p. 181).

In a similar vein, Brice De Ruyver promoted the *instrumental* utilisation of other (international) scientific research. Taking into account that the global description of the situation and trends in drug consumption and drug-related problems in Belgium was still incomplete (BIRN, 2002),[6] several national and international drug policy studies (with special attention to the cannabis policy) were compared (Federal Government, 2001, pp. 57–58). As a result, the analysis of drug policies in other European countries (the Netherlands, France, Germany, Luxembourg, and the UK), included in the attachment of the Federal Drug Policy Note, was very much a result of the promotion by this *observer-turned-player*, as outlined by policy personnel involved at the time:

> I remember that we took into account some international studies of drug policies in European countries and the prevalence rates provided by the EMCDDA. Brice De Ruyver joined the Inter-Cabinet Working Group to stimulate the debate. He also urged more scientific support.
>
> (Respondent 20, policy-maker)

> A permanent dialogue with Brice De Ruyver was used to advance the debate regarding the Federal Drug Policy Note. In particular, he kept close contacts with the policy-makers. He had a very large political

> network. As a policy-maker, I talked with him in order to get a scientific update.
>
> (Respondent 34, policy-maker)

With this in mind, such a public role seems by far the most effective means to advance an *evidence-based* drug policy. This position ensured policy-makers had easy access to and understanding of the evidence base. In this way, having an academic working within government as *observer-turned-player* accords with what Monaghan (2014) described as one of the key elements for *good drug policy governance.*

However, it is important to set realistic expectations about the contributions of scientists in the policy-making process. An *observer-turned-player* is able to inform policy-making, not to make it. Some findings of the evaluation study and international drug policy studies were also used in a more *political/symbolic* way by policy-makers. In the *political/symbolic* model of knowledge utilisation, scientific knowledge is considered as ammunition for political sides (Weiss, 1979). For instance, an important recommendation was that the Federal Drug Policy Note had to resolve the lack of uniformity in prosecutions of cannabis possession between different Public Prosecutor's offices. The evaluation study attributed a large part of this problem to rather vague notions such as 'public nuisance', 'problematic use', and 'limited possession for personal (single or occasional) use' (De Ruyver et al., 2000, p. 41). However, there were important shortcomings in the efforts to address this deficiency. Although the Federal Drug Policy Note introduced new definitions, they still remained too blurry and open to interpretation by police officers, prevention workers, social workers, and the general public. In other words, in the Federal Drug Policy Note reference was made to the Governments' investment in the research, by way of demonstrating commitment and responsiveness. Nevertheless, the vagueness of these notions was not resolved.

Similarly, *political/symbolic utilisation* of the several national and international drug policy studies was also noticed. Although the prevalence rates related to problematic drug use, drug deaths, infectious diseases, and police arrests were presented accurately, these data were accompanied with a rather political interpretation of their level (low, high, or moderate). For instance, numbers related to Dutch drug policy were presented as follows:

> Estimates on national prevalence of problematic drug use in the age category of 15–54 years: 2.8–3.2 per thousand (low); Trend in the number of deaths because of drugs: slightly rising; Prevalence of HIV infections among intravenous drug users: 2.0–2.6% (numbers are vague); Arrests because of infringements on the drug legislation: increasing rapidly.
>
> (Attachment Federal Drug Policy Note)

However, such direct comparisons between national policies cannot be made because these data are affected by differences in definition, methodology, and statistical units (persons, offences, and arrests) and changing drug policies (e.g. introduction of harm reduction measures) or laws (Kraus et al., 2003; Decorte et al., 2009; Cohen, 2016). This resulted in a political debate based on a rather meaningless representation of problematic drug use, drug deaths, infections, diseases, and police arrests in each of these countries.

Non-Government Stakeholders: Practitioners

Widespread consultation with and transparency of stakeholder engagement is also vital in governance processes (UKDPC, 2012; Monaghan, 2014). Through the distribution of the 1999 Policy Memorandum during the intermezzo, practitioners also successfully influenced the development of the Federal Drug Policy Note in the ICWG. In particular, there was a rather large overlap between the Federal Drug Policy Note and the statements included in the 1999 Policy Memorandum (Memorandum Group, 1999). For instance, several issues were (partly or entirely) addressed: the establishment of a forum for better cooperation and coordination between different policy actors (cfr. General Drugs Policy Cell) (Federal Government, 2001, p. 36); better cooperation between judicial actors and treatment workers (Federal Government, 2001, p. 33); the development of initiatives such as needle exchange and methadone substitution (Federal Government, 2001, p. 46); the development of a uniform registration system among treatment centres (Federal Government, 2001, p. 47); and the clarification of the 1998 Ministerial Circular Letter (Federal Government, 2001, p. 64).

> There were a lot of issues integrated in the Federal Drug Policy Note. The 1999 Policy Memorandum strongly influenced the development of the Federal Drug Policy Note in 2001. It became clear that policy-makers listened to the practitioners.
>
> (Internal communication Memorandum Group, 26 October 2000)

Additionally, some practitioners became members of the Ministerial Cabinet (e.g. magistrates and lawyers). Their presence promoted the translation of their particular day-to-day experiences and their needs related to budgets or staff into the policy-making process even more.

> I wrote a large part of the Federal Drug Policy Note. Practitioners had a lot of influence [...]. They succeeded in determining some details and applying their vision [...] I could not delete phrasings but I could influence the particular modalities [...]. This certainly influenced the development of the Federal Drug Policy Note [...]
>
> (Respondent 16, practitioner)

Media and Interest Groups: Increasing Polarisation and Confusion

By 2001, the role of the press and interest groups was growing in the Belgian drug policy debates. The political discussions within the lap of the ICWG appeared to feed into the media by means of policy-makers leaking some internal communication between policy-makers as well as some preliminary versions of the Federal Drug Policy to the media. Simultaneously, through different mechanisms, interest groups sought to affect the policy-making process.

During the Activities of the ICWG: Media Leaks

In anticipation of the decisions to come, media coverage (characterised by a focus on cannabis policy and the harmfulness of cannabis use) gradually increased. In this context, it seemed that the media were not well managed by the ICWG. Even though an embargo was put on the drafts of the Federal Drug Policy Note, a preliminary version of the Federal Drug Policy Note was leaked to the press on 10 November 2000. Leaking to the media was a political strategy of a dissatisfied coalition partner to hamper (and steer) the policy-making process (Gelders, 2006). Even though the Minister of Health Magda Aelvoet (AGALEV, Flemish Greens) repeatedly stated that the leaked note only contained preliminary thoughts, a heavily mediatised and political storm developed. The controversy intensified when MP Frans Lozie (AGALEV, Flemish Greens), as an individual political strategy, announced that the Flemish Green party actually aimed to legalise all illegal drugs. The Green party AGALEV quickly blew the whistle on the MP: the Minister of Health Magda Aelvoet (AGALEV, Flemish Greens) called it a "wrong communication" and a "big mistake". A journalist explained:

> I remember that I received a phone call from their spokesman refuting the statements of Frans Lozie. The spokesman clearly said that these statements were not in accordance with the ideas of the Flemish Green party. They were in favour of the legalisation of cannabis, not of all illegal drugs.
>
> (Respondent 15, journalist)

Additionally, on 25 November 2000, Flemish newspaper *De Morgen* (again a Flemish whistle-blower) published a private letter by Minister of Health Magda Aelvoet (AGALEV, Flemish Greens). In this letter, addressed to the secretary of Ecolo (French-speaking Greens), she supported the *decriminalisation* of cannabis and the *depenalisation* of other illegal drugs. The controversy and the confusion only increased. The general problem with this media communication (especially in the Flemish media) was that it caused confusion between what was only an intention and what had already been decided. "The possession and the production of five grams of cannabis no longer prosecuted" (6 December 2000, Flemish newspaper *De Tijd*). At the same time, media coverage created confusion by juggling with the concepts 'legalisation', 'depenalisation', and 'decriminalisation'. The media clearly were more interested in provoking controversy by emphasising stereotypes and publishing sensational headlines (instead of substantive discussions and reflections). Given the particular characteristics of news production, media coverage is indeed often interlinked with ideology and sensationalism as well as with disclosure and economic concerns that push accuracy way down the list of values (Coomber et al., 2000).

Accordingly, media discourse, issue coverage, and media leaks *framed* the public's (mis)understanding of the debate (Entman, 1989; Lancaster et al., 2011). An opinion poll commissioned by French-speaking newspaper *Le Soir* and conducted by a university team (Prof. Dr. Rene Patesson and Pascale Steinberg) between August and October 2000 (during the discussions in the ICWG) confirmed that 56.2 per cent of the respondents did not know that cannabis use was still prohibited. Flemish (and young) respondents in particular thought that cannabis use was tolerated (Patesson & Steinberg, 2000). While there was no direct influence of the media coverage on the activities of the ICWG, policy-makers were concerned about how the public (and their electorate) (mis)understood policy decisions. An illustration of this point is that, in December 2000, Minister of Public Health Magda Aelvoet tried to produce order out of chaos by hiring a spokesman, Mr. Paul Geerts, for a couple of months. His first assignment was to deal with the ongoing, misleading media communication. Mr. Paul Geerts expressed:

> The decision of the Council of Ministers in December 2000 to postpone the debate increased the controversy [...]. One of my first tasks was to call journalists and to explain the state of the art. In this way, they were well-informed about the developments [...]
>
> (Mr. Paul Geerts, contracted spokesman of Minister of Public Health Magda Aelvoet)

In this context, media clearly played a key role in precipitating decision-making (Scheufele & Tewksbury, 2007; McCombs & Reynolds, 2009). Through media-generated confusion and misunderstanding, the development of the first national drug strategy had shot to prominence in the public attention demanding clear action from the government.

Official Publication of the Federal Drug Policy Note on 19 January 2001

The polarisation and confusion increased even more when the Federal Drug Policy Note was launched officially on 19 January 2001. The press conference was characteristic of the difficulties of the Government in providing clear messages, especially regarding whether and when the possession of cannabis for personal use was allowed or not (Gelders & Vander Laenen, 2007). The Minister of Justice Marc Verwilghen (VLD, Flemish Liberals) stated that "it is wrong to claim that Belgium has implemented a depenalisation" and that "the possession and use of cannabis by minors will always be considered as problematic". The Minister of Public Health Magda Aelvoet (AGALEV, Flemish Greens) softened this statement by saying that "a minor of 16 or 17 who smokes cannabis at home, without causing nuisance or without being in a problematic situation, will not be prosecuted". Clearly, this latter statement was juridically wrong: the particular cannabis regulation in the Federal Drug Policy Note only applied to adults. These confusing and conflicting statements caused huge misunderstandings and it was a source of frustration for the Verhofstadt I Government that the public debate again focused on the cannabis issue (while ignoring the other elements of the Federal Drug Policy Note). Their fear was that the Federal Drug Policy Note would be interpreted as a *tolerance policy* applying a decriminalisation or a legalisation of cannabis. A similar position was taken by the previous Dehaene II Government (1995–1999) when discussing and communicating about the final conclusions and recommendations of the PWG. Their fear was justified: by the end of 2001, the EMCDDA launched a report stating that "in the last year, there has been decriminalisation of all drug use in Portugal, a Policy Note in Belgium to decriminalise cannabis possession, and the start of the process to downgrade the offence of cannabis possession in the UK" (EMCDDA, 2001).

The Belgian media did not hesitate to polarise the discussion even more. While the French-speaking newspapers announced a *depenalisation*, the Flemish newspapers even created headlines that cannabis use was *fully tolerated*: "Depenalised possession and consumption of cannabis" (19 January 2001, French-speaking newspaper *Echo*). "The personal use of cannabis is tolerated. Cannabis depenalised by default" (19 January 2001, French-speaking newspaper *Le Soir*). "The use of cannabis completely free" (19 January 2001, Flemish newspaper *Belang van Limburg*). "Belgian policy of tolerance more tolerant than that of the Netherlands" (19 January 2001, Flemish newspaper *De Morgen*). As a result, the Federal Government, with the Minister of Public Health Magda Aelvoet (AGALEV, Flemish Greens) taking the lead, decided to launch an information campaign to shed some light on both policy and the status of the legislation, and to clarify the future penal policy with regard to cannabis (Federal Government, 2001).[7] In general, the launch of the Federal Drug Policy Note and the information campaign led to a strong increase in media attention to the drug topic (cannabis policy in particular). Concerned about how their electorate would perceive the Federal Drug Policy Note, policy-makers were also actively involved in these debates. The information campaign did not, however, resolve the confusion (Gelders, 2006). For instance, the brochure did not stress that a new bill had yet to be developed and adopted by the Parliament. Several newspapers reported on the positive and negative elements of the new drug law while there was no new law at all. "The new drug law is better than the old one" (6 March 2001, Flemish newspaper *Het Nieuwsblad*).

At the same time, themes such as the increasing THC content in cannabis, the increasing prevalence rates of use, and the health risks of cannabis use were increasingly captured in several quotations. For instance: "Cannabis is twice as strong as 10 years ago" (2 March 2001, Flemish newspaper *Het Laatste Nieuws*). Accordingly, among the public, emotions were still running high. Several readers' opinions were dominated by an emotional discourse (with a mistaken appeal against the legalisation of cannabis and a focus on the stepping-stone theory). Several schools also announced setting-up a campaign against the legalisation and decriminalisation of cannabis. The 'Druglijn', an online contact service as part of the Association for Alcohol and other Drug Problems (VAD), confirmed this public concern. They reported an increasing number of calls in 2001, especially related to the topic of cannabis (VAD, 2003).

Mobilisation of the Interest Group 'Parents against Drugs'

It is also in this context that the creation of the interest group *Parents against Drugs* [*Ouders tegen Drugs*] was noted. The president of the interest group was Mrs. Josefien Smits whose son died from a drug overdose at the end of the 1990s. Several like-minded parents of (ex-)drug users (together with some practitioners and scientists) joined the interest group and the members increasingly and proactively expressed their opinion in the media. Consequently, through the media, this interest group succeeded in heating up and polarising the debate even more. "Mother of a drug-addict angry about the statements of Senator Van Quickenborne of the Flemish Nationalist party" (31 January 2001, Flemish newspaper *Het Nieuwsblad*).

Statements of the Flemish interest group *Parents against Drugs* [*Ouders tegen Drugs*] regularly seeped into the discourse of newspapers. Clearly, the media acted as an important communication tool for interest groups. However, simultaneously, the interest group was often criticised by some (rather progressive) journalists. "Federal Drug Policy Note does not legalise cannabis. J. Smits, president of the interest group Parents against Drugs [Ouders tegen Drugs], is not always well-informed about the goals of the Government" (1 June 2001, Flemish newspaper *Het Nieuwsblad*).

In addition to their use of the media, they employed several other methods to gain more public (and political) attention. The methods used by these groups to influence drug discourse are in accordance with the tools described in the literature earlier on (EMCDDA, 2013; O'Gorman et al., 2014). First, members of *Parents against Drugs* [*Ouders tegen Drugs*] gave lectures and distributed flyers to gain public support. Second, they actively tried to influence policy-making by making contact with (like-minded) members of the Parliament. Within this framework, they succeeded in convincing some MPs to submit questions or interpellations. In particular, the Flemish extreme right party Vlaams Blok was a heavy supporter of a radical interpretation of their message 'say no to drugs'. Several interviewees stressed that the Flemish interest group *Parents against Drugs* [*Ouders tegen Drugs*] was financially and organisationally supported by this political party.

> We had contacts with the interest group, we were their only political representative. But they knew that they risked negative attention by cooperating with the Vlaams Blok [...]. They were careful [...]. They really cooperated with them. Organising meetings, a demonstration etc.
>
> (Respondent 14, policy-maker)

Third, they collected signatures against legalisation and organised a large demonstration on 30 September 2001. Even some political parties were represented: CD&V[8] (Flemish Christian Democrats), Vlaams Blok (Flemish extreme right party), and Front National (French-speaking extreme right party). Several newspapers reported on this demonstration. "More than 90% of the 3,000 demonstrators were Flemish people responding to the appeal of the interest group" (1 October 2001, French-speaking newspaper *Le Soir*). As a result of the petition and demonstration, members of the interest groups were invited by the Prime Minister Guy Verhofstadt and the Minister of Public Health Magda Aelvoet. Even though they were heard and a dialogue was set up, all interviewees (members of interest groups as well as policy-makers) agreed that their efforts did not result in effectively influencing the Ministers (and their representatives) of the Verhofstadt I Government.

> We organised a demonstration and, a couple of days later, we were invited by the Prime Minister Guy Verhofstadt [...]. We were allowed to discuss our worries, but in practice, nothing changed [...]. We were not decisive. We rang a bell but that's it.
>
> (Respondent 3, member of interest group)

> Their emotional discourse influenced some people but it was not structured enough [...]. Each story was touching but, as a group, they did have few impact.
>
> (Respondent 39, policy-maker)

With this in mind, it was often argued that their organisation and arguments were not structured enough and that they united only a small number of citizens who did not necessarily represent the larger public. As Matthew-Simmons articulated (2011), the reality of policy-making dictates that most policy decisions must be acceptable to a majority of the voting population. Additionally, their actions popped up too late; the Federal Drug Policy Note was already developed and politically approved in January 2001. Attempts to influence policy-making therefore remained limited to setting the parliamentary agenda. In other words, they affected policy-makers and the level of the public feasibility of their policy choices instead of at the level of substantive argumentation in the ICWG.

Parliamentary Debates: The Political Struggle Continues

Given the tensions among the coalition partners in the Government, MPs eagerly made use of their capacity to monitor and control its activities. The official launch of the Federal Drug Policy Note immediately provoked some parliamentary activity. Several members of the Chamber of Representatives submitted interpellations regarding the content of the Federal Drug Policy Note (*Hand.* Kamer 2000–2001, 30 januari 2001, 106, 1–56; *Hand.* Kamer 2000–2001, 30 januari 2001, 0025/172, 1–3). Later on, the launch of the information campaign once again led to submission of a high number of parliamentary questions and interpellations.[9]

Similar to the parliamentary debates during the intermezzo (1997–2000), the parliamentary debate was soon narrowed down to one element of the Federal Drug Policy Note: cannabis policy. Again, scientific knowledge brought into the debate by members of Government as well as by MPs competed with other information, as well as with ideology and political interest. For instance, a common statement was that the stipulations regarding cannabis policy in the Federal Drug Policy Note had led to an increase in the prevalence of cannabis use. Several MPs used vague references to scientific research to argue that cannabis use as well as the number of people driving under influence of cannabis had increased in the first half of 2001 (as a result of the Federal Drug Policy Note which was launched in January 2001). "There has been an increase in driving under the influence of cannabis since the launch of the Federal Drug Policy Note in January 2001, hasn't there?" (Mrs. Clotilde Nyssens, MP CVP, Flemish Christian Democrats; *Vr. en Antw.* Senaat, 12 juni 2001, nr. 2/36 (Vr. nr. 1265 C. Nyssen)). Whereas policy issues often rise rapidly to the top of the political agenda and require quick answers, scientific research can take months or years to complete. As the parliamentary debates took place in the months following the launch of the Federal Drug Policy Note, it was not possible to draw conclusions such as "cannabis use increased due to the Federal Drug Policy Note" (Kinable,

2002). Clearly, in accordance with the literature (Lindquist, 2001; Carden, 2004), some MPs drew false conclusions by ignoring the different time frames of science and policy.

Political tactics played an important role too. Opposition parties were very active in formulating *personal insults* and using *metaphors*. These strategies were used to undermine the credibility of the Government and the political majority in the Parliament. Very often MPs presented themselves as honest or aiming for honesty while, at the same time, pointing to the unfairness of political opponents. Having a central position in the drug/cannabis debate, both the Minister of Justice Marc Verwilghen and the Minister of Public Health Magda Aelvoet were blamed. “Mrs Minister, I’m going to be honest with you. In the last year and a half, you have talked nonsense more than once. You have a practically flawless feeling for blunders and inaccurate communication” (Mr. Yves Leterme, MP CVP, Flemish Christian Democrats; *Hand.* Kamer 2000–2001, 30 januari 2001, 106). Moreover, MPs in an oppositional position consciously stimulated the confusion by using *inaccurate terminology*. Many members of the Parliament did not make a distinction between the possession and the use of cannabis and among the concepts legalisation, depenalisation, or decriminalisation. “It is astonishing that the Government has decided to no longer criminalise the use of cannabis” (Mr. Jo Vandeurzen, MP CVP, Flemish Christian Democrats; *Hand.* Kamer 2000–2001, 30 januari 2001, 106). The discourse of the opposition parties and some majority parties often included concepts such as ‘youth’, ‘children’, or ‘minors’. Here, MPs pointed to the increase of cannabis consumption among youth, to the accuracy of the stepping-stone story, and the establishment of *coffee-shops* in Belgium. Such *emotional assumptions* were not based on any scientific knowledge. Likewise, it was sometimes stated that the expertise as a parent was equally as important as the expertise of a scientist.

> You don’t have to be a great psychologist or professor to know this. My children are 20 years old. In a discussion with youngsters about the use of drugs, the argument of ‘authority’ is taken down by the Government [my emphasis].
>
> (Mr. Jos Ansoms, MP CVP, Flemish Christian Democrats; *Hand.* Kamer 2000–2001, 31 januari 2001, COM 373, 1–4)

Finally, arguments related to the renegotiation of the international conventions (referring to the phrase “the Federal Government is an advocate of the need to rethink the international conventions”, Federal Government, 2001, p. 46) were very often observed in the debate. A common strategy here was to project the effects of depenalisation, decriminalisation, or legalisation of cannabis on the basis of *analogies to experiences of other countries* (cf. *policy platonism*; MacCoun & Reuter, 2001). The advantages of prohibition were supported by the American example of the *War on Drugs*. The Dutch *coffee-shop* model was often mentioned to support the idea that liberalisation may lead to drug tourism and an increase in drug use. "Depenalisation of the possession of cannabis may increase the demand. That is obvious. This is confirmed by the current developments in the Netherlands" (Mr. Jo Vandeurzen, MP CVP, Flemish Christian Democrats; *Hand.* Kamer 2000–2001, 30 januari 2001, 106).

Summary

By the mid-2000s, an Inter-Cabinet Working Group (ICWG) had been set up within the lap of the multi-party government coalition to decide on the first national drug strategy. Through the launch of the Federal Drug Policy Note (2001), the drug phenomenon was officially recognised as an ongoing social reality and a matter of public health. Importantly, the rationale for an *evidence-based* policy was also stressed explicitly in the Federal Drug Policy Note and an annual budget was provided to organise and manage a research programme supporting decision-making in the field of illegal drugs (Federal Government, 2001). What followed the launch of the Federal Drug Policy Note was a rather chaotic and confusing political and media debate.

This chapter looked in detail at the work of Prof. Dr. Brice De Ruyver, appointed as the security advisor to Prime Minister Guy Verhofstadt in these processes, and considered his role in relation to the typology established by Loader and Sparks (2011). Being involved in the Inter-Cabinet Working Group (ICWG), the *observer-turned-player* experienced how policy was made and who or what exerted the most influence. This role also enabled him to promote the *instrumental utilisation* (Weiss, 1979) of his own scientific research and that of others in the political arena (i.e. advancing an *evidence-based* drug policy). Despite several media storms, he also acted as a dynamic and proactive mediator between the representatives of the different coalition partners. In this way, he succeeded in creating a kind of 'calm space' in which a sensible debate could be held about the goals of drug policy and what policy options might be part of the compromise. Nevertheless, while he succeeded in adding some 'coolant' to the heated debate, the 'success' of his public engagement was contingent on the rules of politics and competition too. After all, even an *observer-turned-player*, who devotes him- or herself to problem representation or the introduction of acceptable, feasible alternatives, will only stand a chance of influencing policy when the evidence fits with a pre-established stance and if it has engaged sponsors in policy circles. What this example illustrates is the rather obvious but crucial importance of political power.

The role of politics also came to the fore in this chapter in both how Government and Parliamentarians made claims for their side. Debates were clearly overshadowed by the disagreements between coalition partners.

The use of political tactics (e.g. incorrect terminology, personal insults, emotional assumptions, and metaphors) and the examples of *political/symbolic* utilisation of scientific knowledge were a tangible illustration of this point. Throughout, the international framework, international studies or experts on drug policies in other European countries also continued to influence Belgian drug policy development, especially when debating solutions to the direction of cannabis policy.

The launch of the first national drug strategy as well as the information campaign were both heavily debated in the media. It was an interesting observation that in a multi-party government coalition, when agreement could not be reached behind closed doors, the issue erupted into public debate via media leaks. Accordingly, the media was able to further exaggerate the incomplete and contradictory message of the Federal Government at the press conference. This strongly impacted on the public's understanding of the Federal Drug Policy Note, as was witnessed by several opinion polls (Patesson & Steinberg, 2000). Notwithstanding its powerful role in *framing* and *priming* of issues, as put forward by key media theories (McCombs & Shaw, 1972), the media also seemed to play a key role in triggering internal government decision-making by demanding clear action from the government in 2001 (see also Scheufele & Tewksbury, 2007).

By means of several mechanisms (e.g. participation in media debates and demonstrations; EMCDDA, 2013; O'Gorman et al., 2014), interest group *Parents against Drugs* [*Ouders tegen Drugs*] succeeded in heating up and polarising the public debate even more. However, their lack of influence on the internal government decision-making (through the Inter-Cabinet Working Group) appeared to be the result of their deficient organisational and communication structure and that they only represented a small part of public opinion. Furthermore, their mobilisation was initiated too late: the Federal Drug Policy Note was already developed and politically approved.

Chapter 8 covers the implementation of one of the action points of the Federal Drug Policy Note. The adaptation of the drug law (and the Ministerial Circular Letter), the third milestone in the development of Belgian drug policy between 1996 and 2003, is discussed by considering the different accounts where scientific knowledge (and other types of information) have (not) played a role.

Notes

1 The balanced approach was described as an 'integral and integrated policy'. 'Integral' refers to the idea that drug phenomenon is multidimensional and, therefore, all its aspects must consequently be tackled. 'Integrated' means the involvement of and (vertical as well as horizontal) harmonisation among all relevant actors representing the different aspects (De Ruyver et al., 2009).

2 The Minister of Public Health, Food Chain Safety and the Environment, the Minister of Internal Affairs, Minister of Justice, Minister of Social Affairs, Minister for

Social Integration, Minister of Mobility and Transport (traffic safety) and the Minister for Small Businesses, Self-Employed, Agriculture and Science policy.

3 Magda Aelvoet (AGALEV, Flemish Greens) was Vice-Minister and Minister of Consumption Affairs, Public Health and Environment during the Verhofstadt I Government (1999–2003). However, she resigned in 2002 as a result of a scandal related to the controversial supply of weapons to Nepal.

4 As the preparation and writing of the Federal Drug Policy Note really took place in the Inter-cabinet Working Group (as a fundamental preparation of the final discussion in the Council of Ministers (in case of consensus) or the Inner Cabinet (in case no consensus is reached)), it can be perceived as a main actor in the decision-making process. The Inner Cabinet chaired by the Prime Minister constitutes a forum in which coalition parties reach major decisions on conflictual matters, which the Council of Ministers then formally ratifies (Brans, De Winter, & Swenden, 2009). It is important to note that, as a result of the so-called Copernicus reforms of the Government (1999–2003), an Inter-Cabinet Working Group is now called a Policy Coordination Working Group.

5 Flemish and French-speaking Christian Democrats refused to determine a quantity for personal use (see Chapter 5).

6 No general population survey on drugs had been completed until then. The 2001 edition of the national Health Interview Survey (HIS) introduced some questions on cannabis and ecstasy.

7 On 10 February 2001, the Federal Government launched the first part of their information campaign through a media advertisement. Later, in May 2001, an information brochure (i.e. 600,000 leaflets) was circulated through secondary schools, police offices, justice houses, courts, treatment services, post offices, town halls, libraries, and through the website of the Ministry of Public Health. The 24-page brochure presented the Federal Drug Policy Note along the format of Frequently Asked Questions.

8 The CVP became CD&V in September 2001.

9 *Hand.* Kamer 2000–2001, 31 januari 2001, COM 373, 1–4; *Hand.* Kamer 2000–2001, 6 februari 2001, COM 376, 9–11; *Hand.* Kamer 2000–2001, 8 februari 2001, 108, 7–9; *Hand.* Kamer, 2000–2001, 13 februari 2001, COM 390, 4–6; *Hand.* Kamer 2000–2001, 20 februari 2001, COM 394, 17–21; *Hand.* Kamer 2000–2001, 7 maart 2001, COM 410, 12–17; *Hand.* Kamer 2000–2001, 8 maart 2001, 112, 13–15; *Hand.* Kamer 2000–2001, 15 maart 2001, 114, 6–7; *Hand.* Kamer 2000–2001, 29 maart 2001, 119, 12–13; *Hand.* Kamer 2000–2001, 19 april 2001, 121, 5–7; *Hand.* Kamer 2000–2001, 17 mei 2001, 125, 1–3; *Hand.* Kamer 2000–2001, 31 mei 2001, 130, 5–7; *Hand.* Kamer 2000–2001, 7 juni 2001, 132, 9; *Hand.* Kamer 2000–2001, 3 juli 2001, 517, 11–12; *Hand.* Kamer 2000–2001, 19 juli 2001, 158, 18–19; *Hand.* Kamer 2000–2001, 23 oktober 2001, 560, 32–35; *Vr. en Antw.* Kamer, 19 februari 2001, nr. 064 (Vr. nr. 309 A. Colen); *Hand.* Senaat 2000–2001, 1 februari 2001, 2–92, 21–23; *Hand.* Senaat 2000–2001, 8 februari 2001, 2–94, 27–30; *Hand.* Senaat 2000–2001, 15 februari 2001, 2–96, 8–9; *Hand.* Senaat 2000–2001, 22 februari 2001, 2–98, 9–12; *Hand.* Senaat 2000–2001, 8 maart 2001, 2–100, 25–27; *Hand.* Senaat 2000–2001, 29 maart 2001, 2–104, 33–38; *Hand.* Senaat 2000–2001, 17 mei 2001, 2–114, 18–20; *Hand.* Senaat 2000–2001, 31 mei 2001, 2–119, 11–12; *Hand.* Senaat 2001–2002, 6 december 2001, 2–162, 16–18; *Vr. en Antw.* Senaat, 12 juni 2001, nr. 2/36 (Vr. nr. 1265 C. Nyssen); *Vr. en Antw.* Senaat, 9 oktober 2001, nr. 2/42 (Vr. nr. 1509 M. De Schamphelaere); *Vr. en Antw.* Senaat, 6 november 2001, nr. 2/43 (Vr. nr. 1553 V. Van Quickenborne).

Chapter 8

The Reform of Belgian Drug Law 2002–2003

Since the launch of the Federal Drug Policy Note in 2001, the implementation of a coherent, integrated drug policy in Belgium was an ongoing process (De Ruyver et al., 2012). As one of the most discussed action points, the Federal Government modified the criminal policy on drugs in 2003, through the adaptation of the drug law (of 24 February 1921) and the Ministerial Circular Letter of 8 May 1998 (De Ruyver et al., 2012). In doing so, Belgium de facto *depenalised*[1] cannabis possession for personal use – involving maintenance of criminal penalties in the criminal law without any application in practice (Guillain, 2003). At that time, similar debates on the depenalisation or decriminalisation of drugs were also sparked off in other countries (e.g. in Spain, Portugal, the UK, and Luxembourg). Each of these foreign examples clearly demonstrated the political tensions in regard to such a reform and the regular use of arguments based on speculation rather than the available evidence (MacCoun & Reuter, 2001; EMCDDA, 2001; Hughes & Stevens, 2012). This chapter highlights how the reform of the Belgian drug law came along in the light of the *evidence-based* rhetoric put forward by the Federal Government in 1999. Of particular relevance too is that the reform, together with the election of a new Government, marked the closing of the *window of opportunity* (Kingdon, 2002). The new drug law and the new Ministerial Circular Letter were endorsed just before the 2003 elections and the political issue in question faded from the political and public agenda by the end of 2003. Drug policy has not been a contentious issue in Belgium since.

The New Drug Law: Modifications to the 1921 Narcotic Drug Act

The new criminal policy on drugs was anchored through the Law of 4 April 2003 and the Law of 3 May 2003, accompanied by the Royal Decree of 16 May 2003 and the Ministerial Circular Letter of 16 May 2003.[2] In the new drug law[3] and the Royal Decree a criminal approach was suggested, with a focus on the differentiation and the individualisation of the criminal intervention. One of the most important changes concerned the new statute of cannabis being defined as another category of drugs with its own distinct regulations (i.e. the possession of an amount of cannabis, meant for personal use, by an adult (i.e. 18 years or older), without the presence of nuisance or problematic use will only lead to a registration by the police). 'Problematic use' was defined as use that is linked with a level of dependence that prevents the user from controlling his/her use and that is expressed by psychological and physical symptoms. The definition of 'public nuisance' was provided by the broader definition of 'public nuisance' in Art. 135, §2 of the New Community Law.[4] In particular, it was expressly stated that 'public nuisance', in accordance with the 1988 United Nations Convention against illegal traffic in narcotic drugs and psychotropic substances, referred to the "possession of cannabis in a prison, education institute, public institute or in their neighbourhood as well as in meeting places of minors like schools or a sport centre". Other changes implemented by the new drug law were that 'drug use in a group' was no longer punishable and that substances that could be used to produce illicit substances (so-called precursors), under article 8 of a European Council Regulation (n° 3677/90), were now incorporated as well.[5]

In this context, a distinction between infringements for *personal use* or infringements *for profit* (i.e. clear differentiation according to the intent) and between three categories of crimes was explicated. The *first* category involved the importation, production, transport, purchase, possession, and cultivation of cannabis for *personal use*. The *second* category included the behaviour from category 1, but in cases of aggravating circumstances such as the presence of minors,[6] problematic use, or public nuisance. The *third* category included all violations of the drug law that were not included in the first or second category. Both categories 2 and 3 were linked with an imprisonment (of between three months and five years) as well as a fine (of between €5,000 and €500,000). Other penalties were placed in category 1: first infringement (a fine of €15–25), repeated infringement within one year (a fine of €26–50), another repeated infringement within one year after the second infringement (imprisonment of eight days–one month and a fine of €50–100), in case of aggravating circumstances such as involvement of minors or criminal organisations (imprisonment of three months–one year and/or a fine of €1,000–100,000). Obviously, the commerce, production, export, and importation of substances (for profit) remained forbidden, and retained their original punishments.

Furthermore, the new drug law allowed a broader application of the Law of 29 June 1964 concerning the conditional sentence, suspended sentence, and probation (changed by the Law of 10 February 1994).[7] According to this law, a judge can decide to defer the pronouncement of a sentence or to postpone the execution of a sentence. Linking conditions to these decisions results in a 'probationary conditional sentence'[8] or a 'probationary suspended sentence'.[9] While, according to art. 3 and 8, the person concerned should not have been earlier sentenced to a criminal sentence or a prison sentence of more than 12 months, art. 9 of the Law of 9 July 1975 already added that, in particular cases, judicial antecedents were no impediments for probation (see also above). The new drug law (of 3 May 2003) replaced art. 9 of the Law of 9 July 1975 by removing 'drug use in a group' (as this was no longer punishable). Simultaneously, the scope of art. 9 was extended. Art. 9 of the new drug law noted that, in case of offences for personal use (i.e. the possession for personal use as well as the sale to finance one's own use)[10] without aggravating circumstances, judicial antecedents were no impediments for probation (Mahieu, 2004; Geenens, Vanderplasschen, Broekaert, & De Ruyver, 2005). In aiming to reduce users' physical and psychosocial problems that might accompany drug abuse and to protect society, this broader application allowed for guiding problematic drug users more easily towards treatment (*last resort* philosophy).

In a similar vein, as the importance of individualised and continuous care and of cooperation between the criminal justice and the treatment system had been stressed in the Federal Drug Policy Note (Vander Laenen & Dhont, 2003; Geenens et al., 2005), the Royal Decree of 16 May 2003 formally introduced the terms *risk reduction* and *therapeutic advice*.[11] The new concept of case-managers for judicial and health matters, to be appointed by the Federal Ministers of Justice and Health, respectively, was also introduced (see also Federal Government, 2001, pp. 34, 49). On the one hand, the chronic and complex problems of many drug abusers and the lack of coordination and continuity of care were the main reasons for introducing *health case-managers* (Vanderplasschen, Rapp, Wolf, & Broekaert, 2004). A *health case-manager* was said to be responsible for the personal observation of problematic drug users who are guided to treatment (to enhance treatment access, participation, and retention and to improve treatment results concerning drug use, employment, psychological problems, or criminality) (Geenens et al., 2005). Case-managers for health matters were implemented in 2002: a pilot project for the development of crisis units for drug addicts and the implementation of the role of case-manager within these units was initiated (Geenens et al., 2005).

On the other hand, a *judicial case-manager* had to bridge the gap between the criminal justice system and the (drug) treatment system, to inform magistrates about treatment possibilities for drug offenders, and to advise them about the desirability of coercion.[12] In particular, it was determined that, at every stage of criminal justice process, magistrates had the opportunity (through a *judicial case-manager*) to ask for therapeutic advice. The positive or negative advice of an independent *therapeutic advisor* (based on existing scientific, psycho-social, and medical knowledge) was to help the magistrate to assess the extent of problematic use and the need for treatment, taking into account the interests of the user as well as of society. The lack of structural clarity together with limited financial support hampered its implementation for a long time (De Ruyver et al., 2004; De Ruyver, Vander Laenen, & Eelen, 2012).[13]

Towards a Drug Law Reform: An Inter-Cabinet Working Group (ICWG)

The new drug law was developed by an Inter-Cabinet Working Group supervised by the Minister of Justice Marc Verwilghen (VLD, Flemish Liberals), in close cooperation with the Minister of Public Health Magda Aelvoet (AGALEV, Flemish Greens). The ICWG was guided by the same principles described in Chapter 7. It comprised the technically and politically skilled representatives of the Ministers. *Observer-turned-player* Brice De Ruyver, as the security advisor to the Prime Minister, again participated in the ICWG mediating between the opposing points of view to find compromises that were acceptable to the coalition partners. The main issue in the debate was adherence to the international control system and, in particular, if and how cannabis possession should be (de)criminalised. Again, these debates uncovered the recurrent political contradictions between the coalition partners very clearly. From their rather liberal, progressive perspective, the French-speaking Socialists (PS) and Greens (Ecolo) and the Dutch-speaking Greens (AGALEV) did not want criminal prosecution of cannabis possession at all. On the contrary, the French and Dutch-speaking Liberals (MR and VLD) as well as the Dutch-speaking Socialists (SP.A)[14] advocated the criminal prosecution of cannabis possession in case of aggravating circumstances related to the importation, production, transport, purchase, possession, and cultivation of cannabis for personal use such as 'problematic use' or 'public nuisance' (Internal communication Ministerial Cabinet, 16 January 2002). In a response to the rather vague notions that were included in the Federal Drug Policy Note, attempts were made to better define these notions to make it clear how to use these in practice (e.g. by police officers).

> It was a difficult debate. A policy note with intentions is totally different from translating these intentions into a clear text [...]. It was a politically and juridical-technically difficult debate. The discussion consisted of issues like the distinction between categories of crimes, the concepts like 'nuisance' and other 'aggravating circumstances'.
>
> (Respondent 36, policy-maker)

> No criminal prosecution of cannabis possession is inconsistent with the Federal Drug Policy Note. We avoided a tolerance policy. Accordingly, we underlined the importance of notions like 'problematic use'

> and 'nuisance'. The lack of a differentiation is ridiculous and the opposition party Flemish Christian Democrats (CVP) is right when criticising this.
>
> (Internal communication Ministerial Cabinet, 30 April 2002)

In this context, some research projects (commissioned by the Belgian Federal Science Policy) clarifying the concepts of 'problematic drug use' and 'drug nuisance' and gaining insight into the constitutive elements of these concepts, could have supported the determination of the notions 'problematic drug use' and 'public nuisance' in the new drug law (Decorte, Kaminski, Muys, & Slingeneyer, 2005). Likewise, the results of the study Case management in the substance abuse treatment and criminal justice system could have been helpful in determining the position of case-managers for judicial and health matters (Geenens et al., 2005). However, the results of these policy-funded research projects came too late (their reports were published in 2005) to contribute to the development of a legal framework in 2002–2003. Thus, one of the most common barriers between science and policy was observed here: the long time period of conducting research versus the short policy-making time-frames.

> Problematic drug use was a very difficult concept. We encountered the limitations of scientific knowledge. A definition of problematic use was not provided by scientific research in time.
>
> (Respondent 34, policy-maker)

At that time, there was also limited (but developing) evidence surrounding the impacts of the emerging forms of liberalisation in the international context (MacCoun & Reuter, 2001). Within the lap of the Belgians' EU presidency, several Health Ministers (Mrs. Els Borst, the Netherlands; Mrs. Andrea Fischer, succeeded by Mrs. Ulla Schmidt, Germany; Mrs. Ruth Dreifuss, Switzerland; Mr. Bernard Kouchner, France; Mrs. Magda Aelvoet, Belgium) took the initiative to organise an international scientific conference (Brussels, 25 February 2002) on the subject of cannabis to get a good understanding of the scientific state of the art regarding cannabis, its policy, and the effects of cannabis use on health and behaviour. The conference linked discussions in Belgium with those in other European countries and clearly fitted within the sustained concern about the international framework and the increasing importance of scientific knowledge. However, while one of the conclusions of the conference clearly stated: "We sincerely believe that science can help to ensure that cannabis policy gradually develops into an evidence-based policy" (Ministry of Public Health of Belgium, 2002, p. 125), it seemed that, ultimately, the choice to depenalise or to decriminalise was not simply a question of the available research. It remained predominantly a political choice of how one should respond to drug use taking into account the international framework. Right from the start, the great concern to maintain a prohibition against cannabis revealed how much the international framework (e.g. UN treaties of 1961–1971–1988 and the 1990 Schengen Convention) meant to Belgian drug policy-makers. Its power as a framework for the reform of Belgian drug law was strengthened by the activities of the International Narcotics Control Board (INCB) – the body charged with monitoring adherence to the UN Conventions. During the activities of the ICWG, international pressure was felt regularly: the International Narcotics Control Board (INCB) not only published a report in 2001 arguing that "adding another drug to the same category as alcohol and tobacco would be a historical mistake" (INCB, 2001, p. 37), but also contacted the representatives of the Minister of Public Health Magda Aelvoet. An interviewee explained that:

> At the time of the Inter-Cabinet Working Group, a meeting was arranged with the head office of the INCB. We had to counter the misinterpretation and to explain the position of Belgium regarding international and European policy.
>
> (Respondent 55, policy-maker)

Non-Government Stakeholder Engagement: A Juridical-Technical Discussion

The ICWG mainly included a juridical-technical discussion with numerous issues in the field of practicability and feasibility (e.g. registration by the police officer, cooperation between justice and treatment). Therefore, the ICWG involved work from a host of technical experts (e.g. in law or criminal procedure) originating from outside the policy-making process. Also, some prevention and treatment workers were heard by members of the ICWG about the issue of therapeutic advice (Roose, 2002).

> Some lawyers were very helpful and supportive in the juridical translation of the policy options. They had a lot of knowledge about the national and international laws. They helped to decide what was possible, what was not, and how to implement this in practice.
>
> (Respondent 34, policy-maker)

Scientists were less directly involved in the ICWG because of the juridical-technical nature of the discussion. In terms of the *observer-turned-player*, the *evidence-based* policy discourse and movement had given scientists a more overt and direct role in Belgian drug policy-making at the governmental level. Of course not all engagement was 'public'. Much lobbying, discussion, and persuasion took place behind the scenes, and this was a (successful) route to become known as experts in the particular field by policy-makers and to establish an interaction between science and policy. In doing so, some scientists pointed to their public engagements in advising MPs or Ministers informally and establishing contacts with professionals (e.g. police, outreach workers) to influence the policy-making process rather indirectly.

> First, I tried to influence the highest level of the policy-making process but that was not successful. It is better to work bottom-up, talking with professionals and MPs in order to climb up. I also have found other ways to distribute information and get involved, I have attended a lot of conferences, participated in study groups, etc. That is the role of a scientist. Of course, I understand that some scientists do not do this [...]. Eventually, I played a role.
>
> (Respondent 52, scientist)

From Loader and Sparks' (2011) perspective, those *policy advisors* allowed for a certain flow of scientific information into the policy-making process. For example, because of his proactive and long-term involvement as a *policy advisor* in the drug policy-making process (e.g. PWG or policy-funded research), scientist Isidore Pelc was appointed President of the Drug Health Policy Cell, a supporting working cell of the General Drugs Policy Cell. In Belgium, it is the General Drugs Policy Cell that prepares the policy decisions of the Ministers involved in the field of drugs. As a result, in the development of the drug law reform (2003), the Drug Health Policy Cell discussed some preliminary policy documents (bill, Royal Decree, Cooperation agreement, etc.) and eventually formulated some advice which was inspired by scientific knowledge indirectly (Cel Gezondheidsbeleid Drugs, 2002, p. 17).

Media and Interest Groups on the Side-Lines

A clear media communication strategy was considered of particular importance given the ambiguous communication about the Federal Drug Policy Note (January–May 2001) on the one hand, and the looming elections (May 2003) on the other hand. Because of his long-term experience on the topic, *observer-turned-player* Brice De Ruyver was appointed to report about the drug policy issues in the media.

> Prime Minister Verhofstadt learned from the previous communication problems about this topic. Together with the Minister of Justice and the Minister of Public Health, he entrusted this task to Prof. Dr. Brice De Ruyver. The message had to be clear. It was important to know the pitfalls and to know how the media operated.
>
> (Respondent 50, scientist)

However, while the Government was deciding on the stipulations of the bill in the ICWG, the media framings continued to create confusion and polarisation. Representative of this state of affairs was the manipulation of cannabis prevalence rates. For example, some Flemish newspapers (*De Morgen*, *Het Laatste Nieuws*, and *Gazet van Antwerpen*) reported a lifetime prevalence rate of 38 per cent or 40 per cent among the Belgian population (sample of 1,200 respondents), while the report mentioned lifetime prevalence of 21 per cent among a representative sample of 3,311 respondents. As another example, the bill was often incorrectly called the Federal Drug Note and it was implied that a *tolerance* policy was already approved. "Federal Drug Policy Note finally decided" (10 January 2002, Flemish newspaper *De Morgen*). "The Government only tolerates smoking a joint at home [...]. The Government developed a Note and three Royal Decrees to legally formalise the drug policy" (10 January 2002, Flemish newspaper *De Tijd*). The actual influence of media coverage on the ICWG remained limited to a high level of attentiveness of policy-makers towards public opinion and their electorate.

Interest groups also indirectly affected the policy-making process because of their strong link with public opinion (and the electorates of policy-makers). In this context, the Flemish interest group *Parents against Drugs* [*Ouders tegen Drugs*] often made use of media coverage. They stressed their concerns about the increase of cannabis use among youth and the addictive characteristics of cannabis. "A joint is equal to an alcohol dosage of 0.8. Cannabis is addictive, some people use more and more. Accordingly their problems increase" (27 February 2002, Flemish newspaper *De Morgen*). Apart from that, there were hardly any initiatives or actions by interest groups during the activities of the ICWG. An important exception was the active involvement of a member of the interest group *Anti-Prohibition League* [*La Liaison anti-prohibitionniste*] in the ICWG. This particular practitioner became an advisor of the Minister of Public Health Magda Aelvoet and was able to give voice to this interest group. This particular engagement may be the only effective way for interest groups to play a certain role in the policy-making process at the governmental level. However, in this case, having a small voice should be interpreted as having the opportunity to communicate/advise and engage in the *debate* and not as having the means to directly influence the *outcome* of the ICWG.

> Working in the Inter-Cabinet Working Group, I supported the rather radical perspective as a member of the interest group Anti-Prohibition League [La Liaison anti-prohibitionniste]. In the Inter-Cabinet Working Group, I tried to put forward their perspective while discussing the drug law [...]. It was a juridical-technical discussion. In my opinion, the debate was influenced by the discourse of the interest group [...] I tried to get the most out of it [my emphasis].
>
> (Respondent 55, policy-maker)

Parliament: Putting Pressure on the Government

During the debates in the ICWG, MPs from the opposition parties regularly asked questions about the state of the art regarding the new drug law[15] In particular, the opposition party CD&V (Flemish Christian Democrats) sought to give the Government a hard time based on their experiences in the PWG; they were fully aware of the existing pitfalls and the political divergences. The strategy to put some pressure on the Government was a tactic to stimulate controversy among the coalition partners but also a way to keep the item on the political and public agenda (as they believed they could benefit from these disagreements in the following elections). Indeed, an interviewee as well as the arguments of the ICWG showed the indirect influence of the opposition parties on the ICWG.

> The Inter-Cabinet Working Group took a while because of the contradictions between the coalition partners and between several individuals within the same party. The opposition took advantage of these disagreements by regularly asking when the new drug law would be approved.
>
> (Respondent 17, policy-maker)

> Police and judicial actors look like fools. Why do they have to invest in crimes that are punished with a fine of 25 euros? Frankly, this is ridiculous. CD&V (Flemish Christian Democrats) rightly criticised this decision.
>
> (Internal communication Ministerial Cabinet, 30 April 2002)

Passage of a Bill in Parliament: Time Is Almost Up

Eventually, on 21 June 2002, a bill was submitted by the Government to the Parliament's Chamber of Representatives.[16] Both bills and the Royal Decree were treated as a whole in the Chamber of Representatives and the Senate.[17] The power of the Parliament in this particular phase should be put into perspective. On the one hand, the bill had already been heavily discussed and approved in the Inter-Cabinet Working Group (ICWG) and the Council of Ministers. On the other hand, the pressure of the end of the legislature was increasingly felt. "Generally, the parliamentary discussions were less important. There was an agreement in the Inter-Cabinet Working Group. At the same time, the end of the legislature was near. By all means, the new drug law had to be approved" (Respondent 36, policy-maker). The bill was discussed in the Commission of Justice as well as in the Commission of Public Health with the primary role given to the Commission of Public Health (in accordance with the perception of the drug phenomenon as a matter of public health).[18] Similar to the debates in the Commission of Justice (October and November 2002), the Commission of Public Health

(December 2002–February 2003) focused on political issues such as the definitions of 'problematic use' or 'public nuisance' and the compliance with the international drug control system. The internal disagreements between the coalition partners were outlined once more. For instance, they argued differently about the determination of 'quantity for personal use'. While the Minister of Justice mentioned in the Commission of Justice that a 'quantity for personal use' contains maximal five grams, his representative reported a maximum of 2.5 grams in the Commission of Public Health.[19] Minister of Public Health Jef Tavernier declared himself to be against any determination of a number of grams.

In contrast with the Commission of Justice, the Commission of Public Health sought the advice of individuals or institutions which did not belong to the Parliament and asked for some documentation. While the PWG aimed to get a *status questionis* of all aspects of the drug problem, the focus in the Commission of Public Health was primarily on public health issues. Twenty-four experts including five scientists, sixteen practitioners, and three members of the interest group *Parents against Drugs* [*Ouders tegen Drugs*] were heard. These experts were selected according to the same principles as the selection of experts by the PWG (1996–1997): the media and personal contacts/networks played an important role. For instance, the selection of members of the interest group *Parents against Drugs* [*Ouders tegen Drugs*] was clearly supported by MPs from the Flemish extreme right party Vlaams Blok (see also above). They intensively used the media to represent their actions (e.g. demonstrations), to strengthen their position and to become more widely known among the public and policy-makers. Some members of the interest group *Parents against Drugs* reacted emotionally. According to them, the government introduces a tolerance policy but does not mind the drug use among minors (28 November, Flemish newspaper *De Tijd*). Equally, the selected scientists and practitioners had regularly appeared in the media since the launch of the Federal Drug Policy Note (Federal Government, 2001). As an example, "The governmental communication on Belgian drug policy is confusing [...]. That is said by Prof. Dr. Guido Van Hal" (13 November 2002, Flemish newspaper *Gazet van Antwerpen*), and "A joint replaces a cigarette more often, says Prof. Dr. Guido Van Hal" (29 November 2002, Flemish newspaper *Het Volk*). An interviewee explained:

> In the Commission of Public Health, each MP made a list in accordance with the political party [...]. The main issue is: 'unknown, unloved'. Personal contacts played a role. This is also the case with the media. The same experts are selected over and over again. [...]. Accordingly, the public and MPs often adopt the idea that there are only a limited number of experts in this matter.
>
> (Respondent 35, policy-maker)

Furthermore, the selection was also inspired by the 2003 Policy Memorandum. Similar to the previous election in 1999, practitioners united their needs and demands in a Policy Memorandum and distributed the document to the political parties on the eve of the 2003 federal elections (which was at the time of the Commission of Public Health) (Memorandum Group, 2003). As such, the distribution of the Policy Memorandum supported the selection of practitioners in the Commission as well as influenced some arguments of MPs in the parliamentary debates preceding and following the elections.

(Over)focus on the Harmfulness of Cannabis

Comparing the selection of experts with those selected by the PWG, there was some obvious overlap. However, clearly, medical practitioners and psychiatrists were now increasingly considered as experts in this matter. For instance, the selection of Prof. Dr. Jef Hulselmans (Doctor – Head Psychiatry Stuyvenberg Hospital) who elaborated on the issues related to the link between cannabis and psychoses or schizophrenia, has to be understood in the light of the evolution of the Belgian drug policy debate. While none of these issues were discussed or elaborated on in the PWG (most experts seemed to nuance the dangers and risks of cannabis use; see Chapter 5), this particular focus of the Commission of Public Health can be framed within the increasing scientific knowledge (e.g. since the beginning of the twenty-first century, there has been a profusion of writings on the harmfulness of cannabis; Vuillaume, 2008),[20] the recurrent (emotional) public actions (e.g. media presence and demonstrations) of the interest group *Parents against Drugs* [*Ouders tegen Drugs*] and the sustained media coverage on the dangers of cannabis use, the increasing THC concentration, and the increasing prevalence rates since 2000–2001.

Reflecting on the typology of Loader and Sparks (2011), the selected scientists acted as *scientific experts* in the Commission of Public Health. They used their knowledge and methodological skills to give an updated overview of the current state of the art by means of general descriptions (e.g. ‘research shows’, ‘research confirms’, ‘some authors mention’, and ‘the literature shows’) or propositional arguments. Sometimes, footnotes and bibliographies were added. International drug policy studies were often used as a source of information because, as noted above, similar discussions were ignited in various European countries at that time (e.g. Portugal, Spain, and Italy).[21] In doing so, these *scientific experts* did *enlighten* the parliamentary debates with some new scientific knowledge (*conceptual* use or *enlightenment*; Weiss, 1979). In particular, they sensitised MPs to (new) issues such as the harmfulness of cannabis and the connection between cannabis use and psychiatric disorders (e.g. depression, schizophrenia). It was argued that cannabis was more harmful and dangerous than initially thought (e.g. the increasing level of THC was often mentioned).

> In the past, politicians minimised the problems related to the regular use of cannabis. Today, more and more youngsters are into trouble because of their cannabis use. Now, we all know that the level of THC increased drastically [my emphasis].
>
> (Mr. Filip De Man, MP Vlaams Blok, Flemish extreme right party; *Hand.* Kamer 2002–2003, 12 februari 2003, 325, 36)

The media (and interest groups) also seemed to have increased the likelihood of policy-makers being more sympathetic towards the harmfulness of cannabis (linked with schizophrenia, the higher percentage of THC, etc.). As such, the media encouraged refutation of the arguments of the advocates of a liberal policy that cannabis use is harmless (*evolutionary model*; Stevens, 2007a). For instance, the correlation between early and regular cannabis use and the risk of developing schizophrenia, depression, or other psychotic disorders featured increasingly in many parliamentary discussions from 2002 onwards (*Hand.* Kamer 2001–2002, 21 februari 2002, 208, 32–33; *Hand.* Senaat 2001–2002, 19 maart 2002, 2–51, 2692). Similarly, the sustained media focus on the dangers of cannabis, the increasing THC level, and the increasing prevalence rates even continued during the hearings in the Commission of Public Health. Some statements of medical expert Prof. Dr. Jef Hulselmans were manipulated in the Flemish newspaper *Gazet van Antwerpen* (16 January 2003). While the expert stated that "a regular joint contains about 10 mg, the content is now much higher: 150 mg" and "there are differences in how many users become addicted: 9% in one research; 7.7% and 4.8% in other researches", the newspaper reported that "because of the new cultivating techniques, the THC content can be 30 times higher than it used to be [...] Research shows that 10% of the users become addicted [my emphasis]".

Elections Are Looming

The upcoming Federal elections on 18 May 2003 did put a lot of pressure on the activities surrounding the new drug law. The drug law reform was one of the major themes of the 2003 election campaign (Gelders, 2006). MPs and members of the Government were very concerned about how their decisions and actions were viewed by potential voters at the next Federal elections (May 2003). Several opinion polls (e.g. survey on 'Belgians and drugs' (Patesson & Steinberg, 2000)) made clear that drug problems among youngsters was ranked as one of the most important problems in society, and that the poor communication about whether and when the possession of cannabis for personal use was prosecuted, caused a lot of confusion among the public (VAD, 2003; VAD, 2004; Administratie Planning en Statistiek, 2006).

Given that all feared a political defeat, it is unsurprising that scientific knowledge was often used for *political/symbolic* reasons by policy-makers (Weiss, 1979). In the long and controversial discussion in the Parliament, each 'side' highlighted different sets of harms. When making an argument, MPs often *cherry-picked* information that made their case look stronger (also called *trawling*; Stevens, 2007a). The evidence that cannabis use can adversely affect the mental health (e.g. depression, schizophrenia) of some adolescents and young adults had been undermining the simplest argument that cannabis caused no harm. Contradictory information tended to be ignored or criticised. For instance, those concerned to maintain a prohibition against cannabis ignored the social costs of prohibition and the survey results that had failed to find a larger decrease in rates of cannabis use in countries that had severe drug laws (see also Cohen, 2016).

Some MPs from the opposition parties also *misused* or *(consciously) misinterpreted* scientific knowledge. For instance, MP Roel Deseyn (CD&V, Flemish Christian Democrats) exaggerated the number of cannabis addicts. While Prof. Dr. Isidore Pelc stated that 2 per cent of the regular cannabis users became cannabis addicts, this MP argued that "It is now clear that 10% of the cannabis users become addicted" (Mr. Roel Deseyn, MP CD&V, Flemish Christian Democrats; *Hand.* Kamer 2002–2003, 12 februari 2003, 327, 10). In this context, the introduction of the *precautionary principle* in the parliamentary debates was also noted, especially as a way of postponing action and as having a mainly political function. The precautionary principle entails that policy-makers should take precautionary measures to prevent or minimise harm in circumstances where there is uncertainty about the exact nature and extent of the risk. This is a complex question, especially for politics in 'risk societies' (Franklin, 1998; Gelev, 2009). References to precautionary measures in the current context were, however, different and can be considered to be contrary to the principles of *evidence-based* policy (Monaghan et al., 2012; Singleton et al., 2014).

Nonetheless, the parliamentary debates were mainly governed by political considerations. For instance, the discourse of MPs included a large number of propositional arguments (e.g. '*cannabis is a stepping-stone to hard drugs*', '*cannabis is addictive*', '*the level of THC is multiplied by 10*', '*cannabis is very dangerous and harmful*' ...). International examples were often included in the discourse of MPs (*policy platonism*). MPs wrongly used terminology such as *tolerance policy*, *depenalisation*, *decriminalisation*, and *Belgian coffee-shops* while focusing on potential negative consequences of a liberal policy and the lack of compliance with the international conventions. Clearly, the link with the (rejected) Dutch drug policy model was never far away. "The drug law favours a tolerance policy. This policy choice does not take into account the international conventions" (Mr. Filip De Man, MP Vlaams Blok, Flemish extreme right party, Report of the Commission Public Health, p. 270). Additionally, MPs were very active in formulating *personal insults*. Undoubtedly, these actions often originated from self-interest in gaining power and favouring certain electorates. Finally, in a similar vein, some MPs applied a rather *emotive tone*. An appeal to emotions was linked with the strategy of the members of the Parliament to speak from their role as parent or doctor (*dual role*).

Ministerial Circular Letter of 16 May 2003

The new Ministerial Circular Letter detailing the prosecution policy with regard to the possession of and the retail trade in illegal narcotic substances (*B.S.*, 2 June 2003)[22] was implemented by the Minister of Justice Marc Verwilghen, together with the College of Prosecutors-General, on 16 May 2003, only two days before the Federal elections. This brought an end to two years of pervasive uncertainty and legal insecurity concerning what was effectively permitted (Decorte, 2007).

The new Ministerial Circular Letter included the guidelines for the Public Prosecutors' office as to how the possession of cannabis for personal use should be treated. It determined the amount of cannabis for personal use as three grams or one female plant while adding the confusing message that the quantity for personal use was for a single time or for use within a maximum of 24 hours. Conversely, in another paragraph of the Ministerial Circular Letter, it was stated that the Government was not in favour of determining a maximum amount of grams (because the THC level of cannabis products may vary a lot) (Vander Laenen & Dhont, 2003). The determination of a 'quantity for personal use' was innovative taking into account previous debates in the Parliamentary Working Group on drugs (PWG) and in the Inter-Cabinet Working Group (ICWG) deciding on the Federal Drug Policy Note. Despite the contradictions, the Ministerial Circular Letter determined that, provided there were no aggravating circumstances (such as use in the presence of minors, public nuisance, or problematic drug use), the police had to make a simple, anonymous registration of the facts (instead of a regular process-verbal).[23] The Ministerial Circular Letter also contained a set of specific guidelines for police officers in this context (Mahieu, 2005).

Furthermore, related to situations other than the possession of cannabis for personal use outlined above, the 2003 Ministerial Circular Letter emphasised the importance of alternative measures and guidance towards treatment (Dangreau et al., 2012). For instance, in cases of limited possession of other illegal drugs for single or occasional use, the Public Prosecutor has to decide whether or not to prosecute or to apply alternatives (e.g. praetorian probation, transaction). The 2003 Ministerial Circular further asked the Public Prosecutors to be severe in the case of retail sale for profit but to take into consideration alternative measures (e.g. transaction, praetorian probation) in the cases in which the only purpose of the sale was to finance one's own use. In terms of drug-related criminality, the 2003 Ministerial Circular Letter emphasised that addiction can never be a justification for criminal behaviour. It is explicitly stated that the Public Prosecutors in deciding whether or not to prosecute or to apply alternatives always should consider the seriousness of the crime and the individual situation of the offender (i.e. principle of expediency).

With the reform of the Belgian drug law and eventually, the 2003 Ministerial Circular Letter, the cannabis controversy was deemed 'resolved' by the Government. Even though sensitive matters such as the cultivation/supply of cannabis still were not clearly addressed, these decisions introduced the closing of the policy window (Kingdon, 2002). In the following Federal elections of 2003, the Greens suffered significant losses, partly because of their role in the cannabis discussion. While the reform of the drug law was used by the Flemish Greens as a kind of showpiece, the other coalition partners gradually kept their hands off this sensitive issue. They gratefully pointed to the Green party AGALEV. In other words, being the ideal scapegoat, the Minister of Public Health Magda Aelvoet (later on replaced by Mr. Jef Tavernier) became the personification of the debate (even though the bill was a result of a political compromise). The Liberal Prime Minister Guy Verhofstadt reconstituted the Coalition as a *four-party government* with only the Flemish and French-speaking Liberals and the Flemish and French-speaking Socialists in power (Verhofstadt II Government). The Green parties moved from a majority position towards the opposition again.

Summary

This chapter outlined how criminal policy on drugs was anchored through an adaptation of the drug law (of 24 February 1921) and the Ministerial Circular Letter of 8 May 1998 (De Ruyver et al., 2012). The juridical-technical discussion, which made its way through the Government (by means of an ICWG) and the Parliament, was a rather long one (June 2002–May 2003). Compared with the PWG, the persuasive burden in this debate was even far higher for advocates of a drug law reform: the Government had to persuade the community that it is possible to change the law without increasing cannabis use and harm. The new drug law and Ministerial Circular Letter were endorsed just before the 2003 elections. These decisions together with the election of a new government (Verhofstadt II Government; a four-party government without the Green parties) marked the closing of the policy window (Kingdon, 2002) in Belgium.

It has been argued that, in the ICWG, the commitment to an *evidence-based* rhetoric was overshadowed by political disagreements between coalition partners and concerns about the international framework (i.e. UN conventions as well as the limited evidence surrounding the impacts of the emerging forms of liberalisation in the international context). Indeed, reflecting on the typology of Loader and Sparks (2011), the *observer-turned-player* Prof. Dr. Brice De Ruyver (as security advisor to Prime Minister Guy Verhofstadt) mainly acted as a mediator between political divergences. In a similar vein, the *policy advisor* Prof. Dr. Isidore Pelc, appointed the president of the *Drug Health Policy Cell*, was only able to engage the use of scientific knowledge in the ICWG in an indirect way as the *Drug Health Policy Cell* discussed some preliminary policy documents (bill, Royal Decree, Cooperation agreement, etc.).

From this chapter it was also witnessed how the upcoming Federal elections on 18 May 2003 did put a lot of pressure on the activities surrounding the new drug law, especially on the debates in the Parliament. Even though the Commission of Public Health sought the advice of several *scientific experts* (Loader & Sparks, 2011) and they sensitised MPs to 'new' scientific knowledge focusing on the harmfulness of cannabis (e.g. the increasing level of THC, the connection between cannabis use and psychiatric disorders) (*conceptual/enlightenment utilisation*; Weiss, 1979), most examples are to be categorised according to Weiss' *political/symbolic* model. Several instances of *cherry-picking* or *trawling* were observed and some MPs misinterpreted scientific knowledge to support their personal policy narrative (e.g. public health vs. legalistic/repressive framework). Regardless of the position they took, the regular use of propositional arguments and political tactics (e.g. incorrect terminology, personal insults, and emotional assumptions) also illustrated their concerns regarding a potential electoral backlash.

Media communication was often ambiguous and polarising, particularly in the manipulations of prevalence rates or expert opinions, but its role in feeding into political debate (Scheufele & Tewksbury, 2007; McCombs & Reynolds, 2009) was again traced. Media coverage facilitated the *enlightenment* role of scientific knowledge in the Parliament by broadening and even determining frames of reference. Through the sustained media coverage on the dangers and harms of cannabis use, the media encouraged refutation of the argument that cannabis use is harmless (*evolutionary* model; Stevens, 2007a). Likewise, by sharing their discourse in the media and even in the Commission of Public Health, the interest group *Parents against Drugs* [*Ouders tegen Drugs*] increased the likelihood of MPs being more sympathetic towards their arguments on the harmfulness of cannabis. Similar to the media, these stakeholders did not play a key role in the internal government decision-making processes, with one exception. In his capacity as an advisor of the Minister of Public Health Magda Aelvoet, a member of interest group *Anti-Prohibition League* [*La Liaison anti-prohibitionniste*] participated in the ICWG. This may be the only effective way for interest groups to have a small voice in the debate at the governmental level.

Notes

1 The concept *decriminalisation* is often confused with the concept *depenalisation*. In this study, we follow Room et al. (2010) by using the term *decriminalisation* to refer to 'prohibition with civil penalties'. Thus, criminal penalties are removed from the law while administrative penalties are still possible (e.g. Portugal). *Depenalisation* involves maintenance of criminal penalties in the criminal law, yet removing or shortening the periods of incarceration, or reducing fine amounts, as possible sanctions (e.g. Belgium, Germany, Denmark, and the Netherlands). An important distinction between different types of alternatives here is the differentiation between de facto and *de jure*, or in other words, between changing the law that applies (*de jure*), or by modifying the way the law is used or applied in the various stages of the criminal justice system (de facto) (Room et al., 2010). *Legalisation* means that the specified forms of behaviour are no longer offences dealt with under the law, yet they are often still governed by different tools of regulatory law.

2 Because of technical reasons (related to the Articles 77 and 78 of the Constitution), the legislative initiative was divided into two bills (nrs. 1888 and 1889). Both drug laws (of 4 April and 3 May 2003) should also be considered as linked with a Royal Decree (16 May 2003) detailing the categories of infringements and a Ministerial Circular Letter (16 May 2003) determining the prosecution policy of cannabis. Each of the initiatives is complementary to the realisation of the new public health policy. As both laws and the Royal Decree are treated as one entity, this book regularly uses the concept 'new drug law' to refer to this package.

3 Wet van 4 april 2003 tot wijziging van de wet van 24 februari 1921 betreffende het verhandelen van giftstoffen, slaapmiddelen en verdovende middelen, ontsmettingsstoffen en antiseptica (*B.S.* 2 juni 2003), and Wet van 3 mei 2003 tot wijziging van de wet van 21 februari 1921 betreffende het verhandelen van giftstoffen, slaapmiddelen en verdovende middelen, psychotrope stoffen, ontsmettingsstoffen en antiseptica en van de stoffen die kunnen gebruikt worden voor de illegale vervaardiging van verdovende middelen en psychotrope stoffen (*B.S.* 2 juni 2003).

4 This law concerns the local administrative sanctions. It gives the municipalities the possibility of adding behaviours described as public nuisance to their police regulations and responding to those offences with administrative procedures (Wet van 13 mei 1999 betreffende de invoering van de gemeentelijke administratieve sancties, *B.S.* 10 juni 1999).

5 The new drug law changed the title including substances that could be used to produce illicit substances (so-called precursors) as well: Wet van 3 mei 2003 tot wijziging van de wet van 21 februari 1921 betreffende het verhandelen van giftstoffen, slaapmiddelen en verdovende middelen, psychotrope stoffen, ontsmettingsstoffen en antiseptica en van de stoffen die kunnen gebruikt worden voor de illegale vervaardiging van verdovende middelen en psychotrope stoffen, *B.S.* 2 juni 2003. Crimes concerning precursors are subject to the penalties specified in art. 2 quater of the drug law.

6 Even though the concept of aggravating circumstances (e.g. drug use by minors) was implemented by the Law of 9 July 1975, the Royal Decree (of 16 May 2003) underlined the importance of the protection of minors once more (*B.S.* 2 juni 2003, p. 29935).

7 Wet van 29 juni 1964 betreffende de opschorting, het uitstel en de probatie, *B.S.* 17 juli 1964. Wet van 10 februari 1994 tot wijziging van de wet van 29 juni 1964 betreffende de opschorting, het uitstel en de probatie, *B.S.* 27 april 1994.

8 Probationary conditional sentence means a judicial decision according to which the imposition of the sentence is suspended with the condition that the person complies with probation measures.

9 Probationary suspended sentence means that the judge pronounces a sentence but that the execution of the whole or a part of the sentence is suspended for a certain period, during which the person concerned must fulfil certain conditions.

10 This was to stress the distinction between personal use and profit (i.e. clear differentiation according to the intent) (Mahieu, 2004).

11 The title of the Royal Decree of 31 December 1930 was changed and now included the terms risk reduction and therapeutic advice (see also Todts, 2004).

12 While the Royal Decree (16 May 2003) described the role of the *judicial case-manager* as someone who assists in monitoring the drug problem and the people involved and supports the guidance of problematic drug users more easily towards treatment, the Ministerial Circular Letter (16 May 2003) adds that the judicial case-manager should be in charge of the coordination of the treatment network in general (De Ruyver et al., 2008). Within this framework, the importance of agreements considering and respecting the different goals and principles of both sectors (e.g. professional confidentiality) was stressed.

13 Nevertheless, worth mentioning are the pilot-projects such as 'Test Care' (2005–2007) and 'Drug Treatment Court' (2008) which were established recently (De Ruyver et al., 2008; De Ruyver, Lemaître, & Schoenaers, 2009; Luypaert, Françoise, Beyens, Kaminski, & Janssens, 2007). However, the planned and desired generalisation of these projects again faces some capacity and financial obstacles (De Ruyver et al., 2012).

14 The SP became SP.A on 13 October 2001 (while also creating a cartel together with SPIRIT (Flemish Social-Liberal party) in November 2002).

15 (*Hand.* Kamer 2001–2002, 10 januari 2002, 197, 15–16; Hand. Kamer 2001–2002, 21 februari 2002, 208, 32–33; *Hand.* Kamer 2001–2002, 28 februari 2002, 210, 11–13; *Hand.* Senaat 2001–2002, 16 mei 2002, 2–204, 22–23; *Vr. en Antw.* Senaat, 5 maart 2002, nr. 2/50 (Vr. nr. 1544 V. Van Quickenborne); *Vr. en Antw.* Senaat, 19 maart 2002, nr. 2/51 (Vr. nr. 1886 Y. Buysse)).

16 Wetsontwerp tot wijziging van de wet van 24 februari 1921 betreffende het verhandelen van de giftstoffen, slaapmiddelen en verdovende middelen, ontsmettingsstoffen en antiseptica en Wetsontwerp tot wijziging van de wet van 24 februari 1921 betreffende het verhandelen van de giftstoffen, slaapmiddelen en verdovende middelen, ontsmettingsstoffen en antiseptica, en van artikel 137 van het Wetboek van Strafvordering, *Parl.St.* Kamer 2001–2002, nr. 1888/001 en nr. 1889/01.

17 As I treat both bills, the Royal Decree and Ministerial Circular Letter, as one entity, I regularly use the concept bill to refer to this package of initiatives.

18 Verslag namens de Commissie voor de Volksgezondheid, het Leefmilieu en de Maatschappelijke Hernieuwing uitgebracht door de Heren Jacques Germeaux en Luc Paque, *Parl.St.* Kamer 2001–2002, nr. 1888/004.

19 Verslag namens de Commissie voor de Volksgezondheid, het Leefmilieu en de Maatschappelijke Hernieuwing uitgebracht door de Heren Jacques Germeaux en Luc Paque, *Parl.St.* Kamer 2001–2002, nr. 1888/004, 236 and 280.

20 During the 1970s and mid-1980s, many clinical and experimental studies were established to measure the effect of cannabis on different vital organs and functions. Academics studied the somatic effects of cannabis intoxication and chronic cannabis use, the effects of cannabis on human and animal offspring, and the effects on psychomotor and cognitive functions and mental health. As a result, the first studies on the association between intensive cannabis use and psychotic disorders date back from the beginning of the 1970s. Studies on the effect of cannabis use on schizophrenia were established in the late 1980s. The results of all these clinical and experimental studies were hotly debated among researchers at that time. However, these issues were not picked up in the PWG (instead cannabis was considered to be a relatively harmless substance; see above). Since the beginning of the twenty-first century, there has been of profusion of writings on this topic (Vuillaume, 2008).

21 A number of independent Commissions have investigated the cannabis issue during the twentieth century: LaGuardia Commission (1944), British Wootton Commission (1969), Canadian LeDain Commission (1970), Dutch Baan Commission (1972), American Shafer Commission (1972), Commission of the Australian Government (1977), Commission by the Dutch Government (1995), Roques Commission (1997), etc. (Zimmer & Morgan, 1997). These Commissions were appointed to evaluate the scientific evidence on the dangers of cannabis to individuals and society. Each of these Commissions came to the conclusion that the public had been needlessly frightened about the dangers. For instance, in France, the 'Roques report' was commissioned in 1997 by the Minister of Public Health Bernard Kouchner, and conducted by Professor Bernard Roques, an internationally renowned neuropharmacologist. These assumptions and others were extensively used by scientists in the hearings.

22 Ministeriële omzendbrief van 16 mei 2003, betreffende vervolgingsbeleid inzake het bezit van en de detailhandel in illegale verdovende middelen, *B.S.* 2 juni 2003.

23 Art. 16 of the drug law (of 3 May 2003) only stated that a registration by the police forces was required.

Chapter 9

Concluding Thoughts

The *evidence-based policy* message is still spreading and has filtered into the agendas of drug policy-makers in Europe and elsewhere, as witnessed in the EU Drugs Strategy 2013–2020 (Council of the European Union, 2012) and the 2016 United Nations General Assembly (UNGASS, 2016). If the tenets of *evidence-based* policy-making are to be believed, the use of scientific knowledge will result in better (effective) policy (Rich, 1997; Cairney, 2016). However, drug scholars, mainly in the UK and Australia – where the evidence-based movement has been most active – generally provide more critical assessments of the *evidence-based* rhetoric suggesting that drug policy-making is not based on a scientific appeal because it mainly gets in the way of politicians seeking election or authority. Therefore, it is argued that policy-makers should not waste their time in aiming for what they cannot have (Lenton, 2004; Hall, 2008; Ritter, 2009; Monaghan, 2011; Hughes & Stevens, 2012; Cairney, 2016).

This book's primary aim has been to gain a richer understanding of the mechanisms and processes through which drug policy-making is informed by scientific knowledge (and other types of information) to challenge those two extreme views. The book draws on extensive qualitative data regarding the Belgian drug policy development between 1996 and 2003. Even though Belgium is not a drug policy trend-setter such as the USA, the Netherlands, or Portugal, it is clear that the Belgian case has some distinctive features related to the mechanisms or processes through which evidence was mobilised and eventually informed the policy process. Some of the policy issues were generated exogenously or by external pressures such as the international conventions or Dutch drug policy evaluations, while others were generated endogenously or by internal factors such as the change in government in 1999 and the involvement of a particular *policy entrepreneur* and non-governmental stakeholders. In any case, Belgium's development of drug policy shows that a comprehensive, *evidence-informed* drug policy can be built even in an environment of (inter)national disagreements and pressures.

Although a single case-study design requires caution in drawing conclusions or making comparisons, this narrative account is useful in filling the gap of knowledge on this topic in Belgium (for one exception, see Smet, 2013) and, by means of using leading policy and media theories and knowledge utilisation/public scholarship literature as a sound framework for analysis, these insights offer valuable lessons beyond their original context which can be useful in analysing similar cases.

Models of Knowledge Utilisation: Challenges and Opportunities

The utility of the *evidence-based* rhetoric in the messy, complex world of drug policy-making has been questioned in previous research. In these instances, the nature of knowledge utilisation has been called politicised and therefore, points of view, whereby the drug policy-making process is considered an *un-evidenced-based* mess, have been frequently adopted since (Hall, 2008; Monaghan, 2011; Hughes & Stevens, 2012; MacGregor, 2012a; Ritter & Lancaster, 2013). The Belgian case appears to be different in that the findings call for a more nuanced understanding of the role of scientific knowledge in drug policy-making processes, moving more towards *evidence-informed* policy or *evidence-aware* policy concepts (Young, Ashby, Boaz, & Grayson, 2002; Dobrow, Goel, & Upshur, 2004).

Applying Weiss' three-fold typology (1979), the various different forms of knowledge utilisation have been widely documented and covered in each chapter. No part of Weiss three-tiered approach appeared to be dominant and these types of knowledge utilisation were not restricted to specific policy actors; the process was rather random and chaotic. At times there were elements of *instrumental* utilisation which is promoted by the *evidence-based* rhetoric. A policy-funded evaluation study aiming at examining the progress of the Belgian drug policy as well as the experiences of other countries (De Ruyver et al., 2000) led to action/implementation (*instrumental utilisation*). The report fitted with the mood of the time and answered questions at the top of the political agenda since the Parliamentary Working Group on drugs (PWG). Accordingly, the recommendations of the evaluation study were used in determining the specific policy actions by the Federal Government (Federal Government, 2001, pp. 31–68). Scientific knowledge contributed to an overall *enlightenment* too by identifying possible policy options, clarifying issues, and changing the understanding of the drug problem (*conceptual utilisation*). In the Parliamentary Working Group on drugs (1996–1997) and the Commission of Public Health (2002–2003), scientific knowledge contributed to the percolation of (new) ideas and concepts (e.g. related to the prevention projects towards youth or related to the orientation of (problematic) drug users in the criminal justice system towards treatment) and the development of a substantial body of knowledge. There were also a number of examples where the utilisation could be categorised according to Weiss' *political/*

symbolic utilisation. Parliamentary debates consisted of bargaining and negotiation using whatever arguments could be mustered in support of their position. MPs who submitted questions, interpellations, resolutions, bills, or resolutions often selected scientific knowledge as one tool to help win their case (as an instrument to enact power). Scientists or scientific studies which made conflicting opinions more apparent were excluded or criticised (*cherry-picking* or *trawling*; Stevens, 2007a). Similarly, there were examples of political/symbolic use of scientific knowledge among Ministers. For example, when answering questions and interpellations in the Parliament or when addressing the topic in a speech, Ministers readily distorted scientific arguments which were detrimental to the chosen policy direction, by criticising them as irrational or incorrect (a tactic of creating *flak*; Stevens, 2007a).

From the findings of the earlier chapters also came the contribution to the knowledge utilisation literature that the *political/symbolic* category is too broad and needs to be refined. Difficulties in capturing how some examples could be classified according to Weiss' three-fold typology were experienced. In accordance with Stevens (2007a) and Monaghan (2011), Weiss' typology tends to offer only limited descriptions of some modalities through which scientific knowledge was used. First of all, this model fails to distinguish between instances where research is being used appropriately as opposed to research being misused or misinterpreted (see also Stevens, 2007a; Nutley et al., 2007). Instances where scientific knowledge was *misused or misinterpreted* (e.g. making blunt interpretations, false generalisations, and causalities) were often observed in the parliamentary debates. Second, Weiss' political/symbolic model does not cover the occasions where scientific knowledge is cited simply to justify the government's commitment to knowledge utilisation. For example, in accordance with what Cross et al. (2000) termed the *status model* in the literature, policy-makers aim to gain credibility (and *status*) by referring to studies that they (or their predecessor) commissioned or, at the simplest level, by generally stating that they support *evidence-based* policy-making. These references can be categorised as a subtype of *political/symbolic* utilisation as they were used to support personal policy narratives. Thus, Weiss' *political/symbolic* model (Weiss, 1979) seems too simplistic and requires the introduction of clear subcategories.

The book also highlighted that newer models, building on Weiss' three-fold typology, offer significant potential for exploring and explaining the science-policy nexus. The *processual* model (Monaghan, 2011) actually captured the knowledge utilisation processes in Belgium most fully. Its strength lies in the analysis of the selection/power issues in the policy-making processes (as witnessed by mechanisms of *flak* and *trawling*; see *evolutionary* model), but also in the recognition that the nature of scientific knowledge may be contested and that a multiplicity of (f)actors (e.g.

politics and media) may play a role in dynamics of the policy-making process. First, *evidence-based* policy suggests a neat menu from which a government can select the right mix (Cairney, 2016). However, Monaghan (2014, p. 1027) wrote that "one of the true stumbling blocks to the realization of evidence-based policy is that the evidence is rarely definitive". Indeed, as demonstrated in our case, scientific knowledge cannot – and should not be – the only driver of policy. Even where scientific knowledge does influence policy-making, questions about the characteristics of scientific knowledge itself – often contradictory, too late and still evolving, and thus producing uncertainty – remain. For instance, as discussed in several chapters, there was a poor fit between the time needed to complete research and the speed at which policy issues rose to the top of the political agenda. These illustrations further underpin Caplan's *two communities thesis* (1979) – where science and policy are considered as two worlds separated by a huge gap – and criticism of *evidence-based* policy thinking. In a similar vein, analysis revealed that a nuanced account of scientists' discourses is necessary. Scientific knowledge that was brought into the policy process (e.g. in formal advisory structures such as the PWG (1996–1997) or the Commission of Public Health (2002–2003)) by scientists appeared to be largely fed by propositional assumptions (i.e. assumptions about what is or can be or will be the case; 'truth') declared without citations. In their claims to capture truth, scientists were also observed misusing science in several ways. Some neglected the main principles of scientific knowledge by using ambiguous terminology (e.g. a comparison was made between the number of hashish users and the number of cannabis users) or by presenting data regardless of the methodological purity with which it had been developed (e.g. neglecting statistical significance, comparing different methodologies, or ignoring methodological pitfalls). In addition, scientific results were sometimes distorted in several – often subtle – ways, including making simplistic interpretations, false generalisations, and causal inferences. As participating in a formal advisory structure allowed scientists to control which message is provided and how it is absorbed in the political setting, it deserves restatement that scientists offering their expertise in the policy-making process need to accept their responsibility to provide correct information instead of losing sight of their scientific research base (cfr. so-called *airport scientists*; Uggen & Inderbitzin, 2010).

Second, the *processual model* also accepts the inherently unpredictable nature of policy and accepts that evidence is not the only player in the policy-making process with multiple groups interacting and competing in shaping policy (Ingold & Monaghan, 2016). However, building on insights from this case-study and with a critical look at the processual model, little is said about the particular role of the media itself; the role of the media is treated as if it is employed in the same way in each debate. In this regard, the analysis in this book offers significant potential, if only because (il)licit drugs is one of the most polarised subjects of media coverage and it is often distorted or inaccurate construction has been a recurrent concern (Lancaster et al., 2011). As will be elaborated below, the findings about whether and how media coverage did or did not have an impact on the contribution of scientific knowledge in the Belgian drug policy-making process illustrated not only the role of the media as a linking mechanism between science and policy but also how this connection was consolidated, looking at the longer-established knowledge utilisation literature.

Public Scholars Can Play Key Roles

The established models of knowledge utilisation (Weiss, 1979; Stevens, 2007a; Monaghan, 2011) alone cannot explain the subtleties of the science-policy nexus. The second theme that deserves discussion here is that of public scholars. Despite public scholarship being the subject of considerable debate within the discipline of criminology and elsewhere (e.g. Chancer & McLaughlin, 2007; Wacquant, 2011; Ruggiero, 2012), there is a lack of research which examines the outcomes of public engagement. A focus on the individual actions and capacities of key actors is interesting, not least because it informs us about the ways in which scholars can put their body of knowledge at the service of policy-makers alongside other legitimate forms of interests or knowledge (Drake & Walters, 2015). In this context, the longer-established knowledge utilisation literature and the typology on public engagement succinctly and authoritatively captured by Loader and Sparks (2011), have been used as a framework to deepen understanding about the relations between the individual action and the institutional context in the process of policy development or change. Within the 'hot' climate in which the development of Belgian drug policy development unfolded, scientists performed a variety of public roles (e.g. *scientific experts*, *policy advisors*, *observer-turned-players*, or *social movement theorists/activists*), perhaps most clearly illustrated in the Parliamentary Working Group on drugs (Chapter 5) and the development of the Federal Drug Policy Note in 2001 (Chapter 7).

The Belgian case reveals that public academics of diverse persuasions can make strategic incursions that influence and mobilise more open and better informed public and political debate. The public engagement of scientists in the Parliamentary Working Group on drugs (1996–1997) was characterised by awareness raising of ideas and research by scientists embroiled in the process. *Scientific experts* described their input as 'giving information' and presenting 'facts' and 'data'. Even though their engagement did not go beyond rare participation in formal advisory structures, they performed an *enlightenment* role by trying to insert evidence and data into political decision-making. In a similar vein, during the establishment of the national conferences 'Drugs Policy 2000', which brought together practitioners, scientists, politicians, decision-makers, and journalists, the impetus was to stimulate cooperation among key stakeholders and the increasing flow of scientific information into the policy process rather than the outcomes.

At times where scientists became more involved in the process (e.g. *observer-turned-player*), there was a shift in the kinds of influence they sought to achieve. De Ruyver's role in Belgian drug policy is illustrative here. Performing a role as *observer-turned-player* included expanding beyond a rare or rather passive participation in the Parliament or Government. As the hearings of the PWG started, De Ruyver was co-opted as an external expert to integrate scientific findings into a policy document. Altering the tone of the political discussion, the document provided a careful integration of most of the good practices and recommendations of the expert. At this point there is a subtle shift from *conceptual* influence to a more *direct* influence in policy development. Also when bearing in mind the role of De Ruyver in the development of the first national drug strategy ('Federal Drug Policy Note'; Federal Government, 2001), his influence shifted to more *instrumental* use. Being the security advisor to Prime Minister Guy Verhofstadt, De Ruyver was described by policy-makers as 'mediating and encouraging debate' by making sure that politicians and decision-makers took into account scientific findings. Working within the Government was an excellent way to establish oneself and understand how policy is made and who or what exerted the most influence. Given the multidimensional nature of drug policy, it can even be said that in the absence of clear coordination structures to develop and monitor an integral and integrated drug policy at that time, an important explanation for the consistency and transparency regarding Belgian drug policy development can be ascribed to the role of Brice De Ruyver. Without any doubt the influence of this *policy entrepreneur* (Kingdon, 2002), or so-called *observer-turned-player* (a concept used by Loader & Sparks, 2011) on those two important accounts, was that the policy which emerged was more coherent and streamlined than it would have been if there had been more competing or fragmented scientific influences directly involved in the policy-making process. Together with this position ensuring policy-makers had easy access to and understanding of the evidence base, having an academic working within government as *observer-turned-player*, accords with what Monaghan (2014) described as one of the key elements for *good drug policy governance*. However, while De Ruyver clearly succeeded in 'cooling down' the heated debate, this was not always as an independent voice. The 'success' of his public engagement was also contingent on the rules of politics and competition. It was sometimes more to add scientific weight to a pre-established direction of travel (*political/tactical* use of evidence). After all, even an *observer-turned-player*, who devotes him- or herself to problem representation or the introduction of acceptable, feasible alternatives, will only stand a chance of influencing policy when the evidence fits with a pre-established stance and if it has engaged sponsors in policy circles (*evolutionary* model; Stevens, 2007a).

Of course proximity to decision-making is not the only determinant of kinds of influence in the form of evidence used by scientists. Critical voices involved in 'heating up' debates (*social movement theorists/activists*) similarly employed *conceptual* uses of evidence to try and shape the debate. This was done in attempts by scientists to raise some contentious issues (e.g. the largely unproblematic characteristic of drug use or the usefulness of self-control strategies) in debates. As was illustrated in the book, *social movement theorists/activists* generated a large public response: a considerable number of newspaper articles covered these accounts and, simultaneously, several interest groups, campaigning for drug user's rights, were vigorous in promoting these ideas. However, although high-profile, critics of policy had little impact on the overall policy outcome. Indeed, as in the *evolutionary* model advocated by Stevens (2007a), it became clear that some scientific knowledge may fit the interests of the powerful groups, while others may not (which is called 'deviant' knowledge by Walters (2003)). The choice of what counts as usable scientific knowledge and who is considered authoritative or trustworthy involves acts of power (Becker, 1967; Foucault, 1976; Van Swaaningen, 2001; Young, 2011).

In an era in which *evidence-based* policy is promoted, an emphasis on public scholarship in relation to knowledge utilisation is a valuable way to demonstrate the complexity of the science-policy nexus in that it involves multiple steps and multiple actors operating within a wider political context (e.g. Weiss, 1979; Nutley et al., 2007; Ingold & Monaghan, 2016; MacGregor et al., 2014). A more open and better informed public and political debate is not a product derived exclusively from the simple interaction between single key actors or the scholar's skills or actions to take advantage of the *window of opportunity*. Additional exploration in this area, particularly comparisons with other contexts and other policy-making realms, are highly recommended.

Moving Beyond the Science-Policy Nexus: The Role of Media is Significant

Drug policy and media are often closely intertwined and the literature illustrates how media can play a crucial, but often complex, role in drug policy debates (Duke, 2001; Hughes, 2009; Macleod & Hickman, 2010; Monaghan, 2011; MacGregor, 2012a). In casting light on what happened in the media in the Belgian case, the book contributes to both theoretical and empirical understanding of the powerful influence of the media in key policy debates and of whether and how media meaningfully impacts on and shapes knowledge utilisation in policy-making. These findings are particularly relevant in terms of the discussion of the *processual* model of knowledge utilisation (Monaghan, 2011) above.

The Belgian case introduced evidence of the power of the media in defining the public interest (*agenda-setting*), in contextualising issues through selection and prominence (*framing*), and in indirectly shaping individual and community attitudes towards risk (*priming*). Through media-generated panic, drug policy had shot to prominence on the political agenda, demanding action from the Parliament in 1995 (resulting in the PWG in 1996). In a similar vein, the media played a key role in precipitating internal government decision-making. In the light of the development of the Federal Drug Policy Note around 2001, media-generated confusion and misunderstanding triggered the public opinion in demanding clear action from the Verhofstadt I Government. Further, it became clear that the media strongly influenced both the public's and policy-makers' understanding as well as the content of the debate itself. The scope of possible public or political debate was significantly narrowed through the framing of media coverage. In particular, from 1995 onwards, media narrowed down the complexity of the discussion to the legitimacy of the criminalisation of drugs (cannabis in particular) and stimulated further confusion and conflicting interests. As a consequence, MPs (and the public) believed that there were only two positions: either cannabis use is harmless (or at least less harmful than alcohol), and hence it should be decriminalised (if not legalised); or cannabis is harmful to health, and therefore its use should continue to be prohibited.

While previous research mainly focuses on the portrayals of illicit drug issues in the media, the representation and misrepresentation of scientific knowledge within the media and how media may, or may not, have an impact on the contribution of scientific knowledge in the drug policy-making process, is an under-researched area (e.g. Monaghan, 2014; Smith, 2015). Throughout the analysis, it became clear that the evidence base was present in the media reporting of the Belgian drug policy debates. Newspaper articles often included expert opinions, police statistics, prevalence rates, emergency cases, and international studies. On the one hand, newspapers included scientific knowledge as a 'response' to an event that had taken place or was brought to attention. On the other hand, scientific knowledge was presented as factual information by the media itself. However, media was *fact-checking* far less often than scientists would prefer. Media reports have tended to exaggerate scientific knowledge by drawing on research or expert opinions in a selective manner and by describing them in one-sided or in more dramatic terms. The starting point for journalists was what made a story fit in with their particular framework and narrative. As such, media coverage has some well-known drawbacks: space is limited, and it often interlinks sensationalism, disclosure, and economic concerns in a manner that pushes accuracy down the list of priorities (Coomber et al., 2000).

Against a backdrop of calls for *evidence-based* policy-making, the actual role of media as a linking mechanism between science and policy was also covered in the previous chapters. The development of the Belgian drug policy provided a clear case in which the media seemed to have an impact on the contribution of scientific knowledge in the drug policy-making process. First of all, the media played a significant role in empowering the *enlightenment* function of scientific knowledge. It was media coverage which ignited the episode of contention in Belgium and the installation of the PWG in 1996, including a systematic (*evidence-based*) approach with a proper assessment of evidence. In addition, a major way in which policy-makers heard about scientific knowledge was through the media (Weiss & Singer, 1988). More than in internal government decision-making, scientific knowledge which was repeatedly or extensively included in newspaper accounts stood a good chance of playing a role in parliamentary activities. The sustained media focus on the harmfulness of cannabis from 2002 onwards actually increased the likelihood of policy-makers being more sympathetic to this view. Exemplary was the selection of experts for the hearings regarding the new drug-law debates (2002–2003): medical practitioners and psychiatrists were much more considered as experts in this matter.

The media has the necessary platform to quickly put issues on the public agenda and has access to policy-makers, who in turn have easy access to the media. Yet media's role in connecting between those who wish to influence policy (e.g. scientists) and the actual policy-makers was not always straightforward, as the Belgian case illustrated. Media coverage of scientific knowledge was not necessarily a precondition for playing a role in the policy-making process. For instance, the evaluation study conducted by De Ruyver et al. (2000), which gave direction to Belgian drug policy and could be perceived as an example of *instrumental* knowledge utilisation, was not repeatedly or extensively covered by the media. In a similar vein, policy-makers' use of scientific knowledge as represented by the media appeared to be highly prone to *political* utilisation with policy actors picking and choosing what was most supportive of their discourse. The tendency of some outlets towards sensationalism and reporting bias meant that policy-makers did not and often could not seek further information regarding scientific knowledge picked up through the media. Thus, given these findings, scientists still have the final but crucial responsibility in deciding whether the media is the most appropriate mediator in disseminating scientific knowledge, as most research fails to go beyond academic publications (Ritter, 2009).

The Role of Interest Groups Deserves Greater Attention

The case presented in this book also offers an exploration into the ways in which interest groups – defined here as the associations advocating for drug users' rights as well as groups representing parents or ex-drug users who advocate against drug use – influence (knowledge utilisation in) drug policy-making. Several interest groups succeeded in 'heating up' and polarising the debate and in putting and keeping the drug issue on the parliamentary agenda. In this context, they have, together with the media, increased the likelihood of policy-makers to take action, both in the context of the Parliamentary Working Group on drugs (1996–1997) and the Belgian law reform (2002–2003). As such, interest groups also played a role in the empowerment of the *enlightenment* function of scientific knowledge. In contrast, it appeared to be particularly hard for these groups to contribute directly to internal governmental decision-making. Throughout the chapters, it became clear that this was mainly the result of their deficient organisational and communication structure and internal conflicts caused by political and financial squabbles, and that they only represented a small part of public opinion. An important exception was the active involvement of a member of the interest group *Anti-Prohibition League* [*La Liaison anti-prohibitionniste*] in the Inter-Cabinet Working Group developing Belgian drug law (2002–2003). Being an advisor of the Minister of Public Health, this may be the only effective way for interest groups to have a small voice in the debate at the governmental level.

Although Weiss (1986) speculated that interest groups may be a key channel for the flow of scientific knowledge, all of the substantive findings have shown that, given the use of several tools to promote their ideas, their ability to influence the policy-making process or even to allow for the flow of scientific knowledge in these processes is limited. Generally, by employing a rather emotional discourse, interest groups neglected or sometimes consciously misinterpreted scientific knowledge. As Epstein et al. note (2014), these kinds of interest groups tend to experience and discuss policy problems from a very subjective point of view and the barriers to participation by these groups may be closely related to the lack of knowledge and skills needed to engage in a policy-making environment.

As mentioned earlier, more and more players and institutions seem to be engaged in developing and implementing drug policies. The associations advocating for drug users' rights as well as groups representing parents or ex-drug users who advocate against drug use are, of course, not the only type of interest groups that can significantly affect drug policy-making (Bergin, 2013; Duke & Thom, 2014; O'Gorman et al., 2014). A number of international non-governmental organisations (NGOs), such as the International Drug Policy Consortium, are known to monitor the work of the UN agencies and to attempt to influence the international drug policy reform debates, particularly when this is discussed in the United Nations General Assembly (as they did in 2009 or recently in 2016). It would be very interesting to also put this advocacy work in the science-policy nexus to empirical test in the future.

Political Context Matters: Governance vs. Government

A recurrent theme in the literature about the science-policy nexus is the critical need to understand the political context within which policy is formulated and the ideological/institutional frameworks in which evidence is collected and processed (Strassheim & Kettunen, 2014; Hantrais et al., 2015). Indeed, one of the aims of this book was to provide insights and open up thinking about *evidence-based* policy-making by critically analysing policy processes and mechanisms in the Belgian case.

In contrast with the accepted view that drug policy-making is the prerogative of governments, the emerging concept 'governance' points, at the simplest level of distinction, to the growing influence of non-state actors in the policy-making process linking policy-makers to wider networks in a pluralistic and diverse civic society (Weiss, 2000; Sanderson, 2009; MacGregor et al., 2014). Issues of so-called good governance – as outlined in Chapter 2 – may be critical to successful drug policy development or change including but not limited to the extent to which a policy is *evidence-informed* or not (Singleton & Rubin, 2014; Hughes et al., 2014). Consistent with the framework of *good governance* (UKDPC, 2012), some interesting features were found relating to the mechanisms through which evidence was mobilised and eventually informed policy change in Belgium.

First of all, *widespread non-government stakeholder consultation*, through annual conferences and formal advisory structures, was apparent in the Belgian case and can be considered important in good governance too. From the beginning, the development of Belgian drug policy was strongly inspired by a wide range of non-government stakeholders coalescing around particular positions, including practitioners. This is an interesting point, if only because the evidence hierarchy, a concept emerging from *evidence-based* policy thinking and outlined in Chapter 2, assumes that policy-makers are generally best served by studies that use experimental and quasi-experimental research designs with good measures (Randomised Control Trials – RCT) (Wildavsky, 1979), and portrays knowledge derived from practitioners' experiences as unsystematic and not rigorous. It can be argued that the so-called *bottom-up approach*, characterised by public deliberation and participation which challenges the traditional *top-down approach* and recognises the plurality of expert knowledge including informal expertise of practitioners too, has been one of the strong characteristics of the development of Belgian drug policy. Respect for a variety of expert evidence and the existence of a space for deliberative dialogue to understand the problem, set the overarching goal of policy, and identify the intervention options, were core mechanisms in allowing a cross-party agreement on many elements of Belgian drug policy to be reached.

Second, in terms of good governance, several efforts in *considering scientific knowledge as a priority* were identified. The Belgian political context was important in terms of developing an *evidence-based* agenda. This can be seen most clearly with the change in government in 1999 and the emphasis of the new government on accurate scientific evidence, clear objectives, measurable performance targets, and evaluation. Together with their intention to develop a coherent drug policy, the new Verhofstadt I Government (1999–2003) recognised the importance of evidence as a valuable resource in policy-making and in the evaluation of policy choices (so-called *evidence-imbued* leadership). An annual budget was provided to organise and manage a research programme supporting decision-making in the field of illegal drugs (Verhofstadt, 1999). Another example was the appointment of Brice De Ruyver as the security advisor to Prime Minister Guy Verhofstadt. As stated above, assistance in the development of an *evidence-based* coherent Belgian drug policy was one of his main assignments. Generally, *evidence-imbued* leadership seemed to be important in prioritising the role of scientific knowledge in this case, a situation shared with the UK when the Blair Labour government in 1997, as part of its strategy of modernisation, introduced the notion that 'what counts is what works' (Wells, 2007).

However, similar to previous studies (Houborg & Asmussen, 2014; Monaghan, 2014; Zampini, 2014), it became clear that good governance processes were obstructed when discussing issues that concerned law enforcement or the international prohibitive framework. Decriminalisation or legalisation of cannabis possession for personal use often triggered interest and discussion among plenty of stakeholders, but it was never endorsed by the government. Policy-makers were reluctant to undertake a too radical reform. Although most experts in the PWG seemed to nuance the dangers and risks of cannabis use, policy-makers resoundingly rejected a proposal for decriminalisation of cannabis; instead they introduced the recommendation of waiving prosecution in the case of possession of cannabis for personal use. Thus, cannabis policy, as just one of the several action points of the Belgian drug policy, appeared to be a highly politically sensitive issue where cross-party consensus could not be reached. Far more than in debates on other policy issues, *evidence-imbued* leadership or evidence from consultation of non-government stakeholders tended to be balanced by policy-makers against other considerations such as international obligations, ideology, or political interests.

At the macro level, it is well-known that the development of policy in individual countries may be influenced by national and international policy frameworks (MacCoun & Reuter, 1997; Chatwin, 2011; Muscat & Pike, 2012; Hantrais et al., 2015; Beccaria, 2015). Various commentators argued before that the US *War on Drugs* has been exported to other nations, resulting in the development of a punitive and prohibitionist global discourse on drugs as opposed to a treatment, public health-oriented one (Ryan, 1998; Coomber, 1998; Duke, 2003). Belgium's late discovery of the drug phenomenon proved to be an important element as Belgian policy-makers learned from other countries' experiences, positive and negative. On the one hand, the development of a comprehensive, balanced public health policy in Belgium was strengthened by international trends. By the late 1990s, the drug problem was increasingly viewed internationally in a broader social context including drug prevention, reduction of drug-related harm, and crime deterrence (EMCDDA, 2000). Also, the 1997 Amsterdam Treaty determined for the first time that the highest priority should be given to the reduction of drug-related harm (De Ruyver et al., 2002) and the Inter-parliamentary Advisory Council of the Benelux countries clearly showed agreement about the importance of a *normalisation* policy. On the other hand, the central concern of Belgian drug policy-makers to maintain prohibition against all non-medical and non-scientific use of illegal drugs reflected a close adherence to the international control system, revealing how much this meant to Belgian drug policy – more than for drug policies of other countries such as the Netherlands, Switzerland, Portugal, or Australia which have explored the flexibility of the system (MacCoun & Reuter, 2001; Lenton, 2004; Csete, 2010; Hughes & Stevens, 2012). As a signatory to the main international conventions, parallels with the UN conventions framework were of interest to Belgian policy-makers constantly. Here, policy ideas from other countries, particularly from the Netherlands, have been influential. In the Netherlands, it had gradually become clear that the flood of foreign (Belgian) drug tourists resulted in more *coffee shops* and their development into commercial enterprises that did not respect the tolerance criteria (Dutch Government, 2000). Specificities of the Belgian case demonstrated through the book, such as the recurrent fear of being isolated internationally as a result of implementing a too liberal policy (e.g. including the *coffee-shop* model), illustrate the influence of the Dutch example. Another important feed was the recurrent pressure provided by the International Narcotics Control Board (INCB), the body charged with monitoring adherence to the UN Conventions. Throughout several chapters it has been described how the INCB has expressed reservations about the Belgian policy debates. This is in accordance with the activities of the INCB related to decision-making in Portugal (decriminalisation of all drugs) in 2001 and the UK (transfer of cannabis from Class B to Class C) in 2004 (Bewley-Taylor, 2005; EMCDDA, 2005), although the body was clearly less influential in these debates.

Furthermore, many scholars, not at least in the domain of drug policy, have observed that several institutional characteristics of policy-making (e.g. the electoral cycle and the battle between political parties) also shape how scientific knowledge is used, or whether it is used at all at particular points in the policy process (see e.g. Nutley et al., 2010; Flitcroft, et al., 2011; Monaghan, 2011; MacGregor, 2012b). In a context with dominance of two main political parties that have alternated in forming the government,

Monaghan (2011) demonstrated how the reform of the UK cannabis laws displayed an ignorance of the principles of *evidence-based* policy-making for the sake of gaining political capital. As such, *evidence-based* policy-making seems an even less plausible scenario in a political context with a multi-party government coalition where parties are strongly competing for voters and where bargaining and compromise cannot be avoided (Foss Hansen & Rieper, 2008). A multi-party government coalition cannot solely pursue the programme of one of the governing parties. Indeed, in the Belgian case which is characterised by a multi-party government coalition, the political/tactical concerns were visible, especially in the timing of particular policy events, such as the 2003 Federal elections. Policy-makers across competing ideologies were concerned with how their electorate (and public opinion in general) would perceive and respond to policy decisions. Regardless of the position they took, the consistent use of propositional arguments and political tactics (e.g. using incorrect terminology, employing personal insults, or inciting emotional responses) illustrated their concerns of a potential electoral backlash and their aim to gain higher authority. However, in contrast, while competition can be strenuous in determining which items are important or which evidence is examined (or excluded), opportunities arise when problems become widely recognised. It can be said that, once the need to establish a comprehensive national drug policy was commonly accepted, the multi-party government coalition allowed for recruiting and bringing non-government stakeholders together across different political ties. In several instances, whether in the PWG or in the development of the Federal Drug Policy Note, there was multidisciplinary expertise involved as the policy-makers had to compromise on a wide range of competing ideologies. In this way, the Belgian political context encouraged a thorough, cross-political dialogue and the development of a framework on which a broad range of (policy) actors agreed. Clearly, as Weiss (1999) and Zampini (2014) put forward, there is more space for different voices and interests in multi-party political systems when the need to move forward and form compromises is accepted.

The Belgian case can be seen as an encouraging example of *good governance* and even *evidence-informed* policy-making, as scientific knowledge appeared to influence Belgian drug policy development and the distinctive role played by scientists in the Belgian policy process. However, these stories on the political context might still miss some of the complex power structures that exist in policy development. It deserves restatement that the sample of interviewees only included a limited number of civil servants and thus this book lacks detail on routine day-to-day policy-making 'behind the scenes'. In terms of the political context, there is no doubt that the perceptions of more civil servants could have been very interesting to reveal detail on the political context such as intra-political relations, civil service career management, the role of in-house research, etc. (Stevens, 2011).

Policy Windows Open and Close: The Value of Policy Theories

Policy theories, outlined in Chapter 2, conceptualise a wide range of aspects of the policy process. As the examples in this book demonstrate, it is useful to consider policy through the various lenses of small step-by-step advances, active and sustained power and pressure from (policy) actors, entrepreneurial political actions, and the opening of *windows of opportunity* for significant policy change or development.

Policy development or change is often precipitated by major events that simply cannot be ignored, such as the worldwide arrival of the heroin epidemic and HIV in the 1980s. Belgium's late discovery of the drug phenomenon was different. In Belgium, there have been incremental smaller steps prior to the PWG and a period of '*softening up*' between 1997 and 2000, paving the way for policy development. Kingdon's approach (2002) has been illuminating here in demonstrating the fleeting moments where there is potential for change: *windows of opportunity* are opened by compelling problems or by events in the political stream. The involvement of a *policy entrepreneur*, described by Kingdon (2002) as an individual with particular talents of advocacy and the ability to broker power and integrate *evidence-based* policy solutions, was also witnessed by the role of Brice De Ruyver. A policy window, a period of '*softening up*', and a *policy entrepreneur* featuring in this book's case-study shows that key ideas from Kingdon's Multiple Streams model are particularly relevant for understanding policy development as a process that is influenced by many diverse factors and the conditions under which stakeholders can successfully place and negotiate a space for their ideas on the agenda.

In addition, the circumstances of the policy processes and mechanisms show broad similarities with Weiss' iterative model of competing Ideas – Interests – Institutional rules focusing on the power of various actors in the political processes (Weiss, 2001), and the policy network approach which focuses on formal institutional and informal linkages between governmental and other actors with whom they consult and negotiate (Stone, 2001; Cairney, 2016). First, in accordance with Weiss' insights (2001), several examples revealed that scientific knowledge must compete against other kinds of evidence for policy-makers' attention (e.g. political considerations or claims of practitioners). In this context, the dynamics of drug policy development that focused on 'government versus governance' have been elaborated. Second, critical evaluation of the Belgian case in the light of the policy networks revealed a number of formal and informal interactions that may shape knowledge utilisation in policy processes. For instance, widespread non-government stakeholder consultation, through annual conferences and formal advisory structures, can be considered supportive of the policy network approach. It also became clear that an important explanation for the consistency and transparency regarding Belgian drug policy development can be ascribed to the interactive, brokering role of Brice De Ruyver. The particular ideas from the Advocacy Coalition Framework (Sabatier, 1998) also appear helpful, namely in the cannabis policy debates. The debate over cannabis policy was characterised by a battle of ideas or beliefs in which different (groups of) actors sought to gather and interpret evidence. While the cannabis issue involved intensely politicised disputes involving many actors, other issues were not so oppositional or conflictual.

Finally, this book's focus on one single episode of actual policy development limits the ability to understand why policy changes or developments come about (or not) at one particular time, given that policy proceeds in a stable state for most of the time. For this reason, the models of incrementalism and punctuated equilibrium have not been particularly relevant except for their recognition that incremental events may prompt policymakers to shift their attention and punctuate the equilibrium. From this perspective, it would be worthwhile examining the equilibrium of Belgian drug policy from 2003 onwards. For those concerned with good governance, the dynamics of the drug policy-making processes as well as the roles of the different actors, including the interesting position of the *observer-turned-player*, may change over time, across situations, interests, and issues. Another challenge would be if and how these principles can be consolidated in the long term.

Change and Continuity: Drug Policy at a Crossroads?

Policy-making is an endlessly fascinating subject of study characterised by periods of stability and followed by episodes of change. Policy windows, considered the primary means for achieving meaningful (*evidence-based*) policy development or change, mostly open occasionally, and might not stay open very long (Kingdon, 2002; Lenton, 2004; Hyshka, 2009), as was witnessed in our case. From the end of 2003 onwards, Belgian policymakers tended to agree on the need to keep the drug issue marginal. Both the 2001 drug strategy and the 2003 drug law still form the foundations of the Belgian drug policy today. In clear contrast with most European countries (EMCDDA, 2012), there have been no thorough formal (external) evaluations of Belgian drug policy priorities (and accordingly a new drug policy document) since. The Joint Declaration of 25 January 2010 approved by the Inter-Ministerial Conference on Drugs, uniting all Ministers at several policy levels with competence or part competence for aspects of the drug phenomenon (Inter-Ministerial Conference on Drugs, 2010), can be considered an internal up-to-date elaboration of the foundations of Belgian drug policy performed by the national drug coordination body, rather than a replacement of the Federal Drug Policy Note. In this sense, the action points of the Federal Drug Policy Note were evaluated in terms of the extent to which they had been achieved (De Ruyver et al., 2012). For example, the Joint Declaration has indicated that there has been a large increase of policy-funded studies managed by the Research Programme. From 2002 until 2010, 32 drug research projects were commissioned and financed by the Federal Science Policy Office through the Research Programme in support of the Federal Drug Policy Note (Inter-Ministerial Conference on Drugs, 2010, pp. 33–34). Likewise, it has been argued that the structures to develop and monitor an integral and integrated drug policy were established. For instance, the *General Drugs Policy Cell* has been operational since 2010 and prepares the decisions of the Inter-Ministerial Conference and guards the integrated character of the policy measures (Inter-Ministerial Conference on Drugs, 2010, pp. 33–34; De Ruyver et al., 2012). However, none of these (and other) indications has ignited significant media or political attention on the topic of drugs.

One exception, again, is the topic of the criminalisation of drugs (cannabis policy in particular), which clearly has been the underlying but persistent focus in debates from 1996 onwards. In the aftermath of the reform of the Belgian drug law, on 28 November 2003, five non-profit organisations demanded the Court of Arbitration to strike article 16 of the Law of 3 May 2003 (i.e. Article 16 "The possession of an amount of cannabis for personal use by an adult, without the presence of public nuisance or problematic use, will only lead to a registration by the police") because the terms "public nuisance" and "problematic drug use" were too vague and in violation of the principle of legality. The Constitutional Court agreed and article 16[1] of the 2003 drug law (i.e. the article that caused most political commotion) was struck out (Arbitragehof 20 oktober 2004, nr. 158/2004, rolnrs. 2727 en 2850, *B.S.* 28 oktober 2004). This move had implications for the Ministerial Circular Letter of 16 May 2003 which accompanied the new drug law[2] and eventually, a new (transitional) directive was issued by the new Minister of Justice Laurette Onkelinx and the College of Prosecutors-General in 2005 (Gelders and Vander Laenen, 2007). The new Ministerial Circular Letter called for prosecution of an adult in possession of cannabis for personal use (three grams or one plant) only in cases involving disturbance of 'public order' (defined as possession of cannabis in or near educational or similar institutions, possession of cannabis in a prison or institution of child protection, possession of cannabis in a public place or building) or other aggravating circumstances such as the involvement of minors, being a member or leader of an association, or causing severe illness or death. The 2005 Ministerial Circular Letter deleted the concept of 'problematic use' and replaced 'public nuisance' with 'public order' to provide more clarity. On the condition that there are no aggravating circumstances (like use in the presence of minors or disturbance of public order), the police had to make a simplified process-verbal (as was included in the 1998 Ministerial Circular Letter) and an overview was sent to the Public Prosecutors' Office every month. As the new directive still did not give any clear definition of some of the concepts (e.g. 'public order'), both the Minister of Justice Laurette Onkelinx and the Minister of Public Health Rudy Demotte admitted that a new law had to be made to redefine in a clear way the suppressed notions of article 16 (Gelders, 2006). In spite of a few media articles and some parliamentary questions/interpellations on this topic in 2005, a fundamental law reform has not been on the political agenda since.[3] As such, Belgium continues to apply a de facto *depenalisation* of the possession of cannabis for personal use which involves maintenance of criminal penalties in the criminal law without any application in practice.

More recently, however, there has been an increasing collective demand of non-government stakeholders (i.e. treatment practitioners and scientific experts) for a profound change of particular elements of cannabis policy in Belgium (Decorte, De Grauwe, & Tytgat, 2014; FEDITO Wallonne, 2014; FEDITO Bxl, 2014; VAD, 2014). The current international debates about drug policy reform and new approaches being tested such as the legalisation of cannabis supply in Uruguay and some US states (Global Commission on Drug Policy, 2011; Edwards & Galla, 2014; Singleton & Rubin, 2014; UNGASS, 2016) on the one hand, and the revival of a so-called 'local' *drug war*, focussing on harsh law-enforcement actions against those involved in drug use, in some major cities in Belgium on the other hand (Decorte et al., 2014), are playing key roles here. Another important feed is the increasing presence of Cannabis Social Clubs (CSCs) in Belgium. Those non-profit collectives of adult cannabis users who organise the cultivation and distribution of the substance among themselves have been advocating the CSC model as a meaningful middle ground between cannabis prohibition and commercial legalisation (Decorte, 2014, 2015; Fijnaut & De Ruyver, 2014). So far, these requests and initiatives, while triggering some media coverage and parliamentary activity, remain unanswered by national policy-makers. These examples provide a valuable additional dimension to our understanding of precisely how propitious the circumstances need to be before policy windows open and significant change can occur (Sabatier, 1998; Kingdon, 2002). Or as noted by MacGregor (2013):

> for a decisive shift to occur in the overall paradigm within which drug policy is set, other features as well as logic and evidence would also be needed, such as the opening of a window of opportunity through crisis, change in the balance of forces or exceptional leadership.
>
> (MacGregor, 2013, p. 8)

The UNGASS meeting in April 2016 was expected to be such a groundbreaking event opening a global *window of opportunity* for national policy change or development. A steady, progressive evolution of drugs policy towards a more rational, *evidence-based* approach, was the initial ambition, especially because (in)effectiveness of current drug policies, strongly influenced by the member states' commitments to the three principle UN treaties, has been hotly debated in many parts of the world. What the UNGASS example illustrated was that voices from business, politics, and civil society increasingly succeed in capturing the policy agenda and bring reform discussions to the global frameworks that shape the prohibitionist domestic drug policies across the world. Although the drug policy field is still dominated by a *top-down* approach, the promotion of *evidence-based* ideas has successfully generated more opportunities for a larger number of actors to engage in the debates (*bottom-up*). However, instead of offering an opportunity for a thorough evaluation of global drug policy and how to address the most pressing challenges going forward, this event was rather characteristic of much previous policy development or change where a groundswell of *evidence-based* calls for reform were sidestepped in favour of maintaining the policy status quo (Fordham & Jelsma, 2016; Bewley-Taylor & Jelsma, 2016). The story of UNGASS seems similar to many attempts at national drug policy reform the world over. Nonetheless, in the light of a growing sense that global drug policy is at a crossroads, gaining a better understanding of the contours of (*evidence-based*) drug policy developments, is as important as ever.

Notes

1 In discussing the striking out of article 16, some authors speak of the annulment of article 11. Both are right. This conceptual confusion is caused by article 16 of the Law of 3 May 2003 stating that an article 11 must be added to the original Drug Act of 1921. So, both articles refer to the same legislative principles.
2 Legally, the striking out of this chapter implied that the old law had become active again (i.e. a formal report has to be written for every offence instead of an anonymous police registration).
3 Nevertheless, in the framework of the further development of a global and integrated drug policy, the Belgian drug law of 1921 was adapted in 2006 and in 2014. A new Law (20 July 2006) further modified the basic Belgian law (of 24 February 1921). It included two amendments to the Narcotic Drug Act (art. 9 bis and art. 9 ter). This law formally regulated the authority of the mayor in closing drug joints as well as the authority of the police to arrest a person for six hours being under the influence of substances and exposing him/herself and others to dangers. Furthermore, similar to other EU member states, NPS – also known as 'legal highs' – are increasingly becoming an issue in Belgium. In aiming to counter the rapid development of new psychoactive substances (NPS), the law of 7 February 2014 adapted the Belgian drug law of 1921 by defining a generic classification to control psychoactive substances, criminalising preparatory actions, and enabling the instant destruction of seized drugs and materials.

References

Aberbach, J. D., & Rockman, B. A. (2002). Conducting and coding elite interviews. *PS: Political Science and Politics*, *35*(4), 673–676. doi: 10.1017/S1049096502001142.

Acevedo, B. (2007). Creating the cannabis user: a genealogical analysis of cannabis reclassification in the United Kingdom. *International Journal of Drug Policy*, *18*(3), 177–186. doi: 10.1016/j.drugpo.2006.11.008.

Administratie Planning en Statistiek. (2006). *Vlaamse Regionale Indicatoren*. Brussels: APS.

Aguiar, L. L. M. (2012). Redirecting the academic gaze upward. In L. L. M. Aguiar & C. J. Schneider (Eds.), *Researching Amongst Elites. Challenges and Opportunities in Studying up* (pp. 1–28). Surrey: Ashgate Publishing Limited.

Allen, C. (2007). *Crime, Drugs and Social Theory. A Phenomenological Approach*. Hampshire: Ashgate Publishing Limited.

Amara, N., Ouimet, M., & Landry, R. (2004). New evidence on instrumental, conceptual, and symbolic utilization of university research in government agencies. *Science Communication*, *26*(1), 75–106. doi: 10.1177/1075547004267491.

Arbitragehof 20 oktober 2004, nr. 158/2004, rolnrs. 2727 en 2850, B.S. 28 oktober 2004.

Asmussen, V. (2008). Danish drug policy – shifting from liberalism to repression. *Drugs and Alcohol Today*, *8*(2), 26–33. doi: 10.1108/17459265200800015.

Babor, T., Caulkins, J., Edwards, G., Fischer, F., Foxcroft, D., & Humphreys, K. (2010). *Drug Policy and the Public Good*. Oxford: Oxford University Press.

Bacchi, C. (2009). *Analysing Policy: What's the Problem Represented to be?* Frenchs Forest: Pearson Australia.

Bagozi, R. P., & Dabholkar, P. A. (2000). Discursive psychology: an alternative conceptual foundation to means–end chain theory. *Psychology & Marketing*, *17*(7), 535–586. doi: 10.1002/(SICI)1520-6793(200007)17:7<535::AID-MAR1>3.0.CO;2-H.

Bak Jørgensen, M. (2011). Understanding the research–policy nexus in Denmark and Sweden: the field of migration and integration. *The British Journal of Politics & International Relations*, *13*(1), 93–109. doi: 10.1111/j.1467-856X.2010.00441.x.

Barak, G. (1988). Newsmaking criminology: reflections of the media, intellectuals, and crime. *Justice Quarterly*, *5*(4), 565–587. doi: 10.1080/07418828800089891.

Barak, G. (2007). Doing newsmaking criminology from within the academy. *Theoretical Criminology*, *11*(2), 191–207. doi: 10.1177/1362480607075847.

Baumgartner, F. R., & Jones, B. D. (1993). *Agendas and Instabilities in American Politics*. Chicago: University of Chicago Press.

Bauwens, T., De Koster, C., Enhus, E., & Evenepoel, A. (2013). The pains and gains of a social constructionist perspective on policy-supporting research. In K. Beyens, J. Christiaens, B. Claes, S. De Ridder, H. Tournel, & H. Tubex (Eds.), *The Pains of Doing Criminological Research* (pp. 39–57). Brussels: VUB Press.

Beccaria, F. (2015). Evidence and alcohol policy: lessons from the Italian case. *Contemporary Social Science*, *10*(2), 212–220. doi:10.1080/21582041.2015.1061684.

Becker, H. (1967). 'Whose side are we on?'. *Social Problems*, *14*(3), 239–247. doi: 10.2307/799147.

Behague, D., Tawiah, C., Rosato, M., Some, T., & Morrison, J. (2009). Evidence-based policy-making: the implications of globally-applicable research for context-specific problem-solving in developing countries. *Social Science & Medicine*, *69*(10), 1539–1546. doi: 10.1016/j.socscimed.2009.08.006.

Bekkers, V., Fenger, M., Homburg, V., & Putters, K. (2004). *Doorwerking van Strategische Beleidsadvisering*. Rotterdam/Tilburg: Erasmus Universiteit Rotterdam & Universiteit van Tilburg.

Bennett, T., & Holloway, K. (2010). Is UK drug policy evidence based? *International Journal of Drug Policy*, *21*(5), 411–417. doi: 10.1016/j.drugpo.2010.02.004.

Bergin, V. (2013). *Regulating Alcohol Around the World: Policy Cocktails*. London: Ashgate.

Berridge, V. (2002). Epidemiology and policy: the post-war context. *Bulletin on Narcotics*, *1*(3), 143–151.

Berridge, V., & Stanton, J. (1999). Science and policy: historical insights. *Social Science & Medicine*, *49*(9), 1133–1138.

Berridge, V., & Thom, B. (1996). Research and policy: what determines the relationship? *Policy Studies*, *17*(1), 23–34.

Berry, J. M. (2002). Validity and reliability issues in Elite Interviewing. *PS: Political Science and Politics*, *35*(4), 679–682.

Bewley-Taylor, D. R. (2005). Emerging policy contradictions between the United Nations drug control system and the core values of the United Nations. *International Journal of Drug Policy*, *16*(6), 423–431. doi: 10.1016/j.drugpo.2005.06.007.

Bewley-Taylor, D. R., & Jelsma, M. (2016). *UNGASS 2016: A Broken or B-r-o-a-d Consensus? UN summit cannot hide a growing divergence in the global drug policy landscape*. Retrieved October 10, 2016, from www.tni.org/en/publication/ungass-2016-a-broken-or-b-r-o-a-d-consensus.

Beyens, K., Van den Broeck, T., Raes, A., Snacken, S., Eliaerts, C., & De Nauw, A. (2001). *Bouwstenen voor een geïntegreerde criminele politiek*. Brussels: Federale Diensten voor Wetenschappelijke, Technische en Culturele Aangelegenheden.

Bickford, J. J., & Kothari, A. R. (2008). Research and knowledge in Ontario tobacco control networks. *Canadian Journal of Public Health*, *99*(4), 297–300.

BIRN. (2000). *Belgian National Report on Drugs 2000*. Brussels: Scientific Institute of Public Health.

BIRN. (2002). *Belgian National Report on Drugs 2001*. Brussels: Scientific Institute of Public Health.

Bloor, M., & Wood, F. (2006). *Keywords in Qualitative Methods: A Vocabulary of Research Concepts*. London: Sage Publications.

Boekhout van Solinge, T. (1996). Cannabis in Frankrijk. In P. D. A. Cohen & A. Sas (Eds.), *Cannabisbeleid in Duitsland, Frankrijk en de Verenigde Staten* (pp. 136–144). Amsterdam: Centrum voor Drugsonderzoek.

Boekhout van Solinge, T. (2002). *Drugs and Decision-Making in the European Union*. Amsterdam: Mets & Schilt Publishers.

Boekhout van Solinge, T. (2004). *Dealing with Drugs in Europe*. Den Haag: BJU – Boom Juridische uitgevers.

Bogner, A., Littig, B., & Menz, W. (2009). Introduction: expert interviews. Introduction to a new methodological debate. In A. Bogner, B. Littig, & W. Menz (Eds.), *Interviewing Experts. Research Methods Series* (pp. 98–116). New York: Palgrave MacMillan.

Boland, P. (2008). British drugs policy: problematizing the distinction between legal and illegal drugs and the definition of the drugs problem. *Probation Journal*, *55*(2), 171–187. doi: 10.1177/0264550508089120.

Borer, M. I. (2012). Interviewing celebrities: strategies for getting beyond the sound bite. In L. L. M. Aguiar & C. J. Schneider (Eds.), *Researching Amongst Elites. Challenges and Opportunities in Studying up* (pp. 89–102). Surrey: Ashgate Publishing Limited.

Bottoms, A. (1995). The philosophy and politics of punishment and sentencing. In C. Clarkson & R. Morgan (Eds.), *The Politics of Sentencing Reform* (pp. 17–49). Oxford: Clarendon Press.

Bourgois, P. (2000). Disciplining addictions: the bio-politics of methadone and heroin in the United States. *Culture, Medicine and Psychiatry*, *24*(2), 165–195. doi: 10.1023/A:1005574918294.

Bowen, S., & Zwi, A. B. (2005). Pathways to 'evidence informed' policy and practice: a framework for action. *PloS Medicine*, *2*(7), 166–168. doi: 10.1371/journal.pmed.0020166.

Boyd, S., & Carter, C. (2010). Methamphetamine discourse: media, law, and policy. *Canadian Journal of Communication*, *35*(2), 219–237.

Braithwaite, J. (2005). For public social science. *British Journal of Sociology*, *56*(3), 345–353. doi: 10.1111/j.1468-4446.2005.00064.x.

Brambila, C., Ottolenghi, E., Marin, C., & Bertrand, J. T. (2007). Getting results used: evidence from reproductive health programmatic research in Guatemala. *Health Policy and Planning*, 22(4), 234–245. doi: 10.1093/heapol/czm013.

Brans, M., De Winter, L., & Swenden, W. (2009). *The Politics of Belgium. Institutions and Policy under Bipolar and Centrifugal Federalism*. New York: Routledge.

Brans, M., Jacobs, D., Martinello, M., Rea, A., Swyngedouw, M., Adam, I., Balancier, M., Florence, E., & Van der Straeten, T. (2004). *Recherche et Politiques Publiques: le cas de l'Immigration en Belgique – Onderzoek en Beleid: de Gevalstudie van Immigratie in Belgie*. Gent: Academia Press.

Brereton, D. (1996). Does criminology matter? Crime, criminology and the policy process. *Current Issues in Criminal Justice*, *8*(1), 82–88.

Brewster, D. (2014). *Political Polemics and Drugs Debacles: Comparing the Cannabis Policy Process in England & Wales and the Netherlands*. Paper presented at the Eighth Annual Conference of the International Society for the Study of Drug Policy, Rome.

Bright, S., Bishop, B., Kane, R., Marsh, A., & Barratt, M. (2013). Kronic hysteria: exploring the intersection between Australian synthetic cannabis legislation, the media, and drug-related harm. *International Journal of Drug Policy*, *24*(3), 231–237. doi: 10.1016/j.drugpo.2012.12.002.

Brossard, D. (2009). Media, scientific journals and science communication: examining the construction of scientific controversies. *Public Understanding of Science*, *18*(3), 258–274. doi: 10.1177/0963662507084398.

Bullens, F., From, L., Meuwissen, K., Nicaise, P., Warland, O., Pelc, I., Casselman, J., De Ruyver, B., & Noirfalise, A. (1999). *Evaluatie van de MSOC's. Tussentijds Verslag: Fase van de Piloot- en Haalbaarheidsstudie*. Leuven: Katholieke Universiteit Leuven.

Burawoy, M. (2005). For public sociology. *American Sociological Review*, *70*(1), 4–28. doi: 10.1177/000312240507000102.

Burchell, G., & Foucault, M. (1991). *The Foucault effect: studies in governmentality*. London: Harvester Wheatsheaf.

Burssens, D. (2008). Valkuilen van een evidence-based criminaliteitsbeleid. *Panopticon*, *29*(2), 6–20.

Bygnes, S. (2008). Interviewing people-oriented elites. *Eurosphere Online Working Paper Series nr. 10*. Retrieved August 10, 2016, from http://eurospheres.org/files/2010/08/Eurosphere_Working_Paper_10_Bygnes.pdf.

Cabinet of the Prime Minister (1995). Actieplan Toxicomanie Drugs [*Federal Action Plan Toxicomania-Drugs*]. Brussels: Kabinet van de Eerste Minister.

Cairney, P. (2016). *The Politics of Evidence Based Policymaking*. Basingstoke: Palgrave MacMillan.

Caplan, N. (1979). The two-communities theory and knowledge utilization. *American Behavioral Scientist*, *22*(2), 459–470. doi: 10.1177/000276427902200308.

Carden, F. (2004). Issues in assessing the policy influence of research. *International Social Science Journal*, *56*(179), 135–151. doi: 10.1111/j.0020-8701.2004.00480.x.

Carlen, P. (2011). Against evangelism in academic criminology: for criminology as a scientific art. In M. Bosworth & C. Hoyle (Eds), *What is Criminology?* (pp. 95–110). New York: Oxford University Press.

Carrabine, E., Iganski, P., Lee, M., Plummer, K., & South, N. (2004). *Criminology: A Sociological Introduction*. New York: Routledge.

Carrabine, E., Iganski, P., Lee, M., Plummer, K., & South, N. (2009). *Criminology: A Sociological Introduction* (2nd edn). London: Routledge.

Carrabine, E., Lee, M., & South, N. (2000). Social wrongs and human rights in late modern Britain: social exclusion, crime control, and prospects for a public criminology. *Social Justice*, *27*(2), 193–211.

Carrier, N. (2014). On some limits and paradoxes of academic orations on public criminology. *Radical Criminology*, 4. Retrieved October 18, 2016, from http://journal.radicalcriminology.org/index.php/rc/article/view/33.

Cartuyvels, Y., & Hebberecht, P. (2002). The Belgian federal security and crime prevention policy in the 1990s. In P. Hebberecht & D. Duprez (Eds.), *The Prevention and Security Policies in Europe* (pp. 15–49). Brussels: VUB Press.

Cartuyvels, Y., Delpérée, F., & Delwit, P. (1997). *L'Affaire Dutroux: la Belgique Malade de son Systeme*. Bruxelles: Complexe.

Carvalho, A. (2007). Ideological cultures and media discourses on scientific knowledge: re-reading news on climate change. *Public Understanding of Science*, *16*(2), 223–243. doi: 10.1177/0963662506066775.

Caulkins, J. P., Kilmer, B., Kleiman, M., MacCoun, R. J., Midgette, G., Oglesby, P., Pacula, R., & Reuter, P. (2015). *Options and Issues Regarding Marijuana Legalization*. Santa Monica: RAND Corporation.
Cel Gezondheidsbeleid Drugs. (2002). *Activiteitenrapport 2002 van de Cel Gezondheidsbeleid Drugs*. Brussels: Cel Gezondheidsbeleid Drugs.
Cesoni, M. L. (2008). Drug use and possession: the criminalisation-decriminalisation equation. *Crime Prevention*, 7(2), 1–17.
Chan, J. (1995). Systematically distorted communication? Criminological knowledge, media representation and public policy. *Australian and New Zealand Journal of Criminology*, *28*(1), 23–30. doi: 10.1177/000486589502800S103.
Chancer, L., & McLaughlin, E. (2007). Public criminologies: diverse perspectives on academia and policy. *Theoretical Criminology*, *11*(2), 155–173. doi: 10.1177/1362480607075845.
Chari, R., Hogan, J., & Murphy, G. (2010). *Regulating Lobbying: A Global Comparison*. Manchester: Manchester University Press.
Chatwin, C. (2011). *Drug Policy Harmonization and the European Union*. Basingstoke: Palgrave Macmillan.
Clear, T. R. (2010). Policy and evidence: the challenge to the American Society of Criminology: 2009 presidential address to the American Society of Criminology. *Criminology*, *48*(1), 1–25. doi: 10.1111/j.1745-9125.2010.00178.x.
Cohen, M. D., March, J. G., & Olsen, J. P. (1972). A garbage can model of organizational choice. *Administrative Science Quarterly*, *17*(1), 1–25. doi: 10.2307/2392088.
Cohen, P. (2016). Revisiting 'Looking at the UN, smelling a rat. A comment on Sweden's successful drug policy: a review of the evidence' (UNODC, 2006). In A. O'Gorman, G. Potter, & J. Fountain (Eds.), *Evidence in Social Drug Research and Drug Policy* (pp. 19-32). Lengerich: Pabst Science Publishers.
Conti, J., & O'Neil, M. (2007). Studying power: qualitative methods and the global elite. *Qualitative Research*, 7(1), 63–82. doi: 10.1177/1468794107071421.
Coomber, R. (1998). *The Control of Drugs and Drug Users: Reason or Reaction?* Amsterdam: Harwood Academic Publishers.
Coomber, R., Morris, C., & Dunn, L. (2000). How the media do drugs: quality control and the reporting of drug issues in the UK print media. *International Journal of Drug Policy*, *11*(3), 217–225. doi: 10.1016/S0955-3959(00)00046-3.
Council of the European Union (2012). *EU Drugs Strategy 2013–2020*. Brussels: Council of the European Union.
Courtwright, D. T., & Hickman, T. A. (2011). Modernity and anti-modernity: drug policy and political culture in the United States and Europe in the nineteenth and twentieth centuries. In G. Hunt, M. Milhet, & H. Bergeron, *Drugs and Culture: Knowledge, Consumption, and Policy* (pp. 213–224). Burlington: Ashgate.
Cross, M., Henke, R., Oberknezev, P., & Pouilias, K. (2000). *Building Bridges. Towards Effective Means of Linking Scientific Research and Public Policy: Migrants in European Cities. An Exploratory Survey in 10 European Countries by Metropolis International (European Arm) for the European Commission.* Utrecht: Netherlands School for Social and Economic Policy Research (AWSB).
Csete, J. (2010). *From the Mountaintops: What the World Can Learn from Drug Policy Change in Switzerland*. New York: Open Society Foundations.

Currie, E. (2007). Against marginality. Arguments for a public criminology. *Theoretical Criminology*, *11*(2), 175–190. doi: 10.1177/1362480607075846.

Dabrowska, K., & Bujalski, M. (2013). The legal highs problem in the Polish printed media-actors, claims, and its hidden meanings. *Substance Use & Misuse*, *48*(1), 31–40. doi: 10.3109/10826084.2012.720336.

Daems, T. (2008). *Making Sense of Penal Change*. Oxford: Oxford University Press.

Daems, T. (2011). Public criminology? *Panopticon*, *32*(2), 105–111.

Dangreau, J., Deben, L., De Greve, K., Delbrouck, L., De Waele, H., Lambrechts, M., et al. (2012). *Larcier Wetten – Drugwetgeving*. Brussels: Larcier.

Davies, P. (2004). *Is Evidence-Based Government Possible? Jerry Lee Lecture 2004*. Paper presented at the Fourth Annual Campell Collaboration Colloquium, Washington DC.

De Haan, W. J. M. (2008). Publieke criminologie: een criminologie die ertoe doet? *Delikt en delinkwent*, *10*(9), 1051–1060.

De Ruyver, B. (1988). *De Strafrechtelijke Politiek Gevoerd Onder de Socialistische Ministers van Justitie E. Vandervelde, P. Vermeylen en A. Vranckx*. Antwerpen: Kluwer.

De Ruyver, B. (1997). *Synthese: een Drugsbeleid Vanuit een Geïntegreerd Perspectief*. Brussels: Parlementaire Werkgroep Drugs.

De Ruyver, B., Casselman, J., Meuwissen, K., Bullens, F., & Van Impe, K. (2000). *Het Belgisch Drugbeleid Anno 2000: een Stand van Zaken Drie Jaar na de Aanbevelingen van de Parlementaire Werkgroep Drugs*. Gent: Onderzoeksgroep Drugbeleid, Strafrechtelijk beleid en Internationale criminaliteit.

De Ruyver, B., Colman, C., De Wree, E., Vander Laenen, F., Reynders, D., Van Liempt, A., & De Pauw, W. (2008). *Een Brug Tussen Justitie en de Drughulpverlening. Een Evaluatie van het Proefzorgproject*. Antwerpen: Maklu.

De Ruyver, B., Hap, M., Marchandise, T., Schleiper, A., & Vermeulen, G. (Eds.) (1997). *Drugbeleid in 2000 Congresboek*. Antwerpen: Maklu.

De Ruyver, B., Lemaître, A., & Schoenaers, F. (2009). *Onderzoek Naar Essentiële en Bijkomende Randvoorwaarden Voor Interactie Justitie en Drughulpverlening (JUSTHULP). Etude des Conditions Nécessaires et Accessoires a l'Optimalisation de l'Interaction Entre la Justice et le Secteur de l'Aide Sociale et des Soins (JUSTHULP)*. Gent: Academia Press.

De Ruyver, B., Lemaître, A., Born, M., Ponsaers, P., Pauwels, L., Vander Laenen, F., et al. (2009). *Do's and Don'ts in een Integraal en Geïntegreerd Drugbeleid – Faire et ne pas Faire Dans le Cadre d'une Politique Intégrale et Intégrée sur les Drogues*. Gent: Academia Press.

De Ruyver, B., Pelc, I., Casselman, J., Geenens, K., Nicaise, P., From, L., Vander Laenen, F., Meuwissen, K., & Van Dijck, A. (2004). *Drugbeleid in Cijfers*. Gent: Academia Press.

De Ruyver, B., Pelc, I., De Graeve, D., Bucquoye, A., Cornelis, L., & Nicaise, P. (2007). *Drugs in Cijfers II: Studie Naar Betrokken Actoren, Overheidsuitgaven En Bereikte Doelgroepen*. Gent: Academia Press.

De Ruyver, B., Ponsaers, P., Vermeulen, G., & Vander Beken, T. (Eds.) (2010). *Strafrechtshandhaving in België en Nederland: Uitgave ter Gelegenheid van het Eredoctoraat Toegekend Door de Universiteit Gent aan Prof. dr. Cyrille Fijnaut*. Antwerpen: Apeldoorn.

De Ruyver, B., Van Bouchautte, J., & Reisinger, M. (1993). *Les Traitements de Substitution a la Drogue*. Bruxelles: Fondation Roi Baudouin.

De Ruyver, B., Vander Laenen, F., & Eelen, S. (2012). The long road to an integral and integrated policy in Belgium. In R. Muscat & B. Pike (Eds.), *Reflections on the Concept of Coherency for a Policy on Psychoactive Substances and Beyond* (pp. 33–42). Strasbourg Cedex: Council of Europe Publishing.

De Ruyver, B., Vermeulen, G., & Vander Beken, T. (2002). *Multidisciplinary Drug Policies and the UN Drug Treaties*. Antwerpen: Maklu.

De Ruyver, B., Vermeulen, G., De Leenheer, A., & Marchandise, T. (Eds.) (1996). *Veiligheids- en Medisch-Sociale Benadering: Complementair of Tegengesteld?* Antwerpen: Maklu.

De Ruyver, B., Vermeulen, G., De Leenheer, A., & Van Der Straten Waillet, G. (Eds.) (1995). *Op weg Naar een Geïntegreerd Drugbeleid in België?* Antwerpen: Maklu.

De Ruyver, B., Vermeulen, G., Franck, P., & Van Daele, L. (1992). *Kansarmoede, Druggebruik, Criminaliteit*. Gent: Universiteit Gent.

Decorte, T. (2007), Characteristics of the cannabis market in Belgium. In: J. Fountain & D. J. Korf (Eds.), *Drugs in Society: A European Perspective* (pp. 28–38). Oxford: Radcliffe Publishing.

Decorte, T. (2014). De Belgische 'Cannabis Social Clubs': middenweg tussen zwarte markt en commerciële beschikbaarheid? *Panopticon*, *35*(6), 520–537.

Decorte, T. (2015). Cannabis social clubs in Belgium: organizational strengths and weaknesses, and threats to the model. *International Journal of Drug Policy*, *26*(2), 122–130. doi: 10.1016/j.drugpo.2014.07.016.

Decorte, T., & Zaitch, D. (Eds.) (2016). *Kwalitatieve Methoden en Technieken in de Criminologie*. Leuven: Acco.

Decorte, T., De Grauwe, P., & Tytgat, J. (2014). Het Belgisch cannabisbeleid maakt zijn doelstellingen niet waar. *Panopticon*, *35*(2), 151–155.

Decorte, T., Kaminski, D., Muys, M., & Slingeneyer, T. (2005). *Problematisch Gebruik van (Illegale) Drugs: Onderzoek Naar de Operationalisering van het Concept in een Wettelijke Context*. Gent: Academia Press.

Decorte, T., Mortelmans, D., Tieberghien, J., & De Moor, S. (2009). *Drug Use: Overview of General Population Surveys in Europe*. Lisbon: EMCDDA.

Deflem, M. (2005). Public Sociology, Hot Dogs, Apple Pie, and Chevrolet. *The Journal of Public and Professional Sociology*, *1*(1), 4.

Denzin, N. K., & Giardina, M. D. (Eds.) (2008). *Qualitative Inquiry and the Politics Of Evidence*. California: Wallnut Creek.

Denzin, N. K., & Lincoln, Y. S. (Eds.) (1994). *Handbook of Qualitative Research*. Thousand Oaks: Sage.

Devos, C. (2006). *De Kleermakers en de Keizer: Inleiding tot Politiek en Politieke Wetenschappen*. Gent: Academia Press.

Devos, C., Rommel, J., Lannoo, S., & Van Liefferinge, H. (2009). *Politieke Besluitvorming*. Gent: Academia Press.

Devos, C., Rommel, J., Lannoo, S., Van Liefferinge, H., & De Wilde, S. (2010). *Inleiding in de Politieke Besluitvormingstheorie*. Gent: Academia Press.

Devroe, E. (2002). *De Ontmoeting Tussen Criminologisch Onderzoek en Strafrechtelijk Beleid*. Brussel: Politeia.

Devroe, E. (2010). Wetenschap voor beleid of beleid voor wetenschap? Een analyse van 15 jaar politie en justitie onderzoek in België. *Panopticon*, *31*(3), 11–39.

Devroe, E., Deschamps, L., & Hannes, K. (2008). Evidence-based beleidsvoering in de kijker: twee Belgische initiatieven. *Panopticon*, *6*(1), 59–66.

Dienst Strafrechtelijk Beleid. (1996). *Jaarverslag 1995–1996*. Brussel: Ministerie van Justitie.

Dixon, D. (1995). Crime, criminology and public policy. *Australian & New Zealand Journal of Criminology*, *28*(1), 1–5. doi: 10.1177/00048658950280S101.

Dobrow, M. J., Goel, V., & Upshur, R. E. G. (2004). Evidence-based health policy: context and utilisation. *Social Science & Medicine*, *58*(11), 207–217.

Downes, D., Rock, P., & McLaughlin, E. (2016). *Understanding Deviance: A Guide to the Sociology of Crime and Rule-Breaking* (7th Edition). Oxford: Oxford University Press.

Drake, D. H., & Walters, R. (2015). 'Crossing the line': criminological expertise, policy advice and the 'quarrelling society'. *Critical Social Policy*, *35*(3), 414–433. doi: 10.1177/0261018315589448.

Duke, K. (2001). Evidence-based policy making? The interplay between research and the development of prison drugs policy. *Criminology and Criminal Justice*, *1*(3), 277–300. doi: 10.1177/1466802501001003002.

Duke, K. (2002). Getting beyond the 'official line': reflections on dilemmas of access, knowledge and power in researching policy networks. *Journal of Social Policy*, *31*(1), 39–59. doi: 10.1017/S0047279402006505.

Duke, K. (2003). *Drugs, Prisons and Policy making*. Basingstoke: Palgrave.

Duke, K. (2012). From crime to recovery: the reframing of British drugs policy? *Journal of Drug Issues*, *43*(1), 39–55. doi: 10.1177/0022042612466614.

Duke, K., & Thom, B. (2014). The role of evidence and the expert in contemporary processes of governance: the case of opioid substitution treatment policy in England. *International Journal of Drug Policy*, *25*(5), 964–971. doi: 10.1016/j.drugpo.2014.01.015.

Dutch Government (1995). *Het Nederlandse Drugbeleid: Continuïteit en Verandering* [*The Dutch Drug Policy, Continuity and Change*]. Amsterdam: Ministerie van Justitie.

Dutch Government (2000). *Het Pad naar de Achterdeur* [*Pathways to the Back Door*]. Amsterdam: Ministerie van Justitie.

Edwards, C., & Galla, M. (2014). Governance in EU illicit drug policy. *International Journal of Drug Policy*, *25*(5), 942–947. doi: 10.1016/j.drugpo.2014.04.009.

Edwards, G. (2004). *A Matter of Substance*. Penguin Press: London.

Edwards, G., Strang, J., & Jaffe, J. H. (Eds.) (1993). *Drugs, Alcohol, and Tobacco. Making the Science and Policy Connections*. New York: Oxford University Press.

Eisenbach-Stangl, I., Moskalewicz, J., & Thom, B. (Eds.) (2009). *Two Worlds of Drug Consumption in Late Modern Societies*. Surrey: Ashgate Publishing Limited.

El-Jardall, F., Lavis, J. N., Ataya, N., & Jarnal, D. (2012). Use of health systems and policy research evidence in the health policymaking in eastern Mediterranean countries: views and practices of researchers. *Implementation Science*, 7(2), 1–16. doi: 10.1186/1748-5908-7-2.

Elliott, H., & Popay, J. (2000). How are policy makers using evidence? Models of research utilisation and local NHS policy making. *Journal of Epidemiology Community Health*, *54*(6), 461–468. doi: 10.1136/jech.54.6.461.

Embrett, M. G., & Randall, G. E. (2014). Social determinants of health and health equity policy research: exploring the use, misuse, and nonuse of policy analysis theory. *Social Science & Medicine*, *108*(4), 147–155. doi: 10.1016/j.socscimed.2014.03.004.

EMCDDA (1995). *Extended Annual Report on the State of the Drugs Problem in the European Union*. Lisbon: EMCDDA.
EMCDDA (1997). *Extended Annual Report on the State of the Drugs Problem in the European Union*. Lisbon: EMCDDA.
EMCDDA (2000). *2000 Annual Report on the State of the Drugs Problem in the European Union*. Lisbon: EMCDDA.
EMCDDA (2001). *Decriminalisation in Europe? Recent Developments in Legal Approaches to Drug Use*. Lisbon: EMCDDA.
EMCDDA (2004). *Evaluation of 'National Drug Strategies' in Europe. EMCDDA 2004 Selected Issue*. Lisbon: EMCDDA.
EMCDDA (2005). *Illicit Drug Use in the EU: Legislative Approaches*. Lisbon: EMCDDA.
EMCDDA (2008). *Selected Issue 2008. National Drug-Related Research in Europe*. Lisbon: EMCDDA.
EMCDDA (2012). *EMCDDA Trend Report for the Evaluation of the 2005–12 EU Drugs Strategy*. Lisbon: EMCDDA.
EMCDDA (2013). *Drug Policy Advocacy Organisations in Europe*. Luxembourg: Publications Office of the European Union.
Entman, R. (1989). How the Media Affect What People Think: An Information Processing Approach. *The Journal of Politics*, *51*(2), 347–370.
Epstein, D., Farina, C., & Heidt, J. (2014). The value of words: narrative as evidence in policy making. *Evidence & Policy: A Journal of Research, Debate and Practice*, *10*(2), 243–258. doi: 10.1332/174426514X13990325021128.
Epstein, S. (1996). *Impure Science: AIDS Activism and the Politics of Science*. Berkeley: University of California Press.
Erickson, P. G. (1998). Neglected and rejected: a case study of the impact of social research on Canadian drug policy. *Canadian Journal of Sociology*, *23*(2), 263–280. doi: 10.2307/3341968.
Ericson, R. (2005). Publicizing sociology. *British Journal of Sociology*, *56*(3), 365–372.
European Commission (1999). *European Action Plan to Combat Drugs 2000–2004*. Brussels: European Commission.
European Union (1992). *Treaty on European Union. Provisions Amending the Treaty Establishing the European Economic Community with a View to Establishing the European Community*. Maastricht: European Union.
European Union (1997). *The Treaty of Amsterdam Amending the Treaty on European Union, the Treaties Establishing the European Communities and Certain Related Acts*. Amsterdam: European Union.
Fairclough, I., & Fairclough, N. (2012). *Political Discourse Analysis. A Method for Advanced Students*. Abingdon: Routledge.
Fairclough, N. (1998). Political discourse in the media: an analytical framework. In A. Bell & P. Garrett (Eds.), *Approaches to Media Discourse* (pp. 142–162). London: Blackwell.
Fairclough, N. (2003). *Analysing Discourse. Textual Analysis for Social Research*. New York: Taylor and Francis Group.
Farquharson, K. (2005). A different kind of snowball: identifying key policymakers. *International Journal of Social Research Methodology*, *8*(4), 345–353. doi: 10.1080/1364557042000203116.

Farrington, D. (2006). The Maryland scientific methods scale. In D. Farrington, D. L. Mackenzie, L. Sherman, & B. C. Welsh (Eds.), *Evidence-Based Crime Prevention* (pp. 13–21). New York: Routledge.
Federal Government. (1992). *Regeerakkoord Federale Regering*. Brussel: Federale Regering.
Federal Government. (1999). *Regeringsverklaring Federale Regering*. Brussel: Federale Regering.
Federal Government. (2001). *Beleidsnota van de Federale Regering in verband met de drugproblematiek* [*Federal Drug Policy Note*]. Brussel: Federale Regering.
FEDITO Bxl (2014). *Mémorandum FEDITO | FEIAT | CLDB. Février 2014*. Brussel: FEDITO Bxl.
FEDITO Wallonne (2014). *Mémorandum de la Fédito Wallonne. Pour de Meilleurs Accompagnements, Traitements et Soins aux Usagers de Drogues et a Leurs Proches*. Brussel: FEDITO Wallonne.
Fichtelberg, A., & Kupchik, A. (2011). Democratic criminology: the place of criminological expertise in the public sphere. *Journal of Theoretical and Philosophical Criminology*, *3*(1), 57–88.
Fijnaut, C., & De Ruyver, B. (2008). *Voor een Gezamenlijke Beheersing van de Drugsgerelateerde Criminaliteit in de Euregio Maas-Rijn*. Maastricht: Euregio Maas-Rijn.
Fijnaut, C., & De Ruyver, B. (2014). *De Derde weg. Een Pleidooi Voor een Evenwichtig Cannabisbeleid*. Antwerpen: Intersentia.
Fijnaut, C., Huyse, L., & Verstraeten, R. (1998). *Parlementaire Onderzoekscommissies: Mogelijkheden, Grenzen en Risico's*. Leuven: Van Halewyck.
Fitzgerald, J. (2005). The Australian National Council on Drugs (ANCD) and governance in the Australian drug policy arena. *Contemporary Drug Problems*, *32*(2), 259–293.
Flitcroft, K., Gillespie, J., Salkeld, G., Carter, S., & Trevena, L. (2011). Getting evidence into policy: the need for deliberative strategies? *Social Science & Medicine*, *72*(7), 1039–1046. doi: 10.1016/j.socscimed.2011.01.034.
Fordham, A., & Jelsma, M. (2016). *Will UNGASS 2016 be the beginning of the end for the 'war on drugs'?* Retrieved October, 2016, from www.opendemocracy.net/drugpolicy/ann-fordham-martin-jelsma/will-ungass-2016-be-beginning-of-end-for-war-on-drugs.
Foss Hansen, H. F., & Rieper, O. (2008). *The Politics of Evidence-based Policy-making: The Case of Denmark*. Paper presented at the Joint Sessions of Workshops, European Consortium for Political Research, Rennes. Retrieved September 2, 2016, from https://ecpr.eu/Filestore/PaperProposal/97e5166a-e20a-4be3-b99c-89c5229cca4b.pdf.
Foucault, M. (1972). *The Archaeology of Knowledge*. London: Routledge.
Foucault, M. (1976). Truth and power. In P. Rabinow (Ed.), *Essential Works of Foucault, Volume 3* (pp. 111–133). New York: Free Press.
Fountain, J. (Ed.) (2000). *Understanding and Responding to Drug Use: The Role of Qualitative Research*. Luxembourg: Office for Official Publications of the European Communities.
Fountain, J., & Korf, D. (Eds.) (2007). *Drugs in Society. European Perspectives*. Oxon: Radcliffe Publishing Ltd.
Franklin, J. (1998). *The Politics of Risk Society*. Cambridge: Polity Press.

Fraser, S., & Moore, D. (2011). Governing through problems: the formulation of policy on amphetamine-type stimulants (ATS) in Australia. *International Journal of Drug Policy*, *22*(6), 498–506. doi: 10.1016/j.drugpo.2011.09.004.

Fraser, S., Hopwood, M., Treloar, C., & Brener, L. (2004). Needle fictions: medical constructions of needle fixation and the injecting drug user. *Addiction Research & Theory*, *12*(1), 67–76. doi: 10.1080/1606635031000 1606132.

Freiberg, A., & Carson, W. G. (2010). The limits to evidence-based policy: evidence, emotion and criminal justice. *The Australian Journal of Public Administration*, *69*(2), 152–164. doi: 10.1111/j.1467-8500.2010.00674.x.

Garland, D. (2001). *The Culture of Control: Crime and Social Order in Contemporary Society*. Oxford: Oxford University Press.

Garland, D. (2011). Criminology's place in the academic field. In M. Bosworth & C. Hoyle (Eds.), *What is Criminology?* (pp. 298–317). Oxford: Oxford University Press.

Garland, D., & Sparks, R. (2000). Criminology, social theory and the challenge of our times. In D. Garland & R. Sparks (Eds.), *Criminology and Social Theory* (pp. 1–22). Oxford: Oxford University Press.

Geenens, K., Vanderplasschen, W., Broekaert, E., & De Ruyver, B. (2005). *Tussen Droom en Daad: Implementatie van Case Management Voor Druggebruikers Binnen de Hulpverlening en Justitie*. Gent: Academia Press.

Gelders, D. (2006). *Tussen Droom en Daad. Communicatie over Beleidsintenties Door de Overheid*. Brugge: Vanden Broele.

Gelders, D., & Vander Laenen, F. (2007). 'Mr Police Officer, I thought cannabis was legal' – Introducing new policy regarding cannabis in Belgium: A story of good intentions and Babel. *Drugs: Education, Prevention and Policy*, *14*(2), 103–116. doi: 10.1080/09687630600935113.

Gelev, F. (2009). 'Risk society' and the precautionary approach in recent Australian, Canadian and UK judicial decision making. *CLPE Research Paper No. 5/2009*. Retrieved November 3, 2016, from https://ssrn.com/abstract=1346968.

Gerring, J. (2007). *Case Study Research. Principles and Practices*. New York: Cambridge University Press.

Ghodse, H. (2008). *International Drug Control Into the 21st Century*. Hampshire: Ashgate Publishing Limited.

Ginsburg, M. B., & Gorostiaga, J. M. (2001). Relationships between theorists/researchers and. policy makers practitioners? Rethinking the two cultures and the possibility of dialogue. *Comparative Education Review*, *45*(2), 173–196. doi: 10.1086/447660.

Global Commission on Drug Policy. (2011). *War on drugs. Report of the Global Commission on Drug Policy*. New York: Global Commission on Drug Policy.

Goode, E., & Ben-Yehuda, N. (1994). *Moral Panics. The Social Construction of Deviance*. Cambridge: Blackwell Publishers.

Gordon, C. (1991). Governmental rationality: an introduction. In G. Burchell & M. Foucault (Eds.), *The Foucault Effect: Studies in Governmentality*. London: Harvester Wheatsheaf.

Green, D. (2008). *When Children Kill Children: Penal Populism and Political Culture*. Oxford: Oxford University Press.

Greenberg, D. H., & Mandell, M. B. (1991). Research utilization in policymaking: A tale of two series (of social experiments). *Journal of Policy Analysis and Management*, *10*(4), 633–656. doi: 10.2307/3324989.

Gregrich, J. R. (2003). A note to researchers: communicating science to policy makers and practitioners. *Journal of Substance Abuse Treatment*, *25*(3), 233–237. doi: 10.1016/S0740-5472(03)00120-X.

Griffiths, P., & McKetin, R. (2005). A common language for a common problem: the developing role of drug epidemiology in a global context. In Z. Sloboda (Ed.), *Epidemiology of Drug Abuse* (pp. 161–176). New York: Springer.

Groombridge, N. (2007). Criminologists say ...: an analysis of UK national press coverage of criminology and criminologists and a contribution to the debate on 'public criminology'. *The Howard Journal*, *46*(5), 459–475. doi: 10.1111/j.1468-2311.2007.00492.x.

Guillain, C. (2003). *La Politique Pénale du Gouvernement Arc-En-Ciel en Matière de Drogues*. Bruxelles: CRISP.

Guillain, C. (2009). Les facteurs de criminalisation et les résistances à la décriminalisation de l'usage des drogues en Belgique. Du contrôle international aux préoccupations sécuritaires *Revue Interdisciplinaire d'Études Juridiques*, *63*(2), 119–132.

Guillain, C., & Marchand, C. (1998). La réglementation du cannabis à la lumière des conventions internationales. In B. De Ruyver (Ed.), *La Politique en Matière de Drogues en Belgique: Développements Actuels* (pp. 299–318). Bruxelles: Bruylant-Maklu.

Gusfield, J. R. (1975). The (f)utility of knowledge? The relation of social science to public policy toward drugs. *Annals of the American Academy of Political and Social Science*, *417*(1), 1–15. doi: 10.1177/000271627541700102.

Haas, P. (1992). Introduction: epistemic communities and international policy coordination. *International Organization*, *14*(1), 1–36.

Haines, A., Kuruvilla, S., & Borchert, M. (2004). Bridging the implementation gap between knowledge and action for health. *Bulletin of World Health Organization*, *82*(10), 724–731. doi: 10.1590/S0042-96862004001000005.

Hajer, M. (1995). *The Politics of Environmental Discourse: Ecological Modernization and the Policy Process*. Oxford: Clarendon Press.

Hall, W. (2004). The contribution of research to Australian policy responses to heroin dependence 1990–2001: a personal retrospection. *Addiction*, *99*(8), 560–569. doi: 10.1111/j.1360-0443.2004.00717.

Hall, W. (2008). The contribution of research to the development of national cannabis policy in Australia. *Addiction*, *103*(5), 712–720. doi: 10.1111/j.1360-0443.2008.02169.

Hammersley, M. (2013). *The Myth of Research-Based Policy & Practice*. London: Sage.

Hammersley, M., & Gomm, R. (2008). Assessing the radical critique of interviews. In M. Hammersley (Ed.), *Questioning Qualitative Inquiry: Critical Essays* (pp. 89–100). Thousand Oaks, CA: Sage.

Hand. Kamer 1920–1921, 21 december 1920, 108/1.

Hand. Kamer 1995–1996, 13 november 1995, 230/1.

Hand. Kamer 1996–1997, 24 juni 1997, 175.

Hand. Kamer 1996–1997, 26 juni 1997, 178.

Hand. Kamer 1996–1997, 22 september 1997, 393.

Hand. Kamer 1997–1998, 22 maart 1999, 774, 1–2.

Hand. Kamer 1998–1999, 15 juli 1999, 003, 63.

Hand. Kamer 1998–1999, 16 juli 1999, 005, 135.

Hand. Kamer 1999–2000, 15 december 1999, 0025/037.
Hand. Kamer 1999–2000, 15 december 1999, COM 074, 9–13.
Hand. Kamer 1999–2000, 25 januari 2000, COM 094, 5–9.
Hand. Kamer 1999–2000, 13 juni 2000, 716/1.
Hand. Kamer 1999–2000, 15 juni 2000, 061, 16.
Hand. Kamer 1999–2000, 4 juli 2000, COM 255, 18.
Hand. Kamer 1999–2000, 9 november 2000, 081, 12.
Hand. Kamer 2000–2001, 30 januari 2001, 106, 1–56.
Hand. Kamer 2000–2001, 30 januari 2001, 0025/172, 1–3.
Hand. Kamer 2000–2001, 31 januari 2001, COM 373, 1–4.
Hand. Kamer 2000–2001, 6 februari 2001, COM 376, 9–11.
Hand. Kamer 2000–2001, 8 februari 2001, 108, 7–9.
Hand. Kamer, 2000–2001, 13 februari 2001, COM 390, 4–6.
Hand. Kamer 2000–2001, 20 februari 2001, COM 394, 17–21.
Hand. Kamer 2000–2001, 7 maart 2001, COM 410, 12–17.
Hand. Kamer 2000–2001, 8 maart 2001, 112, 13–15.
Hand. Kamer 2000–2001, 15 maart 2001, 114, 6–7.
Hand. Kamer 2000–2001, 29 maart 2001, 119, 12–13.
Hand. Kamer 2000–2001, 19 april 2001, 121, 5–7.
Hand. Kamer 2000–2001, 17 mei 2001, 125, 1–3.
Hand. Kamer 2000–2001, 31 mei 2001, 130, 5–7.
Hand. Kamer 2000 2001, 7 juni 2001, 132, 9.
Hand. Kamer 2000–2001, 3 juli 2001, 517, 11–12.
Hand. Kamer 2000–2001, 19 juli 2001, 158, 18–19.
Hand. Kamer 2000–2001, 23 oktober 2001, 560, 32–35.
Hand. Kamer 2001–2002, 10 januari 2002, 197, 15–16.
Hand. Kamer 2001–2002, 21 februari 2002, 208, 32–33.
Hand. Kamer 2001–2002, 28 februari 2002, 210, 11–13.
Hand. Kamer 2001–2002, 21 februari 2002, 208, 32–33.
Hand. Kamer 2002–2003, 12 februari 2003, 327, 10.
Hand. Senaat 1997–1998, 7 mei 1998, 1–183.
Hand. Senaat 2000–2001, 1 februari 2001, 2–92, 21–23.
Hand. Senaat 2000–2001, 8 februari 2001, 2–94, 27–30.
Hand. Senaat 2000–2001, 15 februari 2001, 2–96, 8–9.
Hand. Senaat 2000–2001, 22 februari 2001, 2–98, 9–12.
Hand. Senaat 2000–2001, 8 maart 2001, 2–100, 25–27.
Hand. Senaat 2000–2001, 29 maart 2001, 2–104, 33–38.
Hand. Senaat 2000–2001, 17 mei 2001, 2–114, 18–20.
Hand. Senaat 2000–2001, 31 mei 2001, 2–119, 11–12.
Hand. Senaat 2001–2002, 6 december 2001, 2–162, 16–18.
Hand. Senaat 2001–2002, 16 mei 2002, 2–204, 22–23.
Hand. Senaat 2001–2002, 19 maart 2002, 2–51, 2692.
Hanney, S., Gonzalez-Block, M., Buxton, M., & Kogan, M. (2003). The utilization of health research in policy-making: concepts, examples and methods of assessment. *Health Research Policy and Systems*, *1*(1), 1–28. doi: 10.1186/1478-4505-1-2.
Hantrais, L., Lenihan, A., & MacGregor, S. (2015). Evidence-based policy: exploring international and interdisciplinary insights. *Contemporary Social Science*, *10*(2), 101–113. doi: 10.1080/21582041.2015.1061687.

Hartman, D. M., & Golub, A. (1999). The social construction of the crack epidemic in the print media. *Journal of Psychoactive Drugs*, *31*(4), 423–433. doi: 10.1080/02791072.1999.10471772.

Hartnoll, R. (1998). International trends in drug policy. In R. Coomber, *The Control of Drugs and Drug Users: Reason or Reaction?* (pp. 233–252). Amsterdam: Harwood Academic Publishers.

Hartnoll, R. (2004). *Drugs and Drug Dependence: Linking Research, Policy and Practice*. Strasbourg: Council of Europe Publishing.

Harvey, W. S. (2010). Methodological approaches for interviewing elites. *Geography Compass*, *4*(3), 193–205. doi: 10.1111/j.1749-8198.2009.00313.x.

Haynes, A. S., Derrick, G. E., Chapman, S., Redman, S., Hall, W. D., Gillespie, J., & Sturk, H. (2011). From "our world" to the "real world": exploring the views and behaviour of policy-influential Australian public health researchers. *Social Science & Medicine*, *72*(7), 1047–1055. doi: 10.1016/j.socscimed.2011.02.004.

Haynes, A. S., Derrick, G. E., Redman, S., Hall, W. D., Gillespie, J., Chapman, S., & Sturk, H. (2012). Identifying trustworthy experts: how do policymakers find and assess public health researchers worth consulting or collaborating with? *PLoS One*, *7*(3), 1–8. doi: 10.1371/journal.pone.0032665.

Head, B. W. (2010). Reconsidering evidence-based policy: key issues and challenges. *Policy and Society*, *29*(2), 77–94. doi: 10.1016/j.polsoc.2010.03.001.

Hebberecht, P. (2009). *De 'Verpaarsing' van de Criminaliteitsbestrijding in België*. Brussel: VUBPress.

Heclo, H. (1978). Issue networks and the executive establishment. In A. King (Ed.), *The New American Political System* (pp. 87–124). Washington, DC: AEI.

Henry, S., & Milovanovic, D. (1996). *Constitutive Criminology. Beyond Post-Modernism*. London: Sage Publications.

Hijmans, E., Pleijter, A., & Wester, F. (2003). Covering scientific research in Dutch newspapers. *Science Communication*, *25*(2), 153–176. doi: 10.1177/1075547003259559.

Hird, J. A. (2009). The study and use of policy research in state legislatures. *International Regional Science Review*, *32*(4), 523–535. doi: 10.1177/0160017609341401.

Hodder, I. (2003). The interpretation of documents and material culture. In N. K. Denzin & Y. S. Lincoln (Eds.), *Collecting and Interpreting Qualitative Materials* (pp. 393–402). London: Sage publications.

Hoppe, R. (1999). Policy analysis, science and politics: from 'speaking truth to power' to 'making sense together'. *Science and Public Policy*, *26*(3), 201–210. doi: 10.3152/147154399781782482.

Hoppe, R. (2005). Rethinking the science-policy nexus: from knowledge utilization and science technology studies to types of boundary arrangements. *Poiesis & Praxis*, *3*(3), 199–215. doi: 10.1007/s10202-005-0074-0.

Hoppe, R. (2009). Scientific advice and public policy: expert advisers' and policymakers' discourses on boundary work. *Poiesis & Praxis*, *6*(3), 235–263. doi: 10.1007/s10202-008-0053-3.

Houborg, E., & Asmussen, V. (2014). Drug consumption rooms and the role of politics and governance in policy processes. *International Journal of Drug Policy*, *25*(5), 972–977. doi: 10.1016/j.drugpo.2014.01.008.

Howlett, M., & Ramesh, M. (1995). *Studying Public Policy: Policy Cycles and Policy Subsystems*. Toronto: Oxford University Press.

Huber, G. P., & Power, D. J. (1985). Retrospective reports of strategic-level managers. *Strategic Management Journal*, *6*(2), 171–180. doi: 10.1002/smj.4250060206.

Hughes, C. E. (2007). Evidence-based policy or policy-based evidence? The role of evidence in the development and implementation of the Illicit Drug Diversion Initiative. *Drug and Alcohol Review*, *26*(4), 363–368. doi: 10.1080/09595230701373859.

Hughes, C. E. (2009). Capitalising upon political opportunities to reform drug policy: a case study into the development of Australian 'Tough on Drugs-Illicit Drug Diversion Initiative'. *International Journal of Drug Policy*, *20*(5), 431–437. doi: 10.1016/j.drugpo.2008.12.003.

Hughes, C. E., & Stevens, A. (2010). What can we learn from the Portuguese decriminalization of illicit drugs? *British Journal of Criminology*, *50*(6), 999–1022. doi: 10.1093/bjc/azq038.

Hughes, C. E., & Stevens, A. (2012). A resounding success or a disastrous failure: re-examining the interpretation of evidence on the Portuguese decriminalisation of illicit drugs. *Drug and Alcohol Review*, *31*(1), 101–113. doi: 10.1111/j.1465-3362.2011.00383.x.

Hughes, C. E., Ritter, A., & Cowdery, N. (2014). Legislating thresholds for drug trafficking: a policy development case study from New South Wales, Australia. *International Journal of Drug Policy*, *25*(5), 992–1000. doi: 10.1016/j.drugpo.2014.03.002.

Hughes, C., Lancaster, K., & Spicer, B. (2011). How do Australian news media depict illicit drug issues? An analysis of print media reporting across and between illicit drugs, 2003–2008. *International Journal of Drug Policy*, *22*(4), 285–291. doi: 10.1016/j.drugpo.2011.05.008.

Hughes, C., Lodge, M., & Ritter, A. (2010). *Monograph No. 18: The Coordination of Australian Illicit Drug Policy: A Governance Perspective*. Sydney, NSW: National Drug and Alcohol Research Centre, University of New South Wales.

Hughes, C., Ritter, A., & Mabbitt, N. (2013). Drug policy coordination: identifying and assessing dimensions of coordination. *International Journal of Drug Policy*, *24*(3), 244–250. doi: 10.1016/j.drugpo.2012.08.004.

Huston, A. C. (2008). From research to policy and back. *Child Development*, *79*(1), 1–12. doi: 10.1111/j.1467-8624.2007.01107.x.

Hyder, A. A., Corluka, A., Winch, P. J., El-Shinnawy, A., Ghassany, H., Malekafzali, H., & Ghaffar, A. (2011). National policy makers speak out: are researchers giving them what they need? *Health Policy and Planning*, *26*(1), 73–82. doi: 10.1093/heapol/czq020.

Hyshka, E. (2009). Turning failure into success: what does the case of Western Australia tell us about Canadian cannabis policy-making? *Policy Studies*, *30*(5), 513–531. doi: 10.1080/01442870902899962.

INCB (2001). *Report of the International Narcotics Control Board for 2001*. Vienna: INCB.

Ingold, J., & Monaghan, M. (2016). Evidence translation: an actor-centred approach to analysing the evidence to policy connection. *Policy & Politics*, *44*(2), 171–190.

Inter-Ministerial Conference on Drugs (2010). *Gemeenschappelijke Verklaring van de Inter-Ministeriële Conferentie Drugs. Een Globaal en Geïntegreerd Drugsbeleid voor België*. Brussel: Inter-Ministeriële Conferentie Drugs.

International Drug Policy Consortium (2016). *The UNGASS on the World Drug Problem: Report of Proceedings*. London: IDPC.

Inter-parliamentary Advisory Council of the Benelux countries. (1998). *Het Drugsbeleid in de Benelux*. Brussel: Inter-parliamentary Advisory Council of the Benelux countries (5 November 1998).

Jack, S. M., Dobbins, M., Sword, W., Novotna, G., Brooks, S., Lipman, E. L., & Niccols, A. (2011). Evidence informed decision-making by professionals working in addiction agencies serving women. *Substance Abuse Treatment, Prevention, and Policy*, *7*(6), 1–13. doi: 10.1186/1747-597X-6-29.

Jacobson, N., Butteril, D., & Goering, P. (2003). Development of a framework for knowledge translation: understanding user context. *Journal of Health Services Research and Policy*, *8*(2), 94–99. doi: 10.1258/135581903321466067.

Jasanoff, S. (1990). *The Fifth Branch: Science Advisers as Policymakers*. Cambridge: Harvard University Press.

Jasanoff, S. (Ed.) (2006). *States of Knowledge. The Co-Production of Science and Social Order*. New York: Routledge.

Jelsma, M. (2008). *The Current State of Drug Policy Debate. Trends in the Last Decade in the EU and UN*. Amsterdam: TNI.

John, P. (2003). Is there life after policy streams, advocacy coalitions, and punctuations: using evolutionary theory to explain policy change? *The Policy Studies Journal*, *31*(4), 1–18. doi: 10.1111/1541-0072.00039.

Jørgensen, M., & Phillips, L. J. (2002). *Discourse Analysis as Theory and Method*. London: Sage Publication.

Kaminski, D. (1998). La directive du 17 avril 1998. La troisième voie ... entre la loi et le débat. *Les Cahiers de Prospective Jeunesse*, *3*(2), 3–6.

Kenis, P. (1997). *Drugs, Research Related Initiatives in the European Union: Synthesis Report (+General Conclusion)*. Lisbon: EMCDDA.

Kinable, H. (2002). *De Nieuwste Trends in het Secundair Onderwijs in Vlaanderen: Syntheserapport Leerlingenbevraging Schooljaar 2000–2001*. Brussel: VAD.

Kinable, H., Casselman, J., Todts, S., & Van Deun, P. (1994). *Drugsgebruikers en AIDS. AIDS-Risico-Gedrag bij Injecterende Drugsgebruikers en Evaluatie van een Preventief Project. Onderzoeksproject in het Kader van het Samenwerkingsakkoord Tussen het Nfwo, de Staat en de Gemeenschappen*. Brussel/Leuven Antwerpen: VAD/Katholieke Universiteit Leuven/Free Clinic.

Kingdon, J. W. (1995). *Agendas, Alternatives and Public Policies*. New York: Addison-Wesely Educational Publishers Inc.

Kingdon, J. W. (2002). *Agendas, Alternatives and Public Policies* (2nd edn). London: Longmans.

Kleiman, M., & Hawdon, J. (2011). *Encyclopedia of Drug Policy* (1st edn). Thousand Oaks: Sage.

Klein Haarhuis, C. M., Hagen, L. L. C., & Scheepmaker, M. P. C. (2009). *Toetsen en Verbinden: Over het WODC in de Tijd en de Relatie Tussen Onderzoek en Beleid in het Bijzonder*. Den Haag: Boom Juridische uitgevers.

Koninklijk besluit van 16 mei 2003 tot wijziging van het koninklijk besluit van 31 december 1930 omtrent de handel in slaap- en verdovende middelen alsmede van het koninklijk besluit van 22 januari 1998 tot reglementering van sommige psychotrope stoffen, teneinde daarin bepalingen in te voegen met betrekking tot risicobeperking en therapeutisch advies, en tot wijziging van het koninklijk besluit van 26 oktober 1993 houdende maatregelen om te voorkomen dat bepaalde stoffen worden misbruikt voor de illegale vervaardiging van verdovende middelen en psychotrope stoffen, *B.S.* 2 juni 2003.

Krastev, I. (2000). Post-communist think tanks: making and faking influence. In D. Stone (Ed.), *Banking on Knowledge: the Genesis of the Global Development Network* (pp. 273–291). London: Routledge.

Kraus, L., & Korf, D. (Eds.) (2005). *Research on Drugs and Drug Policy From a European Perspective.* Lengerich: Pabst Science Publishers.

Kraus, L., Augustin, R., Frischler, M., Kümmler, P., Uhl, A., Wiessing, L. (2003). Estimating prevalence of problem drug use at national level in countries of the European Union and Norway. *Addiction*, *98*(4), 471–85. doi: 10.1046/j.1360-0443.2003.00326.x.

Kübler, D. (2001). Understanding policy change with the advocacy coalition framework: an application to Swiss drug policy. *Journal of European Public Policy*, *8*(4), 623–641. doi: 10.1080/13501760110064429.

Lackey, R. T. (2007). Science, scientists, and policy advocacy. *Conservation Biology*, *21*(1), 12–17. doi: 10.1111/j.1523-1739.2006.00639.x.

Lampinen, O. (1992). *The Utilization of Social Science Research in Public Policy.* Helsinki: VAPK-publishing.

Lancaster, K. (2014). Social construction and the evidence-based drug policy endeavour. *International Journal of Drug Policy*, *25*(5), 948–951. doi: 10.1016/j.drugpo.2014.01.002.

Lancaster, K. (2016). Performing the Evidence-Based Drug Policy Paradigm. *Contemporary Drug Problems*, *43*(2), 142–153. doi: 10.1177/0091450916633306.

Lancaster, K., & Ritter, A. (2014). Making change happen: a case study of the successful establishment of a peer-administered naloxone program in one Australian jurisdiction. *International Journal of Drug Policy*, *25*(5), 985–91. doi: 10.1016/j.drugpo.2014.02.003.

Lancaster, K., Hughes, C. E., Spicer, B., Matthew-Simmons, F., & Dillon, P. (2010). *Curiosity Killed the M-Cat: An Examination of Illicit Drugs and the Media.* Paper presented at the Australian and New Zealand Critical Criminology Conference, Sydney.

Lancaster, K., Hughes, C. E., Spicer, B., Matthew-Simmons, F., & Dillon, P. (2011). Illicit drugs and the media: models of media effects for use in drug policy research. *Drug and Alcohol Review*, *30*(4), 397–402. doi: 10.1111/j.1465-3362.2010.00239.x.

Lancaster, K., Ritter, A., & Stafford, J. (2013). Public opinion and drug policy in Australia: engaging the affected community. *Drug & Alcohol Review*, *32*(1), 60–66. doi: 10.1111/j.1465-3362.2012.00497.x.

Landry, R., Amara, N., & Lamari, M. (1999). *Climbing the Ladder of Research Utilization: Evidence From Social Science Research.* Paper presented at the Annual meeting of the Society for Social Studies of Science, San Diego.

Landry, R., Amara, N., & Lamari, M. (2001). Utilization of social science research knowledge in Canada. *Research Policy*, *30*(2), 333–349. doi: 10.1016/S0048-7333(00)00081-0.

Landry, R., Lamari, M., & Amara, N. (2003). Extent and determinants of utilization of university research in government agencies. *Public Administration Review*, *63*(2), 193-205.

Lasswell, H. D. (1951). The policy orientation. In D. Lerner and H. D. Lasswell (Eds.), *The Policy Sciences* (pp. 3–15). Stanford, CA: Stanford University Press.

Lavis, J. N., Robertson, D., Woodside, J. M., McLeod, C. B., & Abelson, J. (2003). How can research organizations more effectively transfer research knowledge to decision makers? *The Milbank Quarterly*, *81*(2), 221–248. doi: 10.1111/1468-0009.t01-1-00052.

Leiden, W. R. (1995). The role of interest groups in policy formulation. *Washington Law Review*, *70*(1), 715–724.

Lenton, S. (2004). Pot, politics and the press-reflections on cannabis law reform in Western Australia. *Drug and Alcohol Review*, *23*(2), 223–233. doi: 10.1080/09595230410001704226.

Lenton, S. (2007). *Beyond Modelling and Evidence: Bridging the Gap Between Drug Policy Research and Drug Policy Practice.* Paper presented at the First Annual Conference of the International Society for the Study of Drug Policy, Oslo.

Lenton, S., & Allsop, S. (2010). A tale of CIN-the Cannabis Infringement Notice scheme in Western Australia. *Addiction*, *105*(5), 808–816. doi: 10.1111/j.1360-0443.2010.02913.x.

Lenton, S., & Single, E. (1998). The definition of harm reduction. *Drug and Alcohol Review*, *17*(2), 213–219. doi: 10.1080/09595239800187011.

Lester, J. P. (1993). The utilization of policy analysis by state agency officials. *Knowledge: Creation, Diffusion, Utilization*, *14*(3), 267–290. doi: 10.1177/107554709301400301.

Levine, G. H. (2003). Global drug prohibition: its uses and crises. *International Journal of Drug Policy*, *14*(2), 145–153. doi: 10.1016/S0955-3959(03)00003-3.

Lindblom, C. E. (1959). Science of 'muddling through'. *Public Administration Review*, *19*(2), 79–88.

Lindquist, E. A. (2001). *Discerning Policy Influence: Framework for a Strategic Evaluation of IDRC-Supported Research.* Ottawa: IDRC Evaluation Unit.

Littig, B. (2009). Interviewing the Elite – interviewing experts. Is there a difference? In A. Bogner, B. Littig, & W. Menz (Eds.), *Interviewing Experts. Research Methods Series* (pp. 98–116). New York: Palgrave Macmillan.

Loader, I., & Sparks, R. (2010). What is to be done with public criminology? *Criminology & Public Policy*, *9*(4), 771–781. doi: 10.1111/j.1745-9133.2010.00669.x.

Loader, I., & Sparks, R. (2011). *Public Criminology?* New York: Routledge.

Lomas, J. (2000). Using 'linkage and exchange' to move research into policy at a Canadian foundation. *Health Affairs*, *19*(3), 236–240. doi: 10.1377/hlthaff.19.3.236.

Luypaert, H., Françoise, C., Beyens, K., Kaminski, D., & Janssens, C. (2007). *Werken en Leren als Straf: een Onderzoek Naar de Uitvoering van Werkstraffen en Leermaatregelen in België.* Brussel: VUB Press.

MacCoun, R. J., & Reuter, P. (1997). Interpreting Dutch cannabis policy: reasoning by analogy in the legalization debate. *Science*, *278*(5335), 47–52.

MacCoun, R. J., & Reuter, P. (2001). *Drug War Heresies: Learning From Other Vices, Times, and Places.* Cambridge: Cambridge University Press.

MacGregor, S. (2011). The impact of research on policy in the drug field. *Methodological Innovations Online*, 6(1), 41–57. doi: 10.4256/mio.2010.0027.

MacGregor, S. (2012a). *Barriers to the Influence of Evidence on Policy: Are Politicians the Problem?* Paper presented at the Sixth International Society for the Study of Drug Policy, Canterbury.

MacGregor, S. (2012b). Parliamentary committees and drug policy governance. In S. MacGregor, N. McKeganey, & M. Monaghan (Eds.), *Essays on the Governance of Drug Policy* (pp. 5–32). London: UK Drug Policy Commission.

MacGregor, S. (2013). Barriers to the influence of evidence on policy: are politicians the problem? *Drugs: Education, Prevention, and Policy, 20*(3), 225–233. doi: 10.3109/09687637.2012.754403.

MacGregor, S. (2016). *A Critical Discussion of Kingdon's Approach to Policy Analysis: Three Moments of Shifting Policy in English Drugs Policy.* Paper presented at the Tenth Annual Conference of the International Society for the Study of Drug Policy, Sydney.

MacGregor, S., Singleton, N., & Trautmann, F. (2014). Towards good governance in drug policy: evidence, stakeholders and politics. *International Journal of Drug Policy, 25*(5), 931–934. doi: 10.1016/j.drugpo.2014.06.017.

Macleod, J., & Hickman, M. (2010). How ideology shapes the evidence and the policy: what do we know about cannabis use and what should we do? *Addiction, 105*(8), 1326–1330. doi: 10.1111/j.1360-0443.2009.02846.x.

MacMillan, K. (2005). More than just coding? Evaluating CAQDAS in a discourse analysis of news texts. *Forum: Qualitative Social Research, 6*(3), 25.

Mahieu, W. (2004). Drugs: opschorting, uitstel en probatie. *OSS, 45* (4 februari 2004), 19–29.

Mahieu, W. (2005). Drugs: wetgeving. *OSS, 49* (1 juli 2005), 97–106.

Maillé, M., Saint-Charles, J., & Lucotte, M. (2010). The gap between scientists and journalists: the case of mercury science in Québec's press. *Public Understanding of Science, 19*(1), 70–79. doi: 10.1177/0963662509102690.

Marston, G., & Watts, R. (2003). Tampering with the evidence: a critical appraisal of evidence-based policy-making. *The Drawing Board: an Australian Review of Public Affairs, 3*(3), 143–163.

Marteache, N. (2013). The role of public opinion in criminal justice policy making. *Newsletter of the European Society of Criminology, 12*(3), 17–21.

Matthew-Simmons, F. T. (2011). *Public Opinion, the Media, and Illicit Drug Policy* (PhD). Sydney: University of New South Wales.

Matthew-Simmons, F., Sunderland, M., & Ritter, A. (2013). Exploring the existence of drug policy 'ideologies' in Australia. *Drugs: Education, Prevention, and Policy, 20*(3), 258–267. doi: 10.3109/09687637.2012.755494.

Mautner, G. (2008). Analyzing newspapers, magazines and other print media. In R. Wodak & R. Krzyzanowski (Eds.), *Qualitative Discourse Analysis in the Social Sciences* (pp. 30–51). New York: Palgrave Macmillan.

McArthur, M. (1999). Pushing the drug debate: the media's role in policy reform. *Australian Journal of Social Issues, 34*(2), 149–165.

McCann, E. J. (2008). Expertise, truth, and urban policy mobilities: global circuits of knowledge in the development of Vancouver, Canada's 'four pillar' drug strategy. *Environment and Planning, 40*(4), 885–904. doi: 10.1068/a38456.

McCombs, M. E., & Reynolds, A. (2009). How the news shapes our civic agenda. In J. Bryant & M. B. Oliver (Eds.), *Media Effects: Advances in Theory and Research* (pp. 1–16). New York: Routledge.

McCombs, M. E., & Shaw, D. L. (1972). The agenda-setting function of mass media. *The Public Opinion Quarterly*, *36*(2), 176–187. doi: 10.1086/267990.

McLaughlin, E., & Muncie, J. (2013). *The Sage Dictionary of Criminology*. Thousand Oaks: Sage.

McNeill, F., Farrall, S., Lightowler, C., & Maruna, S. (2012). Re-examining evidence-based practice in community corrections: beyond 'a confined view' of what works. *Justice Research and Policy*, *14*(1), 35–60. doi: 10.3818/JRP.14.1.2012.35.

McQuillan, J., & Tse, L. (1996). Does research matter? An analysis of media: opinion on bilingual education, 1984–1994. *The Bilingual Research Journal*, *20*(1), 1–27.

Memorandum Group (1999). *Beleidsmemorandum Belgische Drughulpverlening en Preventie*. Brussels: Memorandum Group.

Memorandum Group (2003). *Memorandum I.V.M. Drugproblematiek (2003–2006)*. Brussels: Memorandum Group.

Miller, D. (1999). Risk, science and policy: definitional struggles, information management, the media and BSE. *Social Science & Medicine*, *49*(9), 1239–1255. doi: 10.1016/S0277-9536(99)00163-X.

Miller, W. R., Sorensen, J. L., Selzer, J. A., & Brigham, G. S. (2006). Disseminating evidence-based practices in substance abuse treatment: A review with suggestions. *Journal of Substance Abuse Treatment*, *31*(1), 25–39. doi: 10.1016/j.jsat.2006.03.005.

Ministerial Circular Letter of 26 May 1993 of the Minister of Justice and the College of General Prosecutors.

Ministerial Circular Letter of 8 May 1998, nr. COL 5/98, of the Minister of Justice and the College of General Prosecutors.

Ministry of Public Health of Belgium (2002). *Joint International Effort at the Initiative of the Ministers of Public Health of Belgium, France, Germany, The Netherlands, Switzerland. Technical Report of the International Scientific Conference Brussels, Belgium, 25/2/2002*. Brussels: Ministry of Public Health of Belgium.

Mitton, G., Adair, C. E., McKenzie, E., Patten, S. B., & Perry, B. V. (2007). Knowledge transfer and exchange: review and synthesis of the literature. *The Milbank Quarterly*, *85*(4), 729–768. doi: 10.1111/j.1468-0009.2007.00506.x.

Monaghan, M. (2008a). *The Turmoil of Evidence: Research Utilisation in UK Drug Classification*. (PhD), University of Leeds, Leeds.

Monaghan, M. (2008b). The evidence base in UK drug policy: the new rules of engagement. *Policy & Politics*, *36*(1), 145–150. doi: 10.1332/030557308783431643.

Monaghan, M. (2009). The complexity of evidence: reflections on research utilization in a heavily politicised policy area. *Social Policy and Society*, *9*(1), 1–12. doi: 10.1017/S1474746409990157.

Monaghan, M. (2011). *Evidence Versus Politics. Exploiting Research in UK Drug Policy Making?* Bristol: Policy Press.

Monaghan, M. (2014). Drug policy governance in the UK: lessons from changes to and debates concerning the classification of cannabis under the 1971 Misuse of Drugs Act. *International Journal of Drug Policy*, *25*(5), 1025–1030. doi: 10.1016/j.drugpo.2014.02.001.

Monaghan, M., Pawson, R., & Wicker, K. (2012). The precautionary principle and evidence-based policy. *Evidence & Policy: A Journal of Research, Debate and Practice*, *8*(2), 171–191. doi: 10.1332/174426412X640072.
Montuschi, E. (2009). Questions of evidence in evidence-based policy. *Axiomathes*, *19*(4), 425–439. doi: 10.1007/s10516-009-9085-0.
Moore, D. (2008). Erasing pleasure from public discourse on illicit drugs: on the creation and reproduction of an absence. *International Journal of Drug Policy*, *19*(5), 353–358. doi: 10.1016/j.drugpo.2007.07.004.
Mosher, C. J., & Akins, S. (2007). *Drugs and Drug Policy: The Control of Consciousness Alteration*. Thousand Oaks: Sage.
Muscat, R. (2008). *From a Policy on Illegal Drugs to a Policy on Psychoactive Substances*. Strasbourg: Council of Europe Publishing.
Muscat, R., & Pike, B. (2012), *Reflections on the Concept of Coherency for a Policy on Psychoactive Substances and Beyond*. Strasbourg: Council of Europe Publishing.
Musto, D. F., & Sloboda, Z. (2003). The influence of epidemiology on drug control policy. *UNODC Bulletin Narcotics*, *55*(1), 9–22.
Nathanson, C. A. (2009). *Disease Prevention as Social Change. The State, Society, and Public Health in the United States, France, Great Britain, and Canada*. New York: Russell Sage Foundation.
National Center for the Dissemination of Disability Research. (1996). *A Review of the Literature on Dissemination and Knowledge Utilization*. Austin: National Center for the Dissemination of Disability Research.
Naughton, M. (2005). 'Evidence-based policy' and the government of the criminal justice system – only if the evidence fits! *Critical Social Policy*, *25*(1), 47–69. doi: 10.1177/0261018305048967.
Neal, S., & McLaughlin, E. (2009). Researching up? Interviews, emotionality and policy-making elites. *Journal of Social Policy*, *38*(4), 689–707. doi: 10.1017/S0047279409990018.
Neilson, S. (2001). *IDRC-Supported Research and its Influence on Public Policy. Knowledge Utilization and Public Policy Processes: a Literature Review*. Ottawa: IDRC Evaluation Unit.
Nelen, H. (2008). *Evidence Maze; het Doolhof van het Evaluatieonderzoek*. Maastricht: Oce-Nederland BV.
Nelen, H. (2010a). Verstrikt in het evidence-based web. *Panopticon*, *31*(3), 72–83.
Nelen, J. M. (2010b). *Gelet op de Wet, de Evaluatie van Strafwetgeving Onder de Loep*. Amsterdam: Vrije Universiteit Amsterdam.
Niemeijer, B. (2009). De ontwikkeling van criminologisch onderzoek voor beleid en praktijk. *Tijdschrift voor Criminologie*, *51*(2), 154–174.
Nilunger Mannheimer, L., Lehto, J., & Östlin, P. (2007). Window of opportunity for intersectoral health policy in Sweden – open, half-open or half-shut? *Health Promotion International*, 22(4), 307–315. doi: 10.1093/heapro/dam028.
Nutley, S. (2003). *Bridging the Policy/Research Divide. Reflections and Lessons from the UK*. Paper presented at the Facing the future: engaging stakeholders and citizens in developing public policy, National Institute of Governance Conference, Canberra.
Nutley, S., Morton, S., Jung, T., & Boaz, A. (2010). Evidence and policy in six European countries: diverse approaches and common challenges. *Evidence & Policy*, *6*(2), 131–144. doi: 10.1332/174426410X502275.

Nutley, S., Walter, I., & Davies, H. T. O. (2003). From knowing to doing. A framework for understanding the evidence-into-practice agenda. *Evaluation*, *9*(2), 125–148. doi: 10.1177/1356389003009002002.

Nutley, S., Walter, I., & Davies, H. T. O. (2007). *Using Evidence: How Research can Inform Public Services*. Bristol: The Policy Press.

O'Gorman, A., Quigley, E., Zobel, F., & Moore, K. (2014). Peer, professional, and public: an analysis of the drugs policy advocacy community in Europe. *International Journal of Drug Policy*, *25*(5), 1001–1006. doi: 10.1016/j.drugpo.2014.04.020.

O'Malley, P. (2002). Globalizing risk? Distinguishing styles of neo-liberal criminal justice in Australia and the USA. *Criminology and Criminal Justice*, 2(2), 205–222. doi: 10.1177/17488958020020020501.

Obama, B. (2009). *Inaugural Address*, transcript, 20 January 2009.

O'Dwyer, L. (2004). *A Critical Review of Evidence-Based Policy Making*. Melbourne: Australian Housing and Urban Research Institute.

Oh, C. H. (1997). Issues for the new thinking of knowledge utilization: introductory remarks. *Knowledge and Policy*, *10*(3), 3–10.

Oliver, K., Innvar, S., Lorenc, T., Woodman, J., & Thomas, J. (2014). A systematic review of barriers to and facilitators of the use of evidence by policy makers. *BMC Health Services Research*, *14*(2), 1–12. doi: 10.1186/1472-6963-14-2.

Olsson, B. (2009). *Dressed for Success?* Paper presented at the Fourth International Society for the Study of Drug Policy, Santa Monica.

Ottoson, J. M., & Hawe, P. (Eds.) (2009). *Knowledge Utilization, Diffusion, Implementation, Transfer and Translation: Implications for Evaluation*. San Francisco: Jossey-Bass.

Parker, H. (2001). *UK Drugs Unlimited: New Research and Policy Lessons on Illicit Drug Use*. Houndmills: Palgrave.

Parker, H., Aldridge, J., & Measham, F. (1998). *Illegal Leisure: The Normalisation of Adolescent Recreational Drug Use*. London: Routledge.

Parl.St. Kamer, 1996–1997, 1062/1–3.

Parl.St. Kamer 1997–1998, nr. 1571/1.

Parl.St. Senaat 2000–2001, nr. 2–585/1.

Parl.St. Kamer 2001–2002, nr. 1888/001 and nr. 1889/01.

Patesson, R., & Steinberg, P. (2000). *Enquête Fondation Rodin, Drogue 2000, Le Soir, ULB sur les Belges et les Drogues: Rapport Concernant les Resultats de l'Enquête*. Bruxelles: ULB.

Pawson, R. (2006). *Evidence Based Policy: A Realist Perspective*. London: Sage.

Pearce, W. (2014). Scientific data and its limits: rethinking the use of evidence in local climate change policy. *Evidence & Policy*, *10*(2), 187–203. doi: 10.1332/174426514X13990326347801.

Petersilia, J. (2008). Influencing public policy: an embedded criminologist reflects on California prison reform. *Journal of Experimental Criminology*, 4(4), 335–356. doi: 10.1007/s11292-008-9060-6.

Pompidou Group (2011). *Policy Paper Providing Guidance to Policy Makers for Developing Coherent Policies for Licit and Illicit Drugs*. Strasbourg: Council of Europe Publishing.

Porter, R. W., & Hicks, I. (1995). *Knowledge Utilization and the Process of Policy Formation: Toward a Framework for Africa*. Washington: U.S. Agency for International Development.

Pryce, S. (2012). *Fixing Drugs: the Politics of Drug Prohibition*. Basingstoke: Palgrave Macmillan.
Radaelli, C. M. (1995). The role of knowledge in the policy process. *Journal of European Public Policy*, 2(2), 159–183. doi: 10.1080/13501769508406981.
Reed, R. (2001). (Un-)Professional discourse? Journalists' and scientists' stories about science in the media. *Journalism*, 2(3), 279–298. doi: 10.1177/146488490100200310.
Reimer, B., Sawka, E., & James, D. (2005). Improving research transfer in the addictions field: a perspective from Canada. *Substance Use & Misuse*, *40*(11), 1707–1720. doi: 10.1080/10826080500224533.
Reinarman, C., & Levine, H. (1997). Crack in context: America's latest demon drug. In C. Reinarman & H. Levine (Eds.), *Crack in America: Demon Drugs and Social Justice* (pp. 1–17). Berkeley: University of California Press.
Reuter, P. (1993). Prevalence estimation and policy formulation. *Journal of Drug Issues*, *23*(2), 167–184. doi: 10.1177/002204269302300203.
Reuter, P. (2011). Assessing global drug problems, policies and reform proposals. In G. Hunt, M. Milhet, & H. Bergeron, *Drugs and Culture: Knowledge, Consumption, and Policy* (pp. 225–240). Burlington: Ashgate.
Rhodes, R. (2000). Governance and public administration. In J. Pierre (Ed.), *Debating Governance: Authority, Steering and Democracy* (pp. 36–54). Oxford: Oxford Press.
Rich, R. F. (1997). Measuring knowledge utilization: processes and outcomes. *Knowledge and Policy*, *10*(3), 11–24. doi: 10.1007/BF02912504.
Rich, R. F. (2001). *Social Science Information and Public Policy Making*. New Jersey: Transaction Publishers.
Richardson, C. (2013). Knowledge-sharing through social interaction in a policy-driven industrial cluster. *Journal of Entrepreneurship and Public Policy*, 2(2), 2045–2101. doi: 10.1108/JEPP-08-2011-0010.
Rist, R. C. (1981). On the utility of ethnographic research for the policy process. *Urban Education*, *15*(4), 485–494.
Ritter, A. (2009). How do drug policy makers access research evidence? *International Journal of Drug Policy*, *20*(1), 70–75. doi: 10.1016/j.drugpo.2007.11.017.
Ritter, A. (2011). The role of research evidence in drug policy development in Australia. *Politicka Misao*, *48*(5), 141–156.
Ritter, A., & Bammer, G. (2010). Models of policy-making and their relevance for drug research. *Drug and Alcohol Review*, *29*(4), 353–357. doi: 10.1111/j.1465-3362.2009.00155.x.
Ritter, A., & Lancaster, K. (2013). Measuring research influence on drug policy: a case example of two epidemiological monitoring systems. *International Journal of Drug Policy*, *24*(1), 30–37. doi: 10.1016/j.drugpo.2012.02.005.
Ritter, A., & McDonald, D. (2008). Illicit drug policy: scoping the interventions and taxonomies. *Drugs: Education, Prevention and Policy*, *15*(1), 15–35. doi: 10.1080/09687630701204344.
Ritter, A., Bammer, G., Hamilton, M., & Mazerolle, L. (2007). Effective drug policy: a new approach demonstrated in the Drug Modelling Program. *Drug and Alcohol Review*, *26*(3), 265–271. doi: 10.1080/09595230701247665.

Ritter, A., Livingston, M., Chalmers, J., Berends, L., & Reuter, P. (2016). Comparative policy analysis for alcohol and drugs: current state of the field. *International Journal of Drug Policy*, *31*(2), 39–50. doi: 10.1016/j.drugpo.2016.02.004.

Rock, P. (2010). Comment on "public criminologies". *Criminology & Public Policy*, *9*(4), 751–767. doi: 10.1111/j.1745-9133.2010.00667.x.

Roe, E. M. (1991). Development narratives, or making the best of blueprint development. *World Development*, *19*(4), 287–300. doi: 10.1016/0305-750X(91)90177-J.

Room, R. (2005). Symbolism and rationality in the politics of psychoactive substances. In B. Lindgren & M. Grossman (Eds.), *Substance Use: Individual Behaviour, Social Interactions, Markets and Politics* (pp. 331–346). Amsterdam: Elsevier.

Room, R., Fischer, B., Hall, W. D., Lenton, S., & Reuter, P. (2010). *Cannabis policy: moving beyond stalemate*. New York: Oxford University Press.

Roose, N. (2002). Therapeutisch advies: hoe zit het nu? Standpunt van de hulpverlenings- en welzijnssector. *VAD-berichten*, *2*(2), 7–8.

Rossi, C. (2002). A critical reading of the World Drug Report. *International Journal of Drug Policy*, *13*(3), 225–235. doi: 10.1016/S0955-3959(02)00074-9.

Rudd, K. (2008). Address to Heads of Agencies and Members of Senior Executive Service, Great Hall, Parliament House, Canberra, April (www.pm.gov.au/media/Speech/2008/speech_0226.cfm).

Ruggiero, V. (2012). How public is public criminology? *Crime, Media & Culture*, *8*(2), 151–160. doi: 10.1177/1741659012444432.

Ryan, K. F. (1998). Clinging to failure: the rise and continued life of US drug policy. *Law and Society*, *32*(1), 221–242. doi: 10.2307/827753.

Sabatier, P. A. (1998). The advocacy coalition framework: revisions and relevance for Europe. *Journal of European Public Policy*, *5*(1), 98–130. doi: 10.1080/13501768880000051.

Sabatier, P. A. (1999). Fostering the development of policy theory. In P. A. Sabatier (Ed.), *Theories of the Policy Process* (pp. 261–275). Boulder: Westview.

Sackett, D., Rosenberg, W., Gray, J. A., Haynes, R. B., & Richardson, W. S. (1996). Evidence-based medicine: what it is and what it isn't. *British Medical Journal*, *312*(7032), 71–72. doi: 10.1136/bmj.312.7023.71.

Sanderson, I. (2009). Intelligent policy making for a complex world. *Political Studies*, *57*(4), 699–719. doi: 10.1111/j.1467-9248.2009.00791.x.

Santisteban, D., Vega, R. R., & Suarez-Morales, L. (2006). Utilizing dissemination findings to help understand and bridge the research and practice gap in the treatment of substance abuse disorders in Hispanic populations. *Drug and Alcohol Dependence*, *84*(1), 94–101. doi: 10.1016/j.drugalcdep. 2006.05.011.

Scheufele, D. A., & Tewksbury, D. (2007). Framing, agenda setting and priming: the evolution of three media effects models. *Journal of Communication*, *57*(1), 9–20. doi: 10.1111/j.0021-9916.2007.00326.x.

Scholten, P. (2011). Constructing Dutch immigrant policy. Research-policy relations and immigrant integration in the Netherland. *British Journal of Politics and International Relations*, *13*(1), 75–92. doi: 10.1111/j.1467-856X.2010.00440.x.

Seddon, T., Ralphs, R., & Williams, L. (2008). Risk, security and the 'criminalization' of British drug policy. *British Journal of Criminology*, *48*(6), 818–834. doi: 10.1093/bjc/azn056.

Shapiro, H. (1999). Dances with drugs: pop music, drugs and youth culture. In N. South (Ed.), *Drugs: Cultures, Controls and Everyday Life* (pp. 17–35). London: Sage.

Singleton, N., & Rubin, J. (2014). What is good governance in the context of drug policy? *International Journal of Drug Policy*, *25*(5), 935–941. doi: 10.1016/j.drugpo.2014.03.008.

Singleton, N., Stevens, A., Ochoa, J. F., & Feilding, A. (2014). *Developing a Framework for Analysing the Impact of Different Regulatory Approaches.* Paper presented at the Eighth Annual conference of the International Society for the Study of Drug Policy, Rome.

Smet, V. (2013). *Sociaal-Wetenschappelijk Onderzoek en Beleid. Een Analyse van de Interactie, Kennisgebruik en Doorwerking in Belgie en Vlaanderen.* Den Haag: Boom Lemma Uitgevers.

Smith, A. (2015). Mind-altering discourse: experts and sources in the news on the UK drug policy reform debate. *Journal of Promotional Communications*, *3*(2), 261–267.

Smith, K. (2006). Problematising power relations in 'elite' interviews. *Geoforum*, *37*(4), 643–653. doi: 10.1016/j.geoforum.2005.11.002.

Smith, K. (2010). Research, policy and funding – academic treadmills and the squeeze on intellectual spaces. *British Journal of Sociology*, *61*(1), 176–195. doi: 10.1111/j.1468-4446.2009.01307.x.

Snertingdal, M., & Basberg Neuman, C. (2010). *Resisting Complexity; Evidence Based Knowledge and the Neglect of Practice.* Paper presented at the 21st Annual Conference of the European Society for Social Drug Research, Dubrovnik.

Sorian, R., & Baugh, T. (2002). Power of information: closing the gap between research and policy. *Health Affairs*, *21*(2), 264–273. doi: 10.1377/hlthaff.21.2.264.

Sorrell, S. (2007). Improving the evidence base for energy policy: the role of systematic reviews. *Energy Policy*, *35*(3), 1858–1871. doi: 10.1016/j.enpol.2006.06.008.

Souchon, A. L., & Dianmantopoulos, A. (1994). A conceptual framework of expert marketing information use: key issues and research propositions. *Journal of international marketing*, *4*(1), 49–71.

South, N. (1999). *Drugs: Cultures, Controls and Everyday Life.* London: Sage.

Standring, A. (2016). A constructivist critique of evidence based drug policy – from depoliticized governance to political metagovernance. In A. O'Gorman, G. Potter & J. Fountain (Eds.), *Evidence in Social Drug Research and Drug Policy* (pp. 33–50). Lengerich: Pabst Science Publishers.

Stevens, A. (2007a). Survival of the ideas that fit: an evolutionary analogy for the use of evidence in policy. *Social Policy & Society*, *6*(1), 25–35. doi: 10.1017/S1474746406003319.

Stevens, A. (2007b). When two dark figures collide: Evidence and discourse on drug-related crime. *Critical Social Policy*, *27*(1), 77–99. doi: 10.1177/0261018307072208.

Stevens, A. (2011). *Drugs Crime and Public Health: The Political Economy of Drug Policy.* London: Routledge.

Stevens, A., & Measham, F. (2014). The 'drug policy ratchet': why do sanctions for new psychoactive drugs typically only go up? *Addiction*, *109*(8), 1226–1132. doi: 10.1111/add.12406.

Stevens, A., & Rhodes, T. (2011). Sociological approaches to the study of drug use and drug policy. *International Journal of Drug Policy*, *22*(6), 399–403. doi: 10.1016/j.drugpo.2011.10.003.

Stevens, A., & Ritter, A. (2013). How can and do empirical studies influence drug policies? Narratives and complexity in the use of evidence in policy making. *Drugs: Education Prevention and Policy*, *20*(3), 169–174. doi: 10.3109/09687637.2013.793892.

Stimson, G. V. (1997). *Estimating the prevalence of problem drug use in Europe*. Luxembourg: EMCDDA.

Stone, D. (2001). *Getting Research Into Policy?* Paper presented at the Third Annual Global Development Network Conference on 'Blending Local and Global Knowledge', Rio De Janeiro.

Stone, D., & Maxwell, S. (Eds.) (2005). *Global Knowledge Networks and International Development*. New York: Routledge.

Storbjörk, J. (2014). A study of a Swedish treatment policy reform proposal. In D. Korf (Ed.), *Snapshots of Social Drug Research in Europe* (pp. 57–59). Lengerich: Pabst Publishers.

Strang, J., Babor, T., Caulkins, J., Fischer, B., Foxcroft, D., & Humphreys, K. (2012). Drug policy and the public good: evidence for effective interventions. *The Lancet*, *379*(1), 71–83. doi: 10.1016/S0140-6736(11)61674-7.

Strassheim, H., & Kettunen, P. (2014). When does evidence-based policy turn into policy-based evidence? Configurations, contexts and mechanisms. *Evidence & Policy*, *10*(2), 259–277. doi: 10.1332/174426514X13990433991320.

Sutton, R. (1999). *The Policy Process: an Overview (Working Paper 118)*. London: Overseas Development Institute.

Swanborn, P. G. (2003). *Case-Study. Wat, Wanneer en Hoe?* Amsterdam: Boom Onderwijs.

Szarka, J. (2004). Wind power, discourse coalitions and climate change: breaking the stalemate. *European Environment*, *14*(6), 317–330. doi: 10.1002/eet.367.

Sznitman, S., Lewis, N., & Taubman, D. (2014). Analysing Twitter as an opportunity to understand substance use. In G. R. Potter, M. Wauters, & J. Fountain (Eds.), *Change and Continuity: Researching Evolving Drug Landscapes in Europe* (pp. 103–122). Lengerich: Pabst Publishers.

Taylor, S. J. (2008). Outside the outsiders: media representations of drug use. *Journal of Community and Criminal Justice*, *55*(4), 369–387. doi: 10.1177/0264550508096493.

Thomas, S. (2009). Newspapers on education policy: constructing an authorative public voice on education. In R. Fitzgerald & W. Housley (Eds.), *Media, Policy and Interaction* (pp. 205–223). Farnham: Ashgate Publishing Limited.

Todts, S. (2004). De drugwet en de hulpverlening: lat-relatie of shotgun wedding? *Orde van de dag*, *26*(7), 5–18.

Tonry, M. (1995). *Malign Neglect: Race, Crime, and Punishment in America (1st Edition)*. New York: Oxford University Press.

Tonry, M. (2010). 'Public criminology' and evidence-based policy. *Criminology & Public Policy*, *9*(4), 783–797. doi: 10.1111/j.1745-9133.2010.00670.x.

Tops, D. (2001). *A Society With or Without Drugs? Continuity and Change in Drug Policies in Sweden and the Netherlands*. Lund: Lunds Universitet.

Torfing, J. (1999). *New Theories of Discourse: Laclau, Mouffe and Žiézek.* Oxford: Blackwell.

Uggen, C., & Inderbitzin, M. (2010). 'Public criminologies'. *Criminology & Public Policy*, *9*(4), 725–750. doi: 10.1111/j.1745-9133.2010.00666.x.

UKDPC. (2012). *How to Make Drug Policy Better: Key Findings from UKDPC Research into Drug Policy Governance.* London: UK Drug Policy Commission.

UNGASS. (1998). *UNGASS Resolutions on the World Drug Problem.* New York: United Nations General Assembly.

UNGASS. (2016). *Our Joint Commitment to Effectively Addressing and Countering the World Drug Problem.* New York: United Nations General Assembly.

United Nations. (1961). *Single Convention on Narcotic Drugs.* Vienna: UNODC.

United Nations. (1971). *United Nations Convention on Psychotropic Substances.* Vienna: UNODC.

United Nations. (1988). *United Nations Convention Against the Illicit Traffic in Narcotic Drugs and Psychotropic Substances.* Vienna: UNODC.

UNODC. (2008). *Drug Policy and Results in Australia.* UNODC: Vienna.

VAD. (2003). *Jaarverslag van 2002 van de Druglijn.* Brussel: VAD.

VAD. (2004). *Jaarverslag van 2003 van de Druglijn.* Brussel: VAD.

VAD. (2014). *Probleemverkennende nota cannabisbeleid VAD.* Brussel: VAD.

Van der Hulst, M. (2010). *Het Federale Parlement. Organisatie en Werking.* Kortrijk: UGA Publishers.

Van Dijk, T. A. (2003). Critical discourse analysis. In D. Schiffrin, D. Tannen, & H. E. Hamilton (Eds.), *The Handbook of Discourse Analysis* (pp. 85–109). Cornwall: Blackwell Publishing.

Van Eijk, D. L., & Hartkamp, J. P. (1992). Van zwarte schapen en vreemde eenden. Een verhandeling over de positie van het WODC. *Justitiële Verkenningen*, *18*(3), 90–118.

Van Hout, M., & Brennan, R. (2011). Plant food for thought: a qualitative study of mephedrone use in Ireland. *Drugs: Education, Prevention & Policy*, *18*(5), 371–381. doi: 10.3109/09687637.2010.537713.

Van Swaaningen, R. (2001). Kritische criminologie. In E. Lissenberg, S. Van Ruller, & R. Van Swaaningen (Eds.), *Tegen de Regels IV* (pp. 251–271). Nijmegen: Ars Aequi Libri.

Van Swaaningen, R. (2009). De criminoloog, het publieke debat en het beleid. In W. Bruggeman, E. De Wree, J. Goethals, P. Ponsaers, P. Van Calster, T. Vander Beken, & G. Vermeulen (Eds.), *Van Pionier Naar Onmisbaar. Over 30 Jaar Panopticon* (pp. 577–588). Antwerpen: Maklu.

Vande Walle, G. (2010). De plaats en betekenis van evaluatieonderzoek in de interbestuurlijke veiligheids- en preventieplannen. *Panopticon*, *31*(3), 40–57.

Vander Laenen, F. (2001). *The Drug and Cannabis Policy of the City of Ghent, Belgium.* Paper presented at the European City Conference on Cannabis Policy, Utrecht.

Vander Laenen, F., & Dhont, F. (2003). Zalven en slaan: een eerste analyse van de nieuwe drugwetgeving. *Tijdschrift voor Strafrecht*, *4*(5), 227–245.

Vanderplasschen, W., Rapp, R., Wolf, J., & Broekaert, E. (2004). The development and implementation of case management for substance use disorders in North America and Europe. *Psychiatric Services*, *55*(8), 913–922. doi: 10.1176/appi.ps.55.8.913.

Vercaigne, C., & Walgrave, L. (1995). *Jeugd Tussen (sub)Cultuur en Business: een Onderzoek Naar Mega-Dancings, House en de Last van Recreatie*. Leuven: Acco.

Verhofstadt, G. (1999). *Governmental Declaration*. Brussels: Federal Government.

Verslag namens de Parlementaire Werkgroep belast met het bestuderen van de drugproblematiek [*Report of the PWG*], *Parl.St.* Kamer, 1996–1997, 1062/1–3.

Vianello, C. (2011). *Injecting New Highs Into Public Policy: Analysis of the Changing Problematisations of Drug Policy Reform: the Case of Safe Injection Facilities and the Decriminalisation of Cannabis*. Auckland: University of Auckland.

Vr. en Antw. Kamer, 9 oktober 1998, nr. 49/B152 (Vr. nr. 951 F. Van den Eynde).

Vr. en Antw. Kamer, 4 februari 2000, nr. 50/22, 2415 (Vr. nr. 67 F. Van den Eynde).

Vr. en Antw. Kamer, 19 februari 2001, nr. 064 (Vr. nr. 309 A. Colen).

Vr. en Antw. Senaat, 12 januari 1999, nr. 1–90, 4733 (Vr. nr. 1479 M. Olivier).

Vr. en Antw. Senaat, 4 januari 2000, nr. 2–6, 201 (Vr. nr. 170 V. Van Quickenborne).

Vr. en Antw. Senaat, 4 januari 2000, nr. 2–6, 203 (Vr. nr. 171 V. Staveaux-Van Steenberge).

Vr. en Antw. Senaat, 18 januari 2000, nr. 2–7, 236 (Vr. nr. 191 V. Van Quickenborne).

Vr. en Antw. Senaat, 20 juli 2000, nr. 2–67, 11 (Vr. nr. 2–333 V. Van Quickenborne).

Vr. en Antw. Senaat, 20 juli 2000, nr. 2–67, 15 (Vr. nr. 2–334 L. Caluwé).

Vr. en Antw. Senaat, 12 juni 2001, nr. 2/36 (Vr. nr. 1265 C. Nyssen).

Vr. en Antw. Senaat, 9 oktober 2001, nr. 2/42 (Vr. nr. 1509 M. De Schamphelaere).

Vr. en Antw. Senaat, 6 november 2001, nr. 2/43 (Vr. nr. 1553 V. Van Quickenborne).

Vr. en Antw. Senaat, 5 maart 2002, nr. 2/50 (Vr. nr. 1544 V. Van Quickenborne).

Vr. en Antw. Senaat, 19 maart 2002, nr. 2/51 (Vr. nr. 1886 Y. Buysse).

Voorstel van wet tot regeling van de teelt, de distributie en de verkoop van cannabis (ingediend door Mr. Vincent Decroly, Mrs. Martine Schüttringer & Mr. Frans Lozie (Flemish and French-speaking Green party)), *Parl.St.* Kamer 1996–1997, nr. 1186/001.

Voorstel van wet tot wijziging van de wet van 24 februari 1921 betreffende het verhandelen van de giftstoffen, slaapmiddelen en verdovende middelen, ontsmettingsstoffen en antiseptica, teneinde het gebruik van cannabis uit het strafrecht te halen (ingediend door Mr. Patrick Moriau & Mr. Thierry Giet (both PS, French-speaking socialists)), *Parl.St.* Kamer 1999–2000, nr. 0727/001.

Voorstel van wet tot wijziging van de wet van 24 februari 1921 betreffende het verhandelen van de giftstoffen, slaapmiddelen en verdovende middelen, ontsmettingsmiddelen en antiseptica, ten einde het bezit van cannabis en derivaten ervan gedeeltelijk uit het strafrecht te halen (ingediend door Mr. Daniel Bacquelaine & Mr. Olivier Chastel (both PRL-FDF, French-speaking liberals)), *Parl.St.* Kamer 1999–2000, nr. 0461/001.

Voorstel van wet tot verstrenging van de straffen zoals bepaald in de wet van 24 februari 1921 betreffende het verhandelen van de giftstoffen, slaapmiddelen en verdovende middelen, ontsmettingsstoffen en antiseptica (ingediend door Mr. Filip De Man & Mr. Gerolf Annemans (both Vlaams Blok, Flemish extreme right party)), *Parl.St.* Kamer 1999–2000, nr. 0389/001.

Voorstel van wet tot regeling van de teelt, de distributie en de verkoop van cannabis (ingediend door Mr. Vincent Decroly, Mr. Paul Timmermans, Mrs. Zoé Genot, & Mrs. Simonne Leen (Flemish and French-speaking Green party)), *Parl. St.* Kamer 1999–2000, nr. 0780/001.

Voorstel van wet tot wijziging van de wet van 24 februari 1921 betreffende het verhandelen van de giftstoffen, slaapmiddelen en verdovende middelen, ontsmettingsstoffen en antiseptica (ingediend door Mr. Vincent Van Quickenborne & Mr. Patrik Vankrunkelsven (both VU&ID, Flemish Nationalists)), *Parl.St.* Senaat 2000–2001, nr. 2–585/1.

Vuillaume, D. (2008). Changing scientific perspectives on cannabis use. In D. Korf (Ed.), *Cannabis in Europe: Dynamics in Perception, Policy and Markets* (pp. 15–29). Lengerich: Pabst Science Publishers.

Wacquant, L. (2011). From 'public criminology' to the reflexive sociology of criminological production and consumption. *British Journal of Criminology*, *51*(2), 438–448. doi: 10.1093/bjc/azr002.

Wagner, P., Weiss, C., Wittrock, B., & Wollmann, H. (Eds.) (1991). *Social Sciences and Modern States: National Experiments and Theoretical Crossroads.* Cambridge: Cambridge University Press.

Walgrave, L. (2008). Criminology, as I see it ideally. *Newsletter of the European Society of Criminology*, *7*(3), 3.

Walgrave, S., & Van Aelst, P. (2006). The contingency of the mass media's political agenda setting power: toward a preliminary theory. *Journal of Communication*, *56*(1), 88–109. doi: 10.1111/j.1460-2466.2006.00005.x.

Walters, R. (2003). *Deviant knowledge. Criminology, politics and policy.* Devon: Willan Publishing.

Webber, D. J. (1991). The distribution and use of policy knowledge in the policy process. *Knowledge and Policy*, *4*(4), 6–35. doi:10.1007/BF02692779.

Webster, C. (2007). Drug treatment. In M. Simpson, T. Shildrick, & R. MacDonald, *Drugs in Britain: Supply, Consumption, and Control* (pp. 141–161). Basingstoke: Palgrave MacMillan.

Weiss, C. H. (1979). The many meanings of research utilization. *Public Administration Review*, *39*(5), 426–431. doi: 10.2307/3109916.

Weiss, C. H. (1986). The circuitry of enlightenment: diffusion of social science research to policy makers. *Science Communication*, *8*(2), 274–281. doi: 10.1177/107554708600800211.

Weiss, C. H. (1991). Policy research: data, ideas or arguments? In P. Wagner, C. Weiss, B. Wittrock, & H. Wollmann (Eds.), *Social Sciences and Modern States: National Experiments and Theoretical Crossroads* (pp. 307–332). Cambridge: Cambridge University Press.

Weiss, C. H. (1995). The haphazard connection: social science and public policy. *International Journal of Educational Research*, *23*(2), 137–150. doi: 10.1016/0883-0355(95)91498-6.

Weiss, C. H. (1999). The interface between evaluation and public policy. *Evaluation*, *5*(4), 468–486. doi: 10.1177/135638909900500408.

Weiss, C. H. (2001). *What kind of evidence in evidence-based policy?* Paper presented at the International Interdisciplinary Evidence-Based Policies and Indicator Systems Conference, London.

Weiss, C. H., & Bucuvalas, M. J. (1980). *Social Science Research and Decision Making*. New York: Colombia University Press.

Weiss, C. H., & Singer, E. (1988). *Reporting of Social Science in the National Media*. New York: Russell Sage Publications.

Weiss, C. H., Murphy-Graham, E., Petrosino, A., & Gandhi, A. G. (2008). The Fairy godmother – and her warts making the dream of evidence-based policy come true. *American Journal of Evaluation*, *29*(1), 29–47. doi: 10.1177/1098214007313742.

Weiss, T. G. (2000). Governance, good governance and global governance: conceptual and actual challenges. *Third World Quarterly*, *21*(5), 795–814. doi:10.1080/713701075.

Welch, C., Marschari-Piekkari, R., Penttinen, H., & Tahvanainen, M. (2002). Corporate elites as informants in qualitative international business research. *International Business Review*, *11*(5), 611–628. doi: 10.1016/S0969-5931(02)00039-2.

Wells, P. (2007). New Labour and evidence based policy making: 1997–2007. *People, Place & Policy Online*, *20*(7), 22–29. doi: 10.3351/ppp. 0001.0001.0004.

Wet van 13 mei 1999 betreffende de invoering van de gemeentelijke administratieve sancties, *B.S.* 10 juni 1999.

Wet van 22 augustus 2002 strekkende tot de wettelijke erkenning van behandelingen met vervangingsmiddelen en tot wijziging van de wet van 24 februari 1921 betreffende het verhandelen van de giftstoffen, slaapmiddelen en verdovende middelen, ontsmettingsstoffen en antiseptica, *B.S.* 1 oktober 2002.

Wet van 24 februari 1921 betreffende het verhandelen van giftstoffen, slaapmiddelen en verdovende middelen, psychotrope stoffen, ontsmettingsstoffen en antiseptica, *B.S.* 16 maart 1921.

Wet van 29 juni 1964 betreffende de opschorting, het uitstel en de probatie, *B.S.* 17 juli 1964.

Wet van 3 mei 2003 tot wijziging van de wet van 21 februari 1921 betreffende het verhandelen van giftstoffen, slaapmiddelen en verdovende middelen, psychotrope stoffen, ontsmettingsstoffen en antiseptica en van de stoffen die kunnen gebruikt worden voor de illegale vervaardiging van verdovende middelen en psychotrope stoffen, *B.S.* 2 juni 2003.

Wet van 4 april 2003 tot wijziging van de wet van 24 februari 1921 betreffende het verhandelen van giftstoffen, slaapmiddelen en verdovende middelen, ontsmettingsstoffen en antiseptica, en van artikel 137 van het Wetboek van strafvordering, *B.S.* 2 juni 2003.

Wet van 20 juli 2006 tot wijziging van de wet van 24 februari 1921 betreffende het verhandelen van giftstoffen, slaapmiddelen en verdovende middelen, psychotrope stoffen, ontsmettingstoffen en antiseptica en van de stoffen die kunnen gebruikt worden voor de illegale vervaardiging van verdovende middelen en psychotrope stoffen, *B.S.* 28 juli 2006.

Wet van 7 februari 2014 tot wijziging van de wet van 24 februari 1921 betreffende het verhandelen van gifstoffen, slaapmiddelen en verdovende middelen, psychotrope stoffen, ontsmettingsstoffen en antiseptica en van de stoffen die kunnen gebruikt worden voor de illegale vervaardiging van verdovende middelen en psychotrope stoffen, *B.S.* 10 maart 2014.

Wetherell, M., Taylor, S., & Yates, S. J. (Eds.) (2001a). *Discourse as Data*. London: Sage Publication.

Wetherell, M., Taylor, S., & Yates, S. J. (Eds.) (2001b). *Discourse Theory and Practice: a Reader*. London: Sage Publications.

Wildavsky, A. (1979). *Speaking Truth to Power. The Art and Craft of Policy Analysis*. New Brunswick: Transaction Publishers.

Wodak, A. (2008). Going soft on evidence and due process: Canada adopts US style harm maximization. *International Journal of Drug Policy*, *19*(3), 226–228. doi: 10.1016/j.drugpo.2008.02.008.

Wodak, R., & Krzyzanowski, M. (Eds.) (2008). *Qualitative Discourse Analysis in the Social Sciences*. New York: Palgrave Macmillan.

Wodak, R., & Meyer, M. (Eds.) (2001). *Methods of Critical Discourse Analysis*. London: Sage Publications.

Wood, E., Kerr, T., Tyndall, M. W., & Montaner, J. S. G. (2008). The Canadian government's treatment of scientific process and evidence: inside the evaluation of North America's first supervised injecting facility. *International Journal of Drug Policy*, *19*(3), 220–225. doi: 10.1016/j.drugpo.2007.11.001.

Woods, M. (1998). Rethinking elites: networks, space, and local politics. *Environment and Planning*, *30*(12), 2101–2119. doi: 10.1068/a302101.

Wouters, M. (2013). *Cannabis Control: Consequences for Consumption and Cultivation*. (PhD), University of Amsterdam, Amsterdam.

Young, J. (2011). *The Criminological Imagination*. Cambridge: Polity Press.

Young, K., Ashby, D., Boaz, A., & Grayson, L. (2002). Social science and the evidence-based policy movement. *Social Policy & Society*, *1*(3), 215–224. doi: 10.1017/S1474746402003068.

Zampini, G. (2014). Governance versus government: drug consumption rooms in Australia and the UK. *International Journal of Drug Policy*, *25*(5), 978–984. doi: 10.1016/j.drugpo.2014.03.006.

Zimmer, L., & Morgan, J. P. (1997). *Marijuana Myths Marijuana Facts: A Review Of The Scientific Evidence*. New York: Lindesmith Center.

Index

Page numbers in *italics* denote tables.

For Product Safety Concerns and Information please contact our EU
representative GPSR@taylorandfrancis.com
Taylor & Francis Verlag GmbH, Kaufingerstraße 24, 80331 München, Germany

www.ingramcontent.com/pod-product-compliance
Ingram Content Group UK Ltd.
Pitfield, Milton Keynes, MK11 3LW, UK
UKHW022119190926
475702UK00013B/1531
9780367136444